VISHVA HINDU PARISHAD AND INDIAN POLITICS

VISHVA HINDU PARISHAD AND INDIAN POLITICS

Second Edition

Manjari Katju

Orient BlackSwan

VISHVA HINDU PARISHAD AND INDIAN POLITICS

ORIENT BLACKSWAN PRIVATE LIMITED

Registered Office
3-6-752 Himayatnagar, Hyderabad 500 029 (Telangana), INDIA
e-mail: centraloffice@orientblackswan.com

Other Offices
Bengaluru, Bhopal, Chennai, Ernakulam, Guwahati, Hyderabad,
Jaipur, Kolkata, Lucknow, Mumbai, New Delhi, Noida, Patna, Vijayawada

First published 2003
Reprinted 2003
Second Edition 2010
Reprinted 2012, 2016

ISBN: 978 81 250 4034 7

Typeset by
Le Studio Graphique, Gurgaon 122 001

Printed in India at
Yash Printographics
Noida

Published by
Orient Blackswan Private Limited
1/24 Asaf Ali Road,
New Delhi 110 002
e-mail: delhi@orientblackswan.com

Contents

List of Tables vii
List of Abbreviations viii
Preface to the Second Edition ix
Preface to the First Edition xix

1. Introduction 1
2. The Early Years 5
3. Transition to Mass Activism 33
4. A Non-Electoral Actor in Indian Politics 61
5. Demolishing the Babri Masjid 88
6. Post-Demolition Consolidation 113
7. Conversions and Reconversions 127
8. Conclusion 142

Appendix I 146
Appendix II 154
Appendix III 161
Appendix IV 163
Appendix V 166
Glossary 169
Bibliography 173
Index 184

Tables

1. Organisational Structure of the VHP 38
2. Deaths in Communal Riots 100
3. Service-Centres Run by the Vanvasi Kalyan Ashram 131
4. Number and Organisational Affiliation of Interviewed Activists 148
5. Name and Occupation of Interviewed Activists 149
   Section 1: Age Group 20 to 40 years 149
   Section 2: Age Group 40 to 60 years 149
   Section 3: Age Group 60 and above 150
6. 1984 Lok Sabha Elections 166
7. 1989 Lok Sabha Elections 167
8. 1991 Lok Sabha Elections 167
9. 1996 Lok Sabha Elections 168
10. 1999 Lok Sabha Elections ix
11. 2004 Lok Sabha Elections x
12. 2009 Lok Sabha Elections x

Abbreviations

BJP	Bharatiya Janata Party
BMCC	Babri Masjid Co-ordination Committee
MP	Madhya Pradesh
NHSF	National Hindu Students' Forum
NF	National Front
OBC	Other Backward Castes
RJB	Ramjanmabhoomi
RSS	Rashtriya Swayamsevak Sangh
SAHMAT	Safdar Hashmi Memorial Trust
SC	Scheduled Caste
UP	Uttar Pradesh
VHP	Vishva Hindu Parishad
VKA	Bharatiya Vanvasi Kalyan Ashram

Preface to the Second Edition

As I write this Preface to the Second Edition, the Sangh Parivar's fortunes lie ebbed. The BJP-led NDA alliance lost both the 14th and 15th Lok Sabha elections, held in the years 2004 and 2009 respectively, to the Congress-led UPA. The BJP's electoral performance makes it clear that the Parivar has been confronted with a weakened popular support. The BJP's seat share declined from 182 in 1999 Lok Sabha elections—when it formed the government—to 138 in 2004 to 116 in 2009. Its vote share went down from 23.8 per cent in 1999 to 22.2 per cent in 2004 to 18.8 per cent in 2009. A look at the general elections in the last twenty-five years shows that the BJP's career graph peaked nationally in 1999. The three tables* show the seats

Table 10: 1999

State	Total Seats	INC	BJP	JD (U)	BSP	CPM+ CPI
AP	42	5(42)	7(8)			
Bihar	54	4(16)	23(29)	18(23)		1(2)+0 (9)
Delhi	7	0(7)	7(7)			
Gujarat	26	6(26)	20(26)			
Haryana	10	0(10)	5(5)			
Himachal	4	0(4)	3(3)			
MP	40	11(40)	29(40)			
Maharashtra	48	10(42)	13(26)			
Rajasthan	25	9(25)	16(24)			
UP	85	10(76)	29(77)		14(85)	
W. Bengal	42	3(41)	2(13)			21(32)+3(3)
Total won in above states		58	154	18	14	22+3
All-India seats won		114	182	21	14	33+4

Note: The NDA coalition, of which BJP was the leading partner, formed the government in 1999 with 298 seats in the Lok Sabha. It completed a successful five-year term.

* *Source:* http://eci.nic.in/eci_main/StatisticalReports/ElectionStatistics.asp; http://indian-electionaffairs.com/parties/; http://www.pib.nic.in/elections2009/default.asp; http://www.pib.nic.in/elections2009/default.asp, as accessed on 8 May 2010.

Table 11: 2004

State	Total Seats	INC	BJP	BSP	SP	CPM	RJD
AP	42	29(34)	0(9)			1(1)	
Bihar	40	3(4)	5(16)				22(26)
Delhi	7	6(7)	1(7)				
Gujarat	26	12(25)	14(26)				
Haryana	10	9(10)	1(10)				
Himachal	4	3(4)	1(4)				
MP	29	4(29)	25(29)				
Maharashtra	48	13(26)	13(26)				
Rajasthan	25	4(25)	21(25)				
UP	80	9(73)	10(77)	19(80)	35(68)		
W. Bengal	42	6(37)	0(13)			26(32)	
Total won in above states		98	91		35	27	22
All-India seats won		145	138	19	36	43	24

Note: The UPA coalition led by the Congress (INC) formed the government in 2004 with 218 seats. The Left Front is among some of the other parties which supported it from outside. The NDA's total tally was 181.

Table 12: 2009

State	Total Seats	INC	BJP	BSP	SP	CPM	RJD
AP	42	33(42)	0(41)				
Bihar	40	2(37)	12(15)				4(28)
Delhi	7	7(7)	0(7)				
Gujarat	26	11(26)	15(26)				
Haryana	10	9(10)	0(5)				
Himachal	4	1(4)	3(4)				
MP	29	12(28)	16(29)	1(28)			
Maharashtra	48	17(25)	9(25)				
Rajasthan	25	20(25)	4(25)				
UP	80	21(69)	10(71)	20(80)	23(75)		
W. Bengal	42	6(14)	1(42)			9(32)	
Total won in above states		139	70	21	23	9	4
All-India seats won		206	116	21	23	16	4

Note: The UPA coalition formed the government in 2009 with 262 seats. It had the backing of parties like the BSP. The NDA coalition's strength came down to 159 seats.

won and contested in eleven major states across India. (I have also pointed out the position of a few other political parties so that one can compare the BJP's electoral strength.) At the state level, the violence on the Muslim community in Gujarat in 2002 followed by the huge victory of the BJP under Narendra Modi in the assembly elections was the highlight of Sangh Parivar politics. Thereafter, its successes have not been as spectacular and overall it has seen a decline. The Vishva Hindu Parishad, in this political context, has once again withdrawn into its shell albeit the occasional violence which it is known for. Rather than a phase of inactivity, this phase describes the VHP as being outside the public eye for it remains active behind the scenes, working quietly, only to surge when *Hindutva* politics demand so.

After its formation in the mid-1960s, the VHP's voice gradually grew and reached its highest point in 1992, the year when the Babri mosque at Ayodhya was demolished. The VHP was at the forefront of this event. The demolition established the VHP as an important player in Indian politics though as a non-electoral participant. The book covers a times span from the middle of 1960s to the late 1990s and looks at how and why the VHP grew from a quiet organisation working under the RSS' shelter to a militant organisation trying to influence the course of Indian politics and nature of the Indian state. It looks at the rise of Hindutva as a political ideology and discusses how the Sangh Parivar operates in the socio-political arena and succeeds in establishing itself among sections as diverse as the tribal communities residing in remote areas and the urban professionals of cities. Through these issues it aims to highlight the larger question: how does extremist religious politics work in a context marked by big income disparities and social divide. Today such disparities have only become much more acute. The book is a reminder of how communal politics manages to come to the centre-stage and influences the course of events. Its electoral reverses notwithstanding, Hindutva retains a substantial presence, both socially and politically and this makes a strong case for the significance of a book on the VHP today.

The research for this book was carried out when the Ayodhya movement was at its height, i.e. the 1990s. The BJP led by the charismatic Atal Bihari Vajpayee was on an ascendance. The politics of the country was amidst the rough and tumble that the *mandal* and *mandir* issues had brought upon it. While the backward classes demanded a bigger pie in education, representation and employment, the Hindutva forces called for Hindu political unity and hinduisation of the state. Caste and communal clashes tore social relations and bred further discord. It was a period of churning as the country moved from a one-party dominant system to coalitional/ alliance politics. This shift is reflective of the deepening politicisation of sections, which were until then outside the fold of formal politics. On the one hand, there was a rise in backward class assertions, on the other, the ascendance of Hindu majoritarian politics. The latter was built upon narrow sectarianism and a fear of the 'other'. There were occasions when the two came together when it proved mutually useful. For one it provided prospects of social and material mobility, for the other, political power. Whether in Gujarat, Madhya Pradesh or Orissa, it was mostly sections of the socially backward communities that participated in the Sangh Parivar sponsored campaigns against minorities. Amidst these happenings, there was also a move towards the roll back of the Indian state from whatever limited role it had played in public welfare. The Indian state had embarked upon neo-liberal economic reforms.

The VHP at this time played a key role to transform Hindutva from a verbal idea, a theoretical formulation, to a broad, militant and forceful movement in the late 1980s and 1990s. The VHP's efforts at mass mobilisation, extremely communal in nature, saw a popular involvement in Hindutva campaigns. This mass involvement also reflected the popular mood of dissatisfaction with the Indian state. The VHP has always been the clamorous and militant sibling of the Sangh Parivar. Its belligerent anti-minority stance and unapologetic participation in overt violence against the minorities is not hidden. Its attempt has always been to present Hindu communalism in a nationalist garb. Through mobilisations on the Ayodhya issue, it succeeded to bring Hindu communalism on the centre-stage of Indian politics.

If one looks back at the last few years of Sangh Parivar's activities, one can see two developments taking shape: first, the Sangh Parivar is trying out strategies to strengthen organisationally and capture the popular imagination, which includes moves to restructure BJP. After the vacillations on Hindutva, the BJP decided to bring it back as its main mobilisational plank. Closely following on the heels were the RSS directed moves to restructure the BJP by bringing in younger, non-controversial, non-Delhi and 'close to the headquarters' leadership to take charge of the organisational affairs of the party. Second, after some years of open involvement in politics, the VHP is going back to its original agenda of silent grass-roots work, which is also the typical way in which the RSS functions. This work has been taken up in states where BJP is in power or has a strong presence. This change of work-tactics has happened because the rabble-rousing, agitational mass programmes of the VHP have not seen much success in recent years.

The VHP tried to replicate the mass mobilisation programmes of the 1980s and 1990s. It attempted campaigns similar to the *ekatmata yatras* of 1983, the *shilanyas* of 1989, Advani's *rathyatra* of 1990 and the Babri demolition of 1992—campaigns which had seen tremendous public response and mass participation. These campaigns which rode on Hindu religious beliefs aimed at Hindu unity and consolidation of the Hindu vote in favour of the BJP. In recent years, the VHP has tried to organise similar events of a popular nature. One should mention two programmes that it took up to build mass support. One of these programmes that began in the late 1990s was the *trishul deeksha* programme or trident-distribution among the public which is an attempt at communal mobilisation on a mass scale. It was intensified in 2002–3 after the Gujarat carnage and the victory of the BJP led by Narendra Modi in Gujarat. From Gujarat it was extended to Rajasthan as also to Madhya Pradesh and Maharashtra. It was reported that this distribution was carried out in localities where Hindutva had a weak hold—the intention being to bring in more and more people in the orbit of Hindutva. However, it remained restricted regionally and could not see the success which the earlier programmes had seen. In Rajasthan, the toughness of the state government led by the Congress, the campaigns of civil rights groups as well as the media helped to contain this programme. The restraint of the BJP at the Centre, due to the adverse publicity it had got over Gujarat, also helped to keep the programme in check. Moreover, a waned popular enthusiasm was a bigger factor in its limited reach.

The second campaign where the VHP tried to build mass fervour, but was not quite effective, was over anti-conversion laws. It took up this issue with great force, especially in Gujarat and Rajasthan. Aimed at the minority communities, the VHP threatened agitations if the laws were not passed on the issue and expected a mass Hindu upsurge in its support. For instance, the VHP threatened agitation if the governor did not give her assent to it in Rajasthan. The anti-conversion bills were passed by both assemblies but did not receive the governors' assent in any of the two states. In Rajasthan, the bill was sent by the governor to the President for his consideration (this is where it still lies). In Gujarat, the refusal of the governor to give assent to the Anti-Conversion Amendment Bill, 2006, made the government go back to the 2003 anti-conversion laws and frame rules for their implementation. However, the governor's decision in both the states, which did not go according to the wishes of the VHP, did not see a mass uprising as declared and expected by the VHP.

While discussing the VHP's current pursuits one should also mention that its aggressive posturings directed towards city-based middle-class youth have also not been very successful in terms of galvanising substantial support for the Sangh Parivar. For instance, its violent stance on Valentine's Day celebrations or pub-visiting women has not gone down well with the professional middle classes whom the VHP constantly tries to woo. The VHP's condemnation of these activities as 'westernisation' or subversion of Hindu culture has in fact caused embarrassment to the BJP. The VHP's involvement in these matters has often caused immediate physical harm and communalised social relations. It has also brought instant publicity to the VHP and helped to maintain its image as a formidable force. But what has been missing is a mass upsurge of the kind the VHP intends.

In this situation, the VHP has had to rework its strategies, which is not unusual for a public organisation based on mass support. Organisations running on public support or claiming to have such support, whether political parties or interest groups, have to constantly evolve and rework strategies to maintain and expand their social base. This applies more to an organisation based on claims of representing the nation and giving expression to the ethos of the land. In a bid to spread its presence, at a time when its mass mobilisation strategies are not working, the VHP has had to re-focus on 'welfare' work. One must remember that the RSS and its family are long-term players. They might be sporadic in their loud and aggressive activities but at the same time work quietly and systematically to expand their social presence. To seep deep into the public psyche is what their aim is.

Accordingly, the VHP-RSS have been devoting attention to welfare work in tribal dominated remote areas. This is a feature of the initial programme of the VHP where aggressive Hindutva campaigns are supposed to run alongside community based work to establish and maintain a social presence especially in areas where the Christian missionaries are working. The emphasis on this grass-root work is for Hinduisation and de-Christianisation, as is discussed in the book. Thus, the VHP is engaged in opening and running cow shelters, *ekal vidyalayas*, health centres and *samskar kendras*. It has also been actively involved in what it calls *paravartan* or reconversion activities, which has become a euphemism to intimidate the minorities. These activities have been going on mainly in Gujarat, Rajasthan, Madhya Pradesh, Karnataka, Chhattisgarh, Jharkhand and Orissa—states where one finds a combination of a substantial tribal population, the presence of Christian missionaries and BJP or its allies in power for a good number of years. The VHP also attempts to establish a local presence through relief work during natural calamities. It contributed to relief work during the earthquake in Gujarat as also during the Orissa floods. It also became active in areas affected by rains and floods in Kurnool, Mahabubnagar and Vijaywada in Andhra Pradesh in October 2009.

This grass-roots work of the VHP pays dividends in the long run. The communalisation in the villages of Gujarat, where substantial numbers of tribal communities reside, became evident in the large-scale anti-Christian violence from the late 1990s and in the violence against Muslims in 2002. Violence and communal polarisation in Kandhamal, Orissa, is another instance of the VHP's long-term invisible work. The VHP-RSS have been active in the villages of Kandhamal district since the late 1960s running schools, hostels, hospitals and temples. Their work over the years has effectively communalised relations between the downtrodden Kui tribals and the dalit Pana communities. Majority of the Panas are Christians. Violence against the Christian community in the villages of these states has become synonymous with the VHP. Since the late 1990s there have been several instances of violence against Christians all on the pretext to stop conversions to Christianity. Intimidation of Christian missionaries, vandalisation of church property, disruption of church services and verbal abuse of the Christian community are the various ways the minority community has been terrorised. This communal venom has been equally effective against the Muslims who stand villianised as 'terrorists' and 'anti-nationals'. What needs to be foregrounded here is that the success of this communal propaganda has had a background of VHP's persistent work among marginal communities and backward areas.

Violence against minorities and incitement of communal passion continue to be the hallmark of the VHP. These it justifies as essential for the protection of Hindu culture and national security. The BJP, the electoral partner, takes a more restrained approach publically. This is not to say that it is opposed to or unwilling to endorse the VHP's anti-minority agenda. It is just that the obligations of coalition politics, where some of the coalition partners may find it difficult to agree with an openly communal agenda, and maintaining a secular-progressive image internationally, make it difficult for the BJP to follow an open Hindu militant position. This public restraint has caused problems in its relations with the VHP. In 2002–3, the VHP felt betrayed by the then prime minister Atal Bihari Vajpayee for not supporting its temple construction plans at Ayodhya. It publicly declared that it had lost trust in him and asked him to step down as prime minister. The VHP's verbal attacks against the BJP have since abated. However, it seems less likely that the VHP is going to forget the betrayal at the hands of the BJP, which it sees as Vajpayee's doing.

The defeat of the BJP at the Centre points towards a decline in right-wing politics, but this does not mean the demise of Hindutva. Reactionary and xenophobic politics sees reverses but comes back during times of discontent and disappointment with the secular state, especially when the latter reneges on its promises. Hindutva is very much present and waiting on the sidelines. It has every chance of becoming politically formidable again. Moreover, one has to note that at present, the BJP is in power in the states of Chhattisgarh, Madhya Pradesh, Gujarat, Himachal Pradesh and Karnataka. It also shares power with its alliance partners in Punjab, Bihar, Jharkhand, Uttarakhand and Nagaland. This might not be a big presence but it is also not insignificant. What this implies is that the VHP, whether through ekal vidyalyas or paravartan, has had ample opportunity and scope to intensify its work in these states. As discussed earlier, its relentless involvement in educational and health services at the ground level is aimed at the long-term goal of establishing a Hindu nation. Sustained efforts are called for to check this sectarian body and its hate driven ideology.

Vishva Hindu Parishad and Indian Politics was written with the hope that Indian democracy, with its plural-secular values, would strengthen from its encounters with reactionary politics. The politicisation of Indian society over the last ten years has kept that hope alive.

Preface to the First Edition

Vishva Hindu Parishad and Indian Politics is a revised and condensed version of my doctoral dissertation. *The Vishva Hindu Parishad and Hindu Nationalism: 1964 to 1996*, that was submitted to the School of Oriental and African Studies, London, in 1998. The spectacular expansion of the popular base of Hindu nationalist politics in the late 1980s and early 1990s, and the centrality of the Vishva Hindu Parishad—or the World Hindu Council, henceforth the VHP—in it, spurred my interest in the VHP organisation. The close association of my grandfather, Shiv Nath Katju (1910–1996) with the VHP, first as a member and then as its president in the late 1980s, led to a deeper involvement in this research, and subsequently this book.

I am indebted to Dr David Taylor of the Department of Political Studies, School of Oriental and African Studies, under whose supervision most of the research on which this book is based was carried out. I must express my gratitude to him for his invaluable help and support. Thanks are due to Dr Sudipta Kaviraj, who as an adjunct supervisor to the thesis offered helpful suggestions on various aspects of this study. I am also grateful to Professor Javeed Alam who patiently looked through the chapters at various points of their preparation and provided insights that clarified my understanding of Hindutva. Professor Tanika Sarkar's suggestions on the dissertation were very useful, and I am indebted to her for sparing time to go through it.

Nalini Vithal and Yoginder Sikand were kind enough to read and comment upon the very first pieces of writing of this work, when it was in its dissertation phase. Kavita, Atul and Amit Singh at Faizabad; Aslesha Shivpuri, Arun Shivpuri along with Mukul Prakash and Sharad Chandra at Lucknow helped immensely during interviews at Faizabad and Lucknow. Annapurna Katju, my grandmother, and Vandana Katju, a dear cousin, have to be thanked for their support during fieldwork at Allahabad. Their presence enabled me to go about my task with minimum difficulties. I am also indebted to Rupinder, Payal and Reena for their help during research at Delhi. My parents, Priti and Rajgopal Katju, and my brothers, Jayant and

Siddharth, were great sources of encouragement and support all along.

I am grateful to the Felix Scholarship Trust for granting me overall financial support to read for a PhD at the School of Oriental and African Studies, without which this work would not have seen its present form. Thanks are also due to the Central Research Fund, the School of Oriental and African Studies Fieldwork Fund, Sir Earnest Cassel Trust, the Leche Trust and the Charles Wallace Trust for their financial support during research.

I must thank the VHP activists at the organisation's various branches for granting me interviews and access to published material without any hesitation. The interviews with VHP activists, as a part of this research, were conduced during November–December 1993, and from September 1995 to May 1996. The willingness of activists to spare time for interviews and their enthusiasm during discussion helped me a great deal in understanding the VHP. I am grateful also to the *Organiser* office at Jhandewalan, New Delhi, for giving me access to the journal copies. Thanks are also due to the staff of the various libraries: SOAS, Senate House (University of London), Jawaharlal Nehru University and Teen Murti. Where would we be without them!

I want to add a special word of thanks for the Orient BlackSwan editorial team, especially Nikhil Bhoopal and Priti Anand, for the time they spent on the manuscript to bring it to its present shape.

Of course, the flows and blunders in this work are my own—however much I would like to, I cannot share them with anyone.

At the end, I must mention that I would not have overcome my reluctance to give this work for publication had it not been for my husband Aniket. His help and encouragement at every stage of research and writing gave this study some sense and coherent shape. His help in going through the various parts of the work and his suggestions proved to be invaluable, not to mention his perseverance during tense and moody phases. This work owes a lot to him and is dedicated to him.

Chapter 1

Introduction

In the early 1960s, organised opposition to the Congress Party had gained considerable confidence and had become distinctly articulate, though not strong enough to dislodge the Congress. The Hindu Right, represented by the Jana Sangh, was experiencing an upward trend in its electoral fortunes and had increased its strength in the Lok Sabha—the lower house of the Indian Parliament—from four to fourteen in 1962. Along with the Swatantra Party it was able to institutionalise opposition to the Congress. The pain and hurt generated by the partition of the subcontinent was always available as an issue to be played upon to spur opposition against the Congress. This apart, nationalist sentiments soared in the 1962 war with China, and again in 1965 during the second confrontation with Pakistan. Congress came under heavy attack from the opposition both for its external and home policies, which were seen as being soft on the Muslims and too trusting of neighbouring powers.

Nehru's death in May 1964 gave another boost to the Hindu Right. The leadership of the Jana Sangh asserted itself more forcefully in both central and state-level politics in the mid-1960s, drawing support primarily from the Hindi-speaking areas of the North, and partly from pockets of the Rashtriya Swayamsevak Sangh's (RSS) influence in Maharashtra. As stated earlier, this support in a large part came from the Partition-affected generations of the North—those who were witnesses to the Partition-related communal violence and churning of populations, and hence saw in Islamic Pakistan a threat to the physical existence of the Indian nation. They saw Nehru's secularism as detrimental to the survival of the country, a policy that amounted to "appeasement" of Muslims who should have been dealt with, in their view, much more firmly.

Leaders belonging to the RSS and Jana Sangh did not look favourably upon demands for separate states of Punjab and Nagaland either. This was all the more so because of the unilingual and uni-religious basis of the former, and the uni-religious nature of the latter,

Sikhism and Christianity, respectively. The Jana Sangh loudly opposed creations of these states within the Indian Union. In this political context the Vishva Hindu Parishad (VHP) was floated—prompted, at the first instance, by the creation of a separate state of Nagaland in 1963—to further strengthen and organise opposition to the Congress at a time when it appeared relatively weak.

At the time of its formation, the VHP seemed more a loose constellation of ideas and membership. It did not reflect signs of strict or tightly defined fundamentals, and certainly did not look geared towards socio-political extremism. Its only aim was to do social spadework towards a non-Congress and non-communist political alternative. It was shaped as a larger non-electoral platform by the RSS to seek the support of those Hindus, both in India and overseas, who identified with the varied strands of self-confessed Hindu traditional ideas and wanted to disassociate themselves from the secular make-up of the Indian state, as represented by the Congress government. These were also the people who did not want to associate openly with the RSS or the Jana Sangh at that juncture in politics. An alternative platform which was ostensibly religious seemed the most feasible means by which to organise the support of this constituency, and the result was the formation of the VHP.

The RSS, the Bharatiya Janata Party (BJP) and the VHP work as three distinct bodies and have separate constitutions, organisational structures and work patterns. It cannot be denied, however, that in terms of membership, ideology and agendas of action, there is an overlap between the three, and that the RSS has played a parenting role in shaping the other two organisations. The *swayamsevaks* (volunteers) of the RSS lent their active contribution in floating the VHP and have worked for it in important organisational capacities. In the politics of the RSS and its *parivar* (family) there does work a "division of labour" (Noorani 2000)—a division of work between the "cultural" RSS, the "political" BJP, and the "religious" VHP. The VHP can be described as a religious front of the RSS, but it definitely has distinctness in terms of membership, forms of functioning, constitution and agendas, which makes an independent study of the VHP organisation possible and important.

As an open challenge to whatever was seen as Nehruvian, the VHP made its own contribution to prioritising the collective over the individual in a proposed project where a well-orchestrated community is geared to a larger "national" cause in highly centralised and hierarchical structures. The VHP came to represent political Hinduism as "a religion of opposition in the strong sense" (Hellman 1993:14), cultivating an attitude of anti-Semitism or complete political subservience of the minority religious communities. A Hindu majoritarian rule with an authoritarian bend came to be seen as perfectly compatible with democratic governance. And all-encompassing moves towards Hinduisation of the polity went along with construction of a specific Hindu self (Basu et al. 1993). The 1990s saw a heightening of propaganda and indoctrination of the majority community that went together with repression of the minorities.

The chapters in this book are chronologically arranged, beginning with a discussion of the formation of the VHP in 1964, and concluding with an analysis of its activities and programmes in 1996 (with a brief look at its present activities). The following chapter explores the VHP's formation in the context of post-1947 politics, and examines the socio-political background of its important founding members, the charter they laid down and the goals they prescribed for the VHP. The chapter also studies the various programmes and activities undertaken by the VHP between 1964 and 1980, which not only articulated its original charter but also crystallised its future outlook and attitude. Chapter three examines the VHP's entry into direct political activism through mass-based programmes such as the country-wide *ekatmata yatra* (journey of unity) and the use of cultural symbols—of which Rama[1] was the most important—to bring about a Hindu militant flavour to Indian politics. The VHP also branched out into organisations like the Bajrang Dal to help it in its mass-based activities. This phase of politics saw the VHP grow in importance to the BJP, whose later success owed much to the former. Between the mid-1980s and the early 1990s, the leadership of the VHP gradually passed from the political elite and religious leaders into the hands of traders, small industrialists and service professionals. This phase is the focus of the fourth chapter. It witnessed the VHP making attempts to become a mass organisation and actually make significant inroads into the middle classes, to the advantage of the BJP. The VHP also took upon itself the task of defining the Hindu and his/her leadership, in a move that remains to be successfully challenged in today's politics in India. The VHP put in efforts to strengthen its organisation and also began involving

[1] An important Hindu deity worshipped mainly in northern India.

the sadhus (ascetics) in mass mobilisation. Chapter five looks at the VHP's programmes immediately before the demolition of the Babri mosque and in its immediate aftermath. The chapter discusses the aggressive and communal idiom employed by the VHP during the early 1990s to take the agenda of Hindu nationalism forward. In chapter six, the VHP's militant contestation of the Indian political institutions and the secular structure of the state is discussed. The VHP's advancement of militant Hindutva by way of negatively politicising the activities of Christian missionaries and thereby leading an attack against the minority Christian community is the subject matter of the seventh chapter. It discusses how the VHP's anti-minority activities, considerably emboldened by the BJP's being in power, has taken the former back to its original charter of "protecting" Hindu dharma from Christianity.

The VHP played a key role in successfully transforming Hindutva from a verbal idea into a broad, militarised and forceful social movement. Through the Ramjanmabhoomi campaigns it succeeded in making Hindutva central to Indian politics. Hindutva, or Hindu nationalist politics, not only contests the principles of pluralism and secularism that form the institutional bedrock of the Indian state, but also poses a challenge to the liberal values that are foundational to Indian democracy.

It is in the light of some of these issues that I discuss the VHP in the following chapters.

Chapter 2

The Early Years

It was in the month of Kumbha[1] in 1966 that delegates gathered at the historic town of Allahabad (Prayagraj) to celebrate the first international assembly of the VHP. This was meant to be the first World Hindu Conference held by the VHP, with the ostensible purpose of integrating all Hindus, by birth or conviction, so as to understand, preserve and practise the principles of Hindu culture and religion. This huge congregation of delegates was the outcome of prolonged deliberations that had taken place at Sandipini *ashram* (hermitage), one of the spiritual centres of Swami Chinmayananda, at Bombay in August 1964. It was on the initiative of the RSS leadership, mainly M. S. Golwalkar and S. S. Apte, that a specific group of religious and political leaders were invited to Bombay. Of the 150 individuals invited, 60 attended the conference, and the rest sent messages welcoming the initiative and extending support to its programme. The main issue of discussion here was a source of much concern to those present. They felt that as public men they had a social responsibility to revitalise Hinduism and "protect" Hindus—religiously, culturally and demographically—to prevent a further partition of India.

When the ban on the RSS was lifted in 1949, K. M. Munshi, a founder member of the VHP, remarked,

> Shri Golwalkar, the RSS chief, is on an all-India tour. The ovation which he received in Delhi, for instance, is an indication that RSS has come to stay. It is no use ignoring the fact. . . . To CPI [Communist Party of India],

[1] Kumbha fair is a religious gathering of Hindu renunciates and pilgrims of all traditions, held in twelve-year cycles, i.e., every three years in rotation at Prayag, Haradwar, Nasik and Ujjain. According to legend some drops of *amrita*—a drink of immortality—fell in these four places when gods and demons fought over it. The name "Kumbha" is derived from the golden pitcher in which amrita was kept. The first historical evidence for this festival dates from the reign of Emperor Harsha.

> Lenin, Stalin and USSR are the Father, Son and Holy Ghost; to RSS, India is the Divine Mother, at whose altar self-immolation is bliss. What is USSR to CPI, ancient Bharat is to RSS. The Church of CPI is materialism; the Church of RSS is Dharma buttressed with ancient traditions. (quoted in Malkani 1980: 58)

This was written long before the formation of the VHP, but gives a clue to the kind of leaders invited in 1964 to Sandipini ashram. The aim of the RSS leadership was to float the idea of the necessity of an organisation like the VHP. The invitees did not seem to require much convincing and could go along smoothly with the RSS's suggestions.

The VHP had inherited the goal of political unity of the Hindus from its parent organisation, the RSS. However, it was unable in this early stage of its formation to clearly formulate and articulate this goal. This in large part can be attributed to three factors: the presence of an influential element of non-RSS leadership in the VHP; the RSS leadership itself preferring a subdued religious front; and popular faith in the Nehruvian and Congress policies of growth and governance, which limited the scope for growth of opposition—especially of a non-secular Hindu alternative.

The Original Charter

The VHP took it upon itself to defend, protect and preserve "the Hindu society from the insidiously spreading clutches of alien ideologies."[2] These "alien ideologies" were declared to be Islam, Christianity and communism (as we shall see later in this chapter). Certain principles of social harmony, organisation, reform and revitalisation were also laid down as guidelines by which the VHP was to function:

> It is the VHP's duty to organise all those people, whether residing in India or abroad, who adhere to the *sampradayas* [religious denominations or sects] that originated in India.
>
> The VHP should work towards freeing Hindu society from meaningless rites and customs which hamper the society's progress. It should restore the self-esteem of Hindu society and make it attune with the present age.

[2] Editorial, *World Hindu Conference 1979* (Bombay: Vishva Hindu Parishad Publication, 1979),vii. This volume is in two sections—English and Hindi; all references are to the English section.

> The VHP must propagate the message of harmony and mutual respect among the adherents of various ways of worship, Sikhism, Jainism, Buddhism etc., within the vast Hindu society.
>
> The VHP is an organisation of Hindus worldwide and is distant from the practice of politics of any type.
>
> In its attempt to serve society the VHP should not discriminate between individuals on the basis of caste, colour, religion, sect, sex etc.
>
> The VHP should try to elicit and encourage support from different regional, community, social and political leaders, industrialists etc.
>
> The VHP should endeavour to bring *sadhus*, *sants* [saints] and *mahatamas* [literally, great souls] of various sects and orders on one platform.
>
> The VHP should make efforts to make the age old Hindu *dharma* [religion, duty] compatible with the present requirements of society so that it is able to face the challenges of the modern world.[3]

Thus, the VHP set out to combine the asceticism of a sadhu with the dynamism of the modern technological age in its endeavour to revitalise Hinduism. While working along these guidelines it was expected to remain detached from politics; however, support of social and political leaders, and of established corporate and business interests was not to be shunned—a clear influence of Golwalkar on the early VHP organisation. Interestingly, the efforts towards revitalisation and modernisation had clearly demarcated social boundaries; it included the Hindu society, with its various *varna*s (castes) and *jati*s (sub-castes), the Sikhs, Jains, Buddhists and the varied tribal groups. These groups were seen as practising varied modes of worship within Hinduism.

Apart from putting down the above mentioned instructions, the early leadership also resolved that no section of society is untouchable and should not be treated so—on the contrary they should be provided a respectable status in society. They should all have the right to temple entry. Temples should be regarded not merely as places of prayer and devotion but also as centres of service and social progress (Vajpayee 1992: 55).

[3] Narayan Rao Tarte, "Vishva Hindu Parishad Ki Kalpana"(Vishva Hindu Parishad: A Vision), *Hindu Vishva*, silver jubilee issue, 1989–90, 14–15, Hindi edition.

The principles adopted did seem socially progressive and did reflect a genuine passion for reform, but the outlook providing them with moral force contained a strong revivalistic energy within itself. Hinduism had to be "protected" against Islam, Christianity and communism, and they were clubbed together as inimical ideologies against whom Hinduism had to be strengthened. This weakened the progressive therein and made the agenda of revitalisation and modernisation prone to extreme revivalism and chauvinism. At the onset of a suitable political climate, the seeds of chauvinism had to just sprout.

The Journey Begins

After its formation, the VHP began working self-assuredly. It was a body scarcely known, and hardly found any mention in the social and political writings of those years. This status continued in the 1970s and somewhat in the early 1980s. The early leadership, for its part, employed the idiom of reform and reconciliation rather than open militancy and belligerence.

The symbol of a banyan tree (*vat vriksha*) was adopted as the insignia of the VHP, to reflect its self-image of a broad-based and all-encompassing Hindu body. The VHP represented a socially conservative movement that stressed strong community ties based on a firm religious belief and adherence to rituals. The RSS, through the VHP, succeeded to some extent in drawing towards itself those who would not have been comfortable to associate with it otherwise, given the notoriety it had acquired as a Hindu communal body. The RSS's own social activity had a limited and exclusively male cadre, and its training programme was a long-term affair. Expansion of its social base and the urge to do some immediate mobilisational work amongst Hindus were the main motives that prompted the RSS to take the lead in the formation of the VHP.

In the 1960s and 1970s, the propagation of Hindu dharma did not produce the fiery and militant traits in the VHP which have become characteristic of the organisation in the post-1983 phase. Also, a uniform conception of the Hindu self and nation, and a clear agenda of action, as represented by the RSS, were absent in the VHP. This gave space for other ideas of Hindu revival and reform to exist within it, coming from its early non-RSS leaders like Swami Chinmayananda, Sushil Muni of the Jains, Sant Tukdoji, Karan Singh,

Jaya Chamraj Wadeyar, K. M. Munshi and C. P. Ramaswamy Aiyar. While these people shared the socio-religious concerns of Shivram Shankar Apte and Madhav Sadashiv Golwalkar of the RSS, who initiated the formation of the VHP, their presence in leadership positions made it impossible to form a unanimity of opinion necessary for the distinctive mass-based political activism of the post-1983 VHP.

What is important about the early VHP is that it was not conceived as a front-ranking, overt and loud political outfit, but as a socio-religious organisation that had to calmly feed into the RSS's agenda of exclusive Hindu nationalism. Evidence suggests that it did not have a clear-cut plan to regenerate the Hindus as a coherent and cemented political community. Its formation reflected an uncertainty about the future socio-political situation. The religious quest was considered by its leadership to be an effective way to rally Hindus together, to bring about some form of stability and certainty to this future. In addition, working for Hindu dharma gave the VHP added legitimacy and did not close to it the support of leaders of other political parties and groups. This also allowed it to function without much political opposition, and drew to it those who were averse to a career of active politics, but shared the VHP's aims.

The early leadership of the VHP was drawn from the intelligentsia, the proprietary classes, the petite bourgeoisie and various religious sects, some of whom were prominent Congress members at a point in their political careers and thus shared its class background. The VHP represented the conservative sections of the bourgeoisie that stood against the ruling Congress Party and somehow could not see themselves as placed within its overarching personality. The formation of the VHP was a response by these sections, conservative in their social outlook and right-wing in their economic programme, against the multi-faceted and large-scale transformation of the country's economy and social structure on the lines of Nehru's "socialistic" vision.

Until the 1960s the Congress was undisputedly the dominant Indian political party, and in these early years of its rule it was possible to see varied ideas and opinions coexist within it. However, gradually, by the mid-1960s the Congress came under growing political strain as a result of the increasing difficulty in maintaining this internal balance of conflicting interests. This was, in a sense, a consequence of a growing resentment on the part of many Congress members, both at the right and left of centre, towards Nehru's political and economic policies. It was in this context that the foundations of the VHP were laid, reflecting the political and economic resentment towards the mainstream and dominant Congress Party. It can be argued that the privileged upper-caste leadership of the VHP saw religiosity as a force that could arrest the tide of "socialism" and prevent a mass upsurge. Thus, the Hindu religion was promoted in order to bring some form of control over society and to restrain it.

At the overall cultural level, the leadership of the VHP reinforced a traditional and conservative perspective that did not give much space to rational analysis and questioning. The work was aimed more against Christianity, which according to them represented modernisation, and also against Nehruvian politics which encouraged a surge in both modernisation and "communism."

Shivram Shankar Apte, the first general secretary of the VHP, explained that its aim was

> to take steps to consolidate and strengthen Hindu society, to protect, develop and spread Hindu values—ethical and spiritual—in the context of modern times, and to establish and strengthen, contact and help all Hindus living abroad. [4]

He went on to say that,

> It will not be challenged if I say that it was the semitic religions which first divided humanity as the Christian world and the Muhammadan world. The declared object of Christianity is to turn the whole world into Christendom—as that of Islam is to make it "Pak." Besides these two dogmatic and proselytizing religions, there has arisen a third religion, communism. For all of these the major target of conquest is the vast Hindu society living in this land and scattered over the globe in small and big numbers. . . . It is therefore necessary in this age of competition and conflict to think of, and organise, the Hindu world to save itself from the evil eyes of all the three.[5]

He felt that such an organisation was an immediate necessity to work as a counterbalance to the three forces: first, the demands for an

[4] Shivram Shankar Apte, "Why Vishva Hindu Parishad," *Organiser*, Diwali issue, 2 November 1964, 15.

[5] Ibid.

independent state by predominantly Christian Naga tribes in the North-East; second, the surge of Islam which kept alive memories of the formation of an Islamic Pakistan; and third, the strengthening of left politics in India, encouraged by the socialistic legacies of the Congress.

Initial Aims

In the beginning, the VHP worked towards two ends. One was to cultivate and preserve Hindu dharma amongst the Indian diaspora—primarily among Indian non-Muslims and non-Christians living abroad—and the other, to check Christian proselytisation among the tribal populace of India. The first, and perhaps more important, was to consolidate the Hindu Indian communities in foreign countries. It was felt that a change in the cultural context brought about by migration to foreign countries would lead to a cultural drift among Hindus. These foreign countries were themselves categorised into two groups: those to which emigration of colonial indentured labour had taken place, and others where Indians had gone due to the economic pull of the booming post-War Western economies. The attempt of the young VHP abroad was to draw the various local Hindu organisations, with membership made up of immigrants from different regional and cultural backgrounds in India, onto common platforms where unified action could be taken.[6] It was felt that the drifting away of substantial numbers, within India and among the economically prosperous diaspora abroad, would lead to a general loss of influence for Hindus as a community. Swami Chinmayananda, founder president of the VHP, was gravely concerned about the Hindu diaspora because he felt that they were contributing their best to all the "highest departments of human endeavour" but many of them did not possess a knowledge of their "cultural duties and spiritual values."[7] Chinmayananda also felt that the children of these Hindus abroad were growing up without any familiarity with Hindu culture. Therefore, he wanted the Parishad to work towards enabling

> these children to have an opportunity to learn, to appreciate and involve themselves in our tradition.[8]

[6] See appendix II for details on the VHP's activities abroad.

[7] Swami Chinmayananda in *World Hindu Conference 1979*, 101.

[8] Ibid., 100–01.

Chinmayananda advocated the construction of temples for Hindus abroad. He believed that these temples "have more duties to perform than the temples in India because each temple has to serve as a total schooling for the growing children to be Indian at heart."[9] In the absence of any other institution he regarded temples as the best community centres and schools for imparting knowledge of Hindu scriptures.

> Our Vishva Hindu Parishad centres abroad should take up this programme of temple building urgently in each of their centres first, and slowly move to the other neighbouring countries, meet people, call meetings and, wherever feasible, start a Temple Building Committee. Wherever it is found necessary, we must have a Prayer Hall or room attending to the needs of the community, where we must encourage all the Hindu families to come and meet together. In this institution the Hindus will include most lovingly Jains, Sikhs, Buddhists.[10]

Shivram Shankar Apte worried about similar issues. According to him,

> Today there are thousands of Hindu brethren in foreign countries whose links from the motherland are either snapped or have become very weak.[11]

The goal was to keep alive Hindu dharma. This was more so at a time when it was believed that the Christians and Muslims were growing in numbers.

The second of the VHP's initial goals was to check the spread of Christianity among the tribal population. It was felt that the spread of Christianity among the tribal populace undermined the cultural unity of India and destroyed the ideological hegemony of Hindu beliefs. Ignoring the socio-economic problems faced by the tribal communities, the VHP read the situation from a narrow religious perspective and interpreted conversions as simple luring away of tribals through monetary means by Christian missionaries. The VHP leadership was of the view that the tribals had become easy victims for conversion to Christianity, being on the periphery of Hindu society and divorced from knowledge of their "Hindu background." These leaders saw education and health services, along with crude monetary temptations, as the tools with which

[9] Ibid., 102.

[10] Ibid., 103.

[11] Shivram Shankar Apte, "VHP, the Confluence of Hindu Society," *Hindu Vishva*, special number, January 1989, 57. The article was written in 1966 and is reproduced in this special issue.

Christian missionaries were attracting tribals. It was felt that unless conversions were curbed, the entire north-eastern border populace would become Christian and threaten the unity of India.

Early Leadership and Activities

Jaya Chamraj Wadeyar (1919–1974), the erstwhile maharaja of Mysore, who served as governor of Karnataka and Madras after Independence, came to head the VHP as its president from 1965 to 1969. He felt that the Hindus were passing through an age of "disastrous situations," which could be met only by "practising our *dharma*, which is unique and as old as our society."[12] He felt the need to "revive and re-emphasise the moral and spiritual values propounded in Hindu *dharma* in the context of modern life," and called upon the VHP to constructively channel the enthusiasm of the people, to "spread the message of Hinduism among the hill tribes and backward groups."[13] Wadeyar also felt that the problems of Hindus could be successfully dealt with only by adhering to the ancient tenets of Hindu dharma. Earlier, speaking at the third meeting of the VHP Executive Council in May 1965, he had said,

> The VHP has come at a stage when we are called upon to face a difficult situation. This can be done successfully only by practising the Dharma, which is unique and which is as old as our society. The concept of Dharma which is the central character of Hindu culture, and its implementation, will be the most useful contribution to the Hindu society as also a unifying force amongst its different sects.[14]

"Diligent practice of religion and morality," according to him, could solve the problems of Hindu society as of other societies of the world.[15] He stressed the cultivation of spirituality and non-violence in everyday life:

[12] At a meeting of the Executive Committee of the VHP held at Mysore on 28 May 1965. Quoted from *Shraddhanjali Smarika* (New Delhi: Vishva Hindu Parishad Publication, 1987), 22.

[13] At a meeting of the Executive Committee of VHP held at Mysore on 27 April 1966. Quoted from *Shraddhanjali Smarika,* 22.

[14] Bangalore correspondent, "Mysore Maharaja becomes Vishva Hindu Parishad president," *Organiser*, 7 June 1965, 13.

[15] Jaya Chamraj Wadeyar, "Grass-Roots of Hinduism," *World Hindu Conference 1979*, 6.

> There are many social and religious problems in Hindu society to be solved without delay. And, this can be done only by the cultivation of ethical and spiritual qualities.
>
> To the Hindu belonging to any sect or creed, the spiritual values of truth (*Satya*) and non-violence (*Ahimsa*) come first; and the biological values like strength and vitality and material values, like wealth and pleasure, occupy only a subordinate place.[16]

One of the VHP's early tasks was to take up the issue of conversion. Concern regarding conversions to Christianity was expressed at a meeting organised by the South Kannada district unit of the VHP to discuss the Freedom of Religion Bill (to which the VHP gave its support):

> The Christians may emulate the tolerant attitude of the Hindus in as much as the Hindus may imbibe the spirit of service of the Christians . . . but if the Christians started converting Hindus in the guise of social service, that would create social disharmony. . . . Conversions and imperialism were respectable during certain period in the past. But at present, just as territorial expansion was an offence so also proselytization.[17]

The activities of Christian missionaries, according to the VHP, were an attempt to divide Hindu society. S. S. Apte cautioned that if the area along the Brahmaputra River (north-eastern India) were culturally alienated from the rest of Hindu society, its—Hindu society's —fate would be threatened.[18] Acting as a pressure group, the VHP called upon the central government to expel all foreign Christian missionaries from the country and ban their entry forthwith. It was also demanded that any special concessions to Scheduled Castes (SCs) or Other Backward Castes(OBCs) should be stopped after their conversion to Christianity.[19] A factor compounding these demands was that the RSS and its partners found it difficult to accept the centre's move to grant statehood to Nagaland in 1963—a move made in order to assuage the demand for regional and political autonomy by the Naga tribes, who were incidentally Christian. Within RSS circles the view was,

[16] Ibid., 6, 8.

[17] Pejawar Swami, "Religious conversions are relics of imperialist days," *Organiser*, 27 May 1979, 14.

[18] Shivram Shankar Apte in *Hindu Vishva*, 5 March 1970, 43.

[19] *Hindu Vishva*, December 1969/1970, 63.

> It is true that Hinduism is not a converting religion but that should not mean that the Hindu population should be looked upon as a quarry to be drawn on indefinitely, and indiscriminately by others to add to their own numbers. After all numbers do count.[20]

Besides working to check the spread of Christianity, the VHP affirmed its support for the countrywide campaign against cow slaughter. In January 1966, the VHP pleaded with the government to ban cow slaughter.[21] The Governing Council of the VHP passed a resolution on 24 August 1966 that read as follows:

> Regarding the demand for a total ban on cow-slaughter which is going to be pressed by some revered Sadhus of our country, the Council felt that the Parishad should try to create a sympathetic atmosphere for the demand by urging on the people to observe a day's fast on 20 November as also to plead with the Government to effect such changes in the Indian Constitution to enable the Central Government itself to promulgate a total ban throughout the country.[22]

The VHP also joined the Hindu Mahasabha, the Jana Sangh, the Arya Samaj and others in organising an anti–cow slaughter demonstration on 7 November 1966 at Delhi. The big demonstration before the Parliament in November 1966 triggered large-scale violence (Vyas 1983: 3). Saffron-robed sadhus armed with spears and tridents barged forward, breaking the police cordon which was protecting the Parliament House. The violence and rioting got out of hand and the police had to use tear gas and lathis (wooden sticks). There were incidents of serious damage to vehicles and property. The police were forced to open fire. Eight people, including a constable, were killed and curfew was imposed.[23] Some who had

[20] R. R. Diwakar, "Vishva Hindu Parishad: Distinctions and Expectations," *Motherland* (New Delhi), 2 May 1971, microfilm, Nehru Memorial Museum and Library, New Delhi. *Motherland* was edited by K. R. Malkani, member of the RSS and Bharatiya Jana Sangh and later of the Bharatiya Janata Party.

[21] "Hindu meet wants ban on cow slaughter," *Hindustan Times*, 24 January 1966, microfilm, Nehru Memorial Museum and Library, New Delhi.

[22] Resolution demanding a total ban on cow slaughter passed at Bombay on 24 August 1966, in Sharma, ed., *Vishva Hindu Parishad Ke Prastav* (The Resolutions of the Vishva Hindu Parishad) (New Delhi: Vishva Hindu Parishad Publication, n.d.), 20.

[23] Reported in *National Herald*, 8 November 1966, 1, 6.

blessed the VHP at its birth took the lead here as well. Prominent among them were Golwalkar of the RSS, Muni Sushil Kumar (a Jain community leader) and the Shankaracharya of Puri.[24]

Hanuman Prasad Poddar, a leading founder member of the VHP, wrote in one of his articles:

> It is saddening indeed that India is free today and yet Indians have to tolerate cruel slaughter of 30,000 and more cows daily and have to request the government to ban this slaughter. Spirituality is at the root of the Indian way of life and yet we have to launch movements and saintly people have to court arrest and sacrifice their lives demanding a ban on cow slaughter. (Verma 1987: 42)

Poddar (1892–1971), affectionately called "Bhaiji" (elder brother) by his acquaintances, had been a member of the Hindu Mahasabha and also of the Congress. He considered himself close to leaders like Tilak, Madan Mohan Malaviya, Rajendra Prasad, Purushottamdas Tandon and also Gandhi. In general, he had a closer rapport with the Hindu conservatives within the Congress. In his own words, "I met some other personalities too in the political field, but I was closer to the above mentioned ones" (Verma 1987: 133). He was the founder of the Gita Press at Gorakhpur, which sold simplified and nominally priced translations, commentaries and interpretations of the Hindu sacred texts (Sharma 1972: 186–87). The press specialised in printing translations of the Gita, the Bhagwat Purana, the Upanishads etc. It tried to popularise these and make them intelligible to the middle-class Hindu by bridging the gap between classical Sanskrit and colloquial Hindi. The press was actually formed in the 1920s to publish a monthly called *Kalyan* which tried to perform a didactic role of *dharmik* (religious) teaching for religious Hindus. The vernacular Gita Press played a major role in shaping a certain understanding of the past, which crucially contributed to the contemporary idea of a glorious and indomitable Hindu era. In 1938, the Gita Press published the Ramacharita Manasa, edited with an introduction, commentary and notes by Poddar himself.

Coming back to the agitation against cow slaughter, its immediate result was that the Jana Sangh reaped a rich political harvest in the general elections that followed, especially in the northern

[24] For details of the agitation see also Graham (1993: 147–55).

Hindi-speaking states. It more than doubled its strength in the Lok Sabha, from fourteen seats in the 1962 elections to thirty-five seats in 1967. Although the VHP strengthened its support among the orthodoxy, it did not seem to have carved a public niche for itself during this agitation. Sadhu extremism still had not become an acceptable form of political protest. Following the agitation, the central government did take upon itself to set up a committee to look into this issue and suggest steps for cow protection. Golwalkar, the Shankaracharya of Puri and Rama Prasad Mukherji (another prominent VHP member) were to be part of this twelve-member committee.

The VHP also lodged complaints demanding clearance of illegal enchroachments on temple lands. It alleged that "more than 1500 acres of temple land have already been encroached upon and still an organised and systematic effort is being made to grab the remaining 5000 acres."[25] However, no organised and planned efforts were made, or agitations launched, to clear these temple lands.

As stated earlier, the main role in the formation of the VHP was played by the RSS—especially by its *sarsanghchalak* (person heading the RSS), Madhav Sadashiv Golwalkar (1906–1973), who led the RSS from 1940 to 1973. Golwalkar's austere lifestyle and his attempt to keep the RSS and the VHP at a low profile partially explain the latter's negligible political activism in its early years. He was able to draw a number of religious leaders towards the VHP on an appeal that the sadhus and sants should work for the unity of Hindu society. This not only enabled the RSS to "lobby for its views among a larger audience" (Andersen and Damle 1987: 163), but also attracted to it sections of the non-RSS Hindu elite such as former *raja*s (rulers) and ex-Congress members. On 12 August 1964, a few days before the launching of the idea of the VHP, Golwalkar had expressed concern that

> the real trouble with us in this country is that we do not have a great goal before us, there is no sense of mission. Without such a sense of high mission no country can become great.[26]

It was felt within the RSS that along with a lack of "sense of mission,"

[25] "VHP is putting new life in Kerala Hindus," *Organiser*, 26 November 1967, 7.
[26] "Shri Guruji says . . . ," *Organiser*, 15 August 1964, 7.

> the reinterpretation of the *Dharmashastras* [the Hindu religious texts] and review of some of its professions and practices in the background of the growing challenges—both internal and external—to the Hindu society and Hindu *dharma* were long overdue. With a view to fulfilling this urgent and paramount need religious leaders came together and decided to form the VHP.[27]

The RSS displayed and exaggerated the fear that the neglected section within Hindu society was being made the special target for proselytisation by Christian and Muslim missionaries.[28] Further, it expressed concern that the *dharmacharyas* (religious leaders or gurus) of the *sanatanis* (adherents of orthodox Hinduisim) had been consistently refusing to take non-Hindus into the Hindu fold "under the deluded notion that our *dharma* does not permit it."[29] According to it, this necessitated restructuring and revitalisation to prevent the weakening of Hindu society.

However, it is important to ask why a separate organisation was required to work for the unity and integrity of the Hindus and for reinterpretation of the Hindu dharma. Could the RSS not take this work upon itself? In the words of the former sarsanghchalak of the RSS, Rajendra Singh,

> It would have been difficult taking up this work too. Guruji [Golwalkar] believed that there were many vices in society and that the message of unity, oneness, equality and harmony could be conveyed more effectively if it were delivered by the *sadhus* and *sants* because people held them in greater reverence. In his opinion an organisation was required in the *dharmik* sphere which would take within its fold the various sects of Hindu society.
>
> Our [RSS's] work is not in the *dharmik* sphere as such but it has more to do with social awareness. It can be called national activity to some extent and it includes building of character, discipline and patriotism. Guruji had an extremely spiritual bent of mind. He was for a long time a member of the Ramakrishna Mission. His name was even proposed for the post of *Shankaracharya* [religious head of one of the four centres established by Adi Shankara], but he did not accept it. He felt that social maladies could be eradicated more effectively through the efforts of *sadhus* and *sants*. Ordinary people like you and I may keep trying to change society

27 *RSS: Spearheading National Renaissance* (Bangalore: Prakashan Vibhag RSS, 1985), 45. This work, though published in 1985, discusses in detail the context of the formation of the VHP and the "internal debates" of the time on these issues.

28 *RSS: Spearheading National Renaissance,* 46.

29 Ibid.

> but it will not make much of a difference. However, when *sadhus* and *sants* say something it is taken seriously by people.[30]

Supplementing Rajendra Singh's explanation of why the VHP was launched when the RSS was already working for Hindu awakening, Gurujan Singh, of the Uttar Pradesh unit of the VHP, and an active *pracharak* (unit organiser at the provincial level in the RSS), told me that

> the RSS's interaction with society is limited to recruiting and training boys and young men. Moreover, changing society through inculcating *samskaras* [cultural and moral conduct], as the RSS does, is a very long-drawn-out and slow process. Therefore, a need was felt for an organisation, which was broad-based and could do immediate work among Hindus, an organisation which could reach out to all—young, old, men, women, employed, unemployed etc. The result was the formation of VHP.[31]

S. S. Apte, an RSS pracharak, took upon himself the responsibility of arranging the meeting in 1964 at the Sandipini ashram, and of bringing various socio-political and religious leaders on one platform. Apte, a Maharashtrian Brahmin, after completing his law studies from Bombay University started legal practice as a junior lawyer under K. M. Munshi. Thereafter, he became a journalist with *Hindustan Samachar*. He was an able organiser, travelled widely and met various sadhus, political leaders and social activists. It was not easy to impress people like Dr Sampurnananda and C. P. Ramaswamy Aiyar.[32] He believed that every Hindu had certain duties to perform towards the ancient and noble Hindu heritage, the most urgent of which was

> to unite the different faiths and sects, creeds and *sampradayas*, sprung up in the holy climate of Bharat [India] and weld together their countless devotees, supporters and followers, who are spread here and abroad. Merely uniting them will not be enough, as a new awakening will have to be brought into their hearts so that they cherish a rightful pride for their *Dharma*, traditions, culture and history.[33]

30 Rajendra Singh, in a personal interview at Allahabad on 5 November 1995.

31 Gurujan Singh, organisational secretary (*sangathan mantri*) of the combined eastern and western Uttar Pradesh units of the VHP, in a personal interview at Allahabad on 17 November 1993.

32 "Shivaram Shankar Apte," *Shraddhanjali Smarika*, 28–29.

33 Shivram Shankar Apte, "VHP, the Confluence of Hindu Society," *Hindu Vishva*, special number, January 1989, 58.

Apte felt that the work of "infusing culture in society," both at home and abroad, had to be accomplished by spreading the teachings of the Vedas and the Smritis, and that the regeneration of values amongst Hindus had to be done on the basis of Hindu dharma.

In the words of Swami Chinmayananda (1916–1993), the motivation behind the formation of the VHP was to

> awake[n] the Hindus and to make them conscious of their proud place in the comity of nations. Once we have made every Hindu conscious of his own identity, the Parishad has done its job and we shall feel fully rewarded.[34]

He was of the opinion,

> Let us convert Hindus to Hinduism, then everything will be all right. (Malkani 1980: 158)[35]

Swami Chinmayananda, in whose ashram the VHP was conceptualised, was a renowned authority on the Bhagavad Gita and the Upanishads, and founder of the well-known Chinmaya Mission, founded to spread the message of *Vedanta* (one of the six schools of traditional Hindu philosophy). He taught the Gita and the Upanishads in English, which enraged the other religious leaders.[36] He rejected ritualistic religion and was critical of caste and gender discrimination. Though he lived the life of a sadhu, he did not belong to any particular sect or monastic order, and was more a teacher of Vedanta philosophy than a preacher. This made his ashram at Bombay an impartial and neutral ground for a meeting of religious preachers of sundry sects and faiths. His headquarters were in Bombay, but he frequently travelled abroad and had a considerable following outside India, both amongst Hindus and non-Hindus. This made him important to an organisation whose aim was to preserve and promote Hinduism among Hindus abroad. Chinmayananda was known to the leadership of the RSS, particularly to Golwalkar and Shivram Shankar Apte. It was Chinmayananda who had first floated the

[34] Ibid., 58–59.

[35] Swami Chinmayananda in *World Hindu Conference 1979*, 100.

[36] Brahmacharini Sadhnaji, *Short Biography of Swami Chinmayananda*, internet, http://www.tazoat.com/-bnaik/biograph.html.

idea of an organisation to protect Hindu culture outside India.[37] He emphasised that Hindus must at least know their scriptures, if not study them in all their finer details—an awareness which, according to him, had to be fostered from early childhood. Knowledge of the Hindu *shastras* [scriptures] was in his view necessary not only for one to be conscious of oneself as a Hindu, but also for one to be "nationalistic." By way of giving direction to the VHP, Chinmayananda said,

> There are very many ways by which we must work out our programme to rouse the individual and national consciousness in the glory and splendour of our heritage. We will have to conceive schemes and plans to start this education from the child onwards in gradual intensity until young men—stalwarts in body, balanced in mind, precise in thinking— grow up to become willing workers in this noble cause.[38]

K. M. Munshi (1887–1971), a Gujarati Brahmin who had been Bombay's home minister as member of the Congress Party, also played a significant role as a founder member of the VHP. He resigned from the Congress in 1959, and along with some others, formed the Swatantra Party. It was the Congress' Nagpur Resolution of 1959, calling for land-reforms (collectivisation and cooperative land relations), which provoked a great deal of criticism from the Swatantra Party, on the grounds that the resolution was not in the interests of political and economic liberalism. Munshi felt that the Congress had come under the overwhelming influence of Nehru and felt uneasy about it. According to him, "Pandit Jawaharlal Nehru has wielded a power greater than that enjoyed by any statesman in the world, and the policies of the Congress have been his policies."[39] Munshi could never reconcile himself to the partition of the subcontinent and the formation of a separate state of Pakistan. He gradually took up political positions against Nehru and the dominant centre-left position of the Congress Party. Interestingly, he gave up his resolve of non-violence after the demand for Pakistan gathered momentum, and supported the idea of civil war to compel the

[37] As I was informed by Ashok Singhal, president of VHP, in a personal interview at New Delhi on 4 February 1997.

[38] Swami Chinmayananda in *World Hindu Conference 1979*, 100.

[39] K. M. Munshi, *Inaugural speech delivered by Munshi at the Madras State Conference of the Swatantra Party,* 14 August 1960, Private Papers, Nehru Memorial Museum and Library, New Delhi.

Muslims to give up their demand.[40] He believed that the Congress would be appeasing the Muslim League's unreasonable attitude if it conceded to the demand for Pakistan. He felt that the salvation of Hindus and Muslims did not lie in disunity as separate nations but in unity, and his idea of *Akhand Hindustan* reflected this unity:[41]

> Again and again, we, Hindus, Sikhs and Muslims alike, have expressed ourselves through a single collective will. India, as a nation, *Akhand Hindustan* [undivided India], is, therefore, a living reality.[42]

Munshi felt closer to Sardar Patel than to Nehru. About Patel he used to say, "Of all the leading men with whom I have come into close contact, he has been the nearest to me, I admire his extraordinary gifts."[43] Munshi also desired Kashmir's full integration with India and the abrogation of Article 370 to hasten the process[44]—a demand still vociferously articulated by the VHP. Munshi also chaired the Committee for Reconstruction of the Somnath temple. In August 1964 he attended the meeting at Sandipini ashram and was appointed the president of the VHP for that meeting.

K. M. Munshi upheld the usage of the English language for both official and educational purposes until such a time when all Indians voluntarily agreed to learn Hindi (Jhangiani 1967: 193). This suggestion of his that English must continue along with Hindi until all parts of the country cheerfully accepted Hindi as the national language[45] made him vulnerable to accusations from the RSS that

> he [Munshi] has yoked Hindi with English in a new fellowship but finds himself ploughing a lone furrow. . . . Two languages cannot be yoked

[40] K. M. Munshi, *The Civil and Military Gazette*, 9 November 1941, Private Papers, Nehru Memorial Museum and Library, New Delhi.

[41] K. M. Munshi, "Mr Munshi's Address," *Tribune*, 3 November 1941, Private Papers, Nehru Memorial Museum and Library, New Delhi.

[42] K. M. Munshi, "'Hindustan is One', Its Significance," *Amrit Bazar Patrika*, 3 November 1941, Private Papers, Nehru Memorial Museum and Library, New Delhi.

[43] K. M. Munshi, "The Indomitable Sardar," *Social Welfare*, 2 November 1945, Private Papers, Nehru Memorial Museum and Library, New Delhi.

[44] K. M. Munshi in an interview to *Gujarat Samachar*, 18 April 1964, see *Swatantra Newsletter*, no. 43, April–May 1964, Private Papers, Nehru Memorial Museum and Library, New Delhi.

[45] Reported in *Leader* (Allahabad), 3 September 1961.

> together and kept indefinitely separate and distinct; this is an elementary fact about the growth of language which he seems unaware of.[46]

Munshi rejected the pro-Hindi fanaticism of many (Erdman 1967: 101), and this led him to have differences with the leadership of the Jana Sangh, an ardent advocate of the use of Hindi as an official language and as the medium of instruction in schools. In fact, all the paperwork of the VHP, including the minutes of its various meetings, was done in the English language. It was only from the mid-1980s that emphasis was laid on Hindi as the language of official work.

In the meeting of the Executive Committee of the VHP held on 21 January 1966, Justice Ramaprasad Mookerjee (1896–?) was appointed as a member of the committee to draft the constitution of the organisation; he became the first working president of the VHP on 28 April 1966. He also presided over the VHP *sammelan* (meeting) held in Prayag in 1966.[47] Ramaprasad Mookerjee had been the chief justice of India in 1956 and the president of the Asiatic Society of Bengal, besides holding other important posts. He also happened to be the elder brother of Dr Shyama Prasad Mookerjee (1901–1953) who formed the Jana Sangh in 1951.

Sir C. P. Ramaswamy Aiyar (1879–1966), a former Congress member, was another founder of the VHP. He started his political career by taking an active part in the Home Rule agitation launched by Annie Besant in 1915. He became the diwan of Travancore state in 1936 and had also been one of the secretaries of the Indian National Congress during the freedom struggle. He was appointed the vice chancellor of Banaras Hindu University in 1955 and the chairman of the Committee on the Reform of Hindu Temples in 1961. Once a reporter asked him, "Do you know that RSS people are behind the Vishva Hindu Parishad?" He replied, "I know that I am in front of them."[48]

Another invitee to the 1964 conference was the Akali leader, Master Tara Singh (1885–1967). He had led a relentless campaign for the creation of a *Punjabi suba* (a distinct area for the Punjabi-speaking populace) in the mid-1950s, on the grounds that the Sikhs

[46] P. Mahadevan, "Blimps of Indian politics," *Organiser*, Diwali issue, 29 October 1967, 27.

[47] In *Shraddhanjali Smarika*, 56.

[48] Ibid., 36.

have a culture different from that of the Hindus (Dua 1992: 95), and called upon the Sikhs "to get ready for the final struggle."[49] While the Akali Dal demanded a Punjabi suba, the Hindu organisations and parties, primarily the Jana Sangh, opposed the demand and asked for the expansion of Punjab's boundaries. The tension that resulted raised the possibility of violent communal clashes between Hindus and Sikhs. Hindu organisations, including the Jana Sangh and the Arya Samaj, declared that no settlement between the central government and the Akali Dal would be acceptable to the Hindus of Punjab if it directly or indirectly involved further vivisection of the state.[50] The Congress itself was not in favour of creation of such a state.

After seeing some ups and downs, the agitation for a Punjabi suba spilled over into the decade of the sixties. A major friction developed within the ranks of the Akali Dal itself, which was leading the agitation. Differences between Master Tara Singh and his once-trusted lieutenant, Sant Fateh Singh, deepened over strategy and the nature of the suba demand. Master emphasised the demand in the name of religion, whereas for Sant it was primarily a linguistic demand based on the principle of Hindu-Sikh unity, and secular values. An urban-rural and also a class divide were visible in the support that the two leaders received. In the face of dwindling public support, Tara Singh began a fast unto death in August 1961 to revive the suba demand, but was not able to generate enough support from his own Akali ranks. Nehru, for his part, was also not moved. To him the demand for a Punjabi suba was nothing more than a "purely communal demand" (Parthasarathi 1989: 450).

Following the termination of Tara Singh's fast, the All India Representative Body of the RSS (the Akhila Bharatiya Pratinidhi Sabha) passed a resolution in October 1961 saying,

> Now that the fast has ended and the tension has eased, it should be possible to consider all issues in a calmer atmosphere. The Sabha [conference or congress] earnestly appeals to Master Tara Singhji to realise the basic unity of Hindus and work for the same. The Sikh sect is an integral part of the Hindu society. Cut off from the latter it can neither flourish nor fulfil the

[49] "Tara Singh on talks with Nehru," *National Herald* (Lucknow), 29 December 1955.

[50] "Punjab Hindus oppose Akali demand," *Leader* (Allahabad), 5 July 1960.

> objective for which the great Gurus dedicated their lives. As past history has shown, the Sikh Panth[sect], as a living limb of the Hindu *Dharma*, can never be in danger of losing its distinct identity.
>
> The Sabha also appeals to the people of Punjab to realise the intrinsic oneness and harmony of the Hindu people and take a sympathetic and tolerant view of the various issues. Such an approach will strengthen the forces of unity and nationalism and ensure that no section of the society will fall prey to disruptive and fissiparous tendencies.[51]

The RSS, as this resolution reveals, did not look favourably upon the demand for a Punjabi suba. It saw this demand as damaging to Hindu nationalism, which considered Sikhs an integral part of Hindu society. It assured the Sikhs that they were in no danger of losing their identity, even though it came within a larger Hindu national identity. The counter-propaganda of the RSS–Jana Sangh, however, gradually began losing its effectiveness as a result of the growing demand for a separate Hindi-speaking state of Haryana. This demand, in fact, held the threat of factionalism within the Jana Sangh itself.

In 1963, the differences between Master Tara Singh and Sant Fateh Singh forced a split in the Akali Dal. Sant's faction got the upper hand and its popularity soared.[52] Under Master's leadership, the Akali Dal had become very critical of the Congress, especially after the Nagpur Resolution (1959), and had become close to the newly formed right-wing Swatantra. After the split, Master's group maintained its understanding with Swatantra and also developed a close relationship with the Jana Sangh. Master was clearly opposed to the Congress' socialism, something he shared with the Swatantra and the RSS. Sant, though opposed to land reforms, favoured the Congress' viewpoint regarding nationalisation of banks and insurance. The urban-rural divide was also visible in the two Akali factions. While Master's drew support from urban-based big business and industrial capital (again a fact that took him closer to Swatantra and Jana Sangh), the other group was backed by village-based landed interests.

However, at that juncture the advocates of a separate Punjabi suba had managed to achieve little success. The events caused an

[51] *RSS Resolves.... Full Text of Resolutions from 1950 to 1983* (Bangalore: Prakashan Vibhag, RSS, 1983), 25.

[52] For details of reasons for this popularity see Nayar (1966) and Narang (1983).

irreparable blow to the leadership of Master Tara Singh (Nayar 1966: 262), and hastened the end of his political career. His closeness to both Swatantra and Jana Sangh at this juncture seem to have been instrumental in taking him to Sandipini ashram. Taking part in the deliberations there in 1964 he declared,

> Protection of *Dharma* is our *Dharma*. The Khalsa Panth [community of Sikhs] was born for that purpose. Never have I left Hinduism. Guru Gobind Singh has produced a lot of Gurumukhi [a variation of Devnagri script] literature based on Vedas, Puranas and the like. Are we to leave all that? Infact [*sic*] Hindus and Sikhs are not two separate communities .... If Sikhs live Hinduism lives. They are not two separate communities. They are one indeed. Lack of mutual confidence has been a small problem. The situation must be put to an end. I want to see that. A Hindu revival movement is very necessary and it will certainly come up. If Guruji Golwalkar takes it up it could be easily built up.[53]

The presence of a Sikh leader in a Hindu conference was a considerable achievement for the RSS. It gave credence to its idea that Sikhs formed an organic part of Hindu society as did the Jains and Buddhists; that Sikhism, Jainism, Buddhism, Arya Samaj and the various tribal groups were basically sects (panths) within the fold of Hindu dharma. Tara Singh's involvement with the VHP was very brief, however, as he died on 22 November 1967 while the VHP was still in its infancy.

Pre–Hindutva Phase

In the early 1970s, the VHP engaged itself in community service and religious proselytisation as a non-political organisation. Its sense of service, although prompted by the worry of a possible Islamisation or Christianisation of society, was cast on the lines of Christian missionary work. In the 1970s, it opened community centres, primary schools and dispensaries, and worked in neighbourhood localities through small regional centres dispersed all over the country. In 1971, the Vanvasi Kalyan Kendra forum was formed by the VHP to counter Christian missionary work. Taking a thoroughly communal posture, the VHP propagated the view that the main function of Christian missions was

[53] Master Tara Singh in *Hindu Vishva*, silver jubilee issue, 1990, 21, English edition.

to "target backward tribals, lure them in their nets and together with improving their economic status subject them to conversions; tens of thousands of tribals as a consequence are alienated from the national mainstream."[54] It also straightforwardly stated that Christian conversions had prompted it to make the tribal belt its primary focus of attention.[55]

In 1977 the Bharatiya Vanvasi Kalyan Ashram (VKA) was revived by the RSS to work amidst the tribals, and many VHP activists joined in its efforts. The attempt was to direct all activities towards discouraging the socially alienated and economically deprived tribals from adopting Christianity, and to "de-Christianise" those who had already done so. The tribals were also consistently urged to give up those customs that identified them as Christian. For instance, they were made to say "Jai Sita Rama" instead of "Jai Isu" (Seshadri 1988: 52), and their customs and traditions were labelled Hindu culture. Moreover, reference was made to them as having a "common *Bharatiya* [Indian] identity" (Seshadri 1988: 67). The work of Christian missionaries was such a cause of indignation for the VHP and VKA that a proposal came from within for the formation of a non-Christian front to face the "Christian manoeuvrings" in Nagaland (Seshadri 1988: 62).

The 1977 parliamentary elections, following the Emergency, saw the defeat of the Congress Party, hugely discredited for the institutional debasement, economic mismanagement and personalisation of governance at its hands. The Janata Party, a merger of anti–Indira Gandhi parties and individuals, was voted to power at the centre.[56] The Jana Sangh, with ninety parliamentary seats, was the largest party within this merged group. In this political setting, in 25–27 January 1979, the VHP organised the second World Hindu Conference, at Allahabad, where its principles of unity and integrity of Hindu society spread the world over were reiterated. If, on the one hand, the late 1970s was a period of growing political awareness and participation, it was also a time of ambiguity in politics, and decay and fragmentation within parties. In this context, Chinmayananda remarked in 1979,

[54] Editorial, *Vanvasi Kalyan Kendra* (Sonbhadra (U.P.): Vishva Hindu Parishad Publication, 1992), 20.

[55] Ibid.

[56] This coalition was headed by Morarji Desai, a former Congress man, whose political rivalry with Indira Gandhi went back to 1967 when he was defeated by her in the Congress parliamentary party leadership elections.

> At this moment the government of India is very much preoccupied with our endless national problems — political, economic and social. We should not expect them to provide any active vigilance over us to secure for us our rights and to protect us when we are threatened by the selfish desires of the nations in foreign countries.[57]

It is evident that this was a mild criticism of the government and not a scathing attack on it. That the Janata Party was an anti-Congress coalition and had the partnership of the Bharatiya Jana Sangh (consciously pro-Hindu) within it explains the VHP's sympathies with the government at that time. Moreover, considering the RSS's noticeable presence in both the Jana Sangh and the VHP, the latter stood to gain much at this juncture. It is said that a considerable amount of money was sanctioned to the VHP by the government, supposedly for social welfare schemes (Vyas 1983: 5).

The VHP in the '60s and '70s, under the decisive influence of its non-RSS leadership and the restraining role of the RSS, approached the Hindu community more as a religious congregation than as a political community, and was unable to link the two conceptions in a meaningful manner. Hindutva politics, as a goal of militant Hindu nationalism, had already been conceptualised by the Hindu Mahasabha under Savarkar. Although this was within the larger discourse of Hindu politics, its pursuit could not become the aim of the VHP in this period. This was because political representation of the Hindus as a community had still not been coherently conceptualised within the VHP. Therefore, we find that the VHP at this time was not able to mobilise single-mindedly on the terrain straddling religion and politics, and remained uncertain about its place in the larger Hindu movement. The uncertainty it embodied was most clearly visible on the question of "internal" Hindu social reform. There was the realisation that Hindu society over the centuries had come to be afflicted with maladies like untouchability, which, if not corrected, could lead on to make those on the lower rungs of society embrace Islam or Christianity, leading to further partition of the country. This was seen as more of a religious question than a political one. There was a lurking fear, which continues at the present, that this massive social inequality and oppression might lead to the irreparable weakening of Hindus as a community and of Hinduism as a religion. Therefore, an important

[57] Swami Chinmayananda in *World Hindu Conference 1979*, 101.

objective of the early VHP was the (re)integration of those on the social margins into the larger fold of Hinduism.

The VHP leaders saw themselves as members of the educated and historically conscious Hindu intelligentsia—publicly high-profile, distinguished and upper-caste—who felt compelled to take steps to check a mass drift not only towards Christianity and Islam, but also towards some sort of leftist ideals. They adopted the socio-religious path and saw in the VHP a device that could help achieve this goal. It was feared that if these problems were not promptly dealt with, the future of Hindu society would be jeopardised. In S. S. Apte's words,

> [The] Hindu religion and *samaj* [society] are still vulnerable from inside also as much as or rather more than from outside. But there should be no dispute if it is said that the dust and the cobwebs of debasing customs and dishonourable practices have to be brushed off the bunch of resplendent principles to lead the humanity in general and Hindu society in particular to light.[58]

The RSS believed that Hinduism had to change its non-proselytising image to save itself from extinction. The aim of its restraining hold over the VHP in the beginning was to buy time and establish the VHP as an acceptable religious organisation before it took on a much more serious goal. The development of a wide network of VHP-affiliated schools, orphanages, hostels and dispensaries, especially in the tribal areas, and programmes for the promotion of Sanskrit, cow protection, festival celebrations etc. in urban localities, was an answer to this perceived crisis. In 1966, Golwalkar remarked,

> It used to be said that a person who has left the Hindu *dharma* once, is gone for ever. But this cannot be. He has to be brought home again. If somebody tries to take away our own people, it is our first duty to be careful that hereafter nothing of the kind will happen, and if it does, we must take every step to reclaim him and bring him home.[59]

With a leadership belonging to disparate backgrounds, the VHP could not acquire an ideological coherence and a militant

[58] Shivram Shankar Apte, "Modernising the Hindu *Samaj* and *Dharma*," *World Hindu Conference 1979*, 96.

[59] Sri Guruji (Golwalkar), "Hindus must wake up," (speech delivered at Assam Vishva Hindu Parishad Conference held at Gauhati on 2 October 1966); extracts in *World Hindu Conference 1979*, 16.

communal stance in its early years. Also, such a stance would have been counterproductive in an atmosphere where Congress still had enormous social support and Jana Sangh had a struggling political career. It cannot be denied, however, that the seeds of antagonistic sectarianism and Hindu militancy were always present in the organisation that had a strong revivalist agenda. Also one cannot deny that its ideas of dharmik intervention in society were largely Brahminical, reflecting the views of a class which was privileged both economically and socially. The Brahmins feared the extinction of Hindu dharma and of their own privileged status, along with all other social institutions of "Indian tradition." And, of course, the constant presence of the RSS in the VHP organisation also increased the chances of a move towards an extreme form of Hindu nationalism.

Golwalkar, while explaining the purpose behind the formation of the VHP, tried to emphasise that their work should not be "reactionary in its nature nor its contents."[60] This, while serving as camouflage, went very well with his belief that the organisation should stay politically low-profile. In his own words,

> It is not because Christians and Muslims are active against us, that we have to work for our society and the Dharma. . . . For remember that even if there were not a single Christian Mission or a Muslim Majlis [congregation] to work against us, it would always be necessary to work for our religion, society and the nation. With this positive idea the VHP has come into being.[61]

As Golwalkar's comment suggests, the Sangh brotherhood considered it necessary that at least initially, it should not only be discreet about the real nature of its outfits, but also allow considerable amount of dilution, so that the organisation might gain legitimacy.

Taking the discussion further, it seems important to mention what one of the founding leaders had to say of the contemporary VHP and one of its members after the Babri mosque was destroyed. This is the view of one of the very few surviving founder members, and it does give us some insights into how the early VHP differed in its perceptions from the contemporary VHP. After the demolition of the Babri mosque, Karan Singh remarked,

[60] Ibid.
[61] Ibid.

> It is indeed shocking to see such a way of hatred and aggressive behaviour suddenly overtaking sections of the Hindu community in some parts of the country. This attitude is well portrayed by one Swami Vamdev,[62] whose name I read for the first time when, at a press conference at New Delhi, he reportedly denounced the Constitution as "anti-Hindu" and laid claim to the Jama Masjid because, according to him, it was built on the ruins of a Hindu temple! (Singh 1993: 44)

Karan Singh had served as the governor of Jammu and Kashmir state from 1965 to 1967, a position he again came to hold after elections in 1995. He took a lead in the various sammelans organised by the VHP for the promotion of Sanskrit, but from the late 1980s gradually distanced himself from the organisation. According to him,

> At their highest all religions are so many different paths leading to the same goal, the ineffable and indescribable union between the human and the divine . . . strife and hatred in the name of religion is therefore the very antithesis of spirituality and a gross slur on the name of humanity.
>
> I believe that we must work for political integration, economic growth, social transformation, and secular democracy not merely as ends in themselves but because this combination can best provide the framework within which the people of our ancient land can fulfil their destiny. (Singh 1974: 5)

He later came to advocate "Hindu renaissance," which he distinguished from "Hindu revival." He appealed for a renaissance of social reform and spiritual regeneration (Singh 1983: 14–17), a renaissance which had nothing to do with Hindu-Muslim confrontation or even Hindu revivalism (Singh 1983: 18). Hindu revivalism, according to him, meant doing away with the Indian Constitution and reintroducing the *Manu Smriti* going 2,500 years back, which is uncalled for (Singh 1983: 15). In Karan Singh's words,

> What is required is a restatement and reaffirmation of these truths [of Vedanta] so that narrow-minded, superstitious and undesirable social customs that have developed in Hinduism over many centuries of servitude can be cleansed. (Singh 1983: 16)

62 A member of the VHP who chaired a VHP committee to rework the Constitution of India.

The VHP in the mid-1980s, from relatively moderate socio-religious aims, moved to a political agenda that was militant and revivalist. As an organisation with a political agenda its concerns have become inextricably linked with the questions of power and identity. The changes within the RSS leadership and the passing away of most of the early leaders of the VHP by the late 1960s and early 1970s brought about many significant changes in the nature of the VHP. The alterations in the politico-economic scenario in the country as a whole, and the broadening of the VHP's base in the 1980s also contributed to this transformation.

Chapter 3

Transition to Mass Activism

Meenakshipuram

In February 1981 Meenakshipuram, a village in Tirunelveli district of Tamil Nadu with a population of 1,300, almost all of whom were "untouchables," became a centre of controversy when large-scale conversions to Islam were reported. For the VHP and its associate organisations, the Meenakshipuram conversions were not an outburst of local grievances, but "a small experience of an old conspiracy to destroy Hindus, Hinduism and Hindusthan," financed by petrodollars.[1] It was reported that around 1,000 of 1,250 untouchables had converted to Islam,[2] a step to protest against the denial of social equality. The rules of social conduct were laid down by the high-caste Thevars, and their infringement prompted harsh retaliation. Conversions to Islam had taken place in 1980–81 in some adjoining areas, but they did not provoke much of an outcry from the VHP or any other Hindu outfit; this was probably because the number was not as great as in Meenakshipuram, and also because bitter intercaste relations prevented reaction on the part of higher castes. The conversions in these areas seem to have been a reaction to the social and political humiliation suffered by the untouchables at the hands of the higher castes like the Thevars.

1 Editorial, *Organiser,* 5 July 1981, 3.

2 Statistics from Tooshar Pandit, "Tamil Nadu's Converted Harijans," *Sunday*, 7 June 1981, 40–43; also see Raj (1981: 60). The Harijans (untouchables) of Meenakshipuram were better placed than many other untouchables in the country. More than 40 per cent of them were educated. Eighty families out of one hundred and eighty owned land, and the biggest landholder in the village was an untouchable. The Harijans of the village included twenty-six graduates, one of whom was a district agricultural officer, and another a district superintendent officer; four were doctors, seven trained teachers and one an engineer. With education and a certain amount of prosperity came the aspiration for social equality, which was being denied to them.

The incident was communally interpreted by the RSS and VHP as "an act performed by several thousand Muslims, both men and women, from the surrounding areas, who invaded the village and forced the Harijans to convert."[3] It seems clear, however, that the VHP could not reconcile itself to the issues which were brought to the fore by the Meenakshipuram mass conversions, despite the linkages it had drawn in its early years between casteism (rules of purity and pollution) and conversions. The agenda of social reform contained in the original charter had become overshadowed. The VHP's socially privileged and conservative character had much to do with this. That continued oppression by the high-caste Hindus could lead to a point when untouchables would make a total break from the Hindu fold was something that had little place in the VHP social understanding. This understanding also denied agency to the socially depressed classes, who, of their own volition, could detach from a community and join another. It is this break that a conservative upper-caste Hindu seemed unable to bear and accept—primarily because, it can well be argued, this reveals a store of embarrassments and uncovers many unpleasant facts within Hindu society structured by Brahminical Hinduism (Rai 1993: 233).

The Meenakshipuram episode was widely publicised by the VHP and other organisations like the Hindu Munnani and the Arya Samaj, after which, it is reported, seven of the converts reconverted to Hinduism (Khan 1991: 49). The VHP floated the Sanskriti Raksha Yojana (Programme to Protect Culture) immediately after the incident. In November and December 1982, it launched the Jana Jagrana Abhiyana (Campaign for People's Awakening) to "warn" the Hindus about "the international conspiracy to devour Hinduism." During this campaign the VHP managed to collect some funds from the public as donations. However, apart from making monetary contributions people generally remained indifferent to the issue.

The 1980s thereafter saw the VHP preoccupied with planning and holding campaigns, conferences and processions at a regional level for "national integration." The issue of religious conversion was much hyped, and was projected as a grave threat to national security and integrity.[4] State intervention was demanded by the VHP to supplement its efforts to check the activities of Christian missionaries. The VHP's Marg Darshak Mandal, a committee of

[3] "How Meenakshipuram has become Rehmatnagar," *Organiser*, 21 June 1981, 6.
[4] *Hindu Vishva*, July 1981, 3.

sadhus to guide the VHP in formulating its policies and programmes, formed the Dharma Sansad, a kind of Hindu religious parliament, in 1982. This body consisted of sadhus and sants of diverse Hindu sects who were willing to come together on a single platform to agitate for specific issues across the whole range of demands of the VHP. The Dharma Sansad, as a religious congregation, was expected to give society a "Hindu" perspective on social and political matters.

After the Meenakshipuram incident, the VHP intensified its drive against conversions. Its interest in tribal areas found renewed fervour, which brought it in direct contact with Christian missionary work. Now, once again after the 1960s, its ire turned towards Christian missionaries. In 1985, the VHP Board of Trustees resolved that there should be a legal ban on the conversion of Hindus, and that the inflow of foreign money in the name of service projects and various other social, cultural and charitable purposes should be stopped.[5] In 1986, the VHP Governing Council pushed forth the above resolution, demanding that the government should

> impose a total ban on the inflow of large foreign funds into the country in the name of Service Projects; turn out of the country all such foreign missionaries who are engaged in anti-national activities and withdraw the facilities being given to the various Christian Organisations in the name of Minority Rights.[6]

The scale of Christian conversions was repeatedly publicised as unpardonable and as having left even Islamic conversions behind. They were dubbed as being backed by more solid political support—as the note below, though poorly written, indicates:

> Eight percent population of Bharat reside in Vananchal [tribal areas]. The medical facility, employment, education and other facility are scarcely available. On the other hand British supported missionaries wanted to convert all of them. Proselitization [*sic*] politics of the area ashamed even Islamic conversion of India. Vanvasi's fought British for their existence,

5 "Ban on Conversion of Hindus and on inflow of foreign money used for conversion," (resolution of the Board of Trustees in a meeting at Pune on 13 January 1985), in Sharma, *Vishva Hindu Parishad ke Prastav*, 55.

6 "Christian missionaries' conspiracy in India," (demand of the Governing Council of the VHP in a meeting at Bhopal on 3 May 1986), in Sharma, *Vishva Hindu Parishad Ke Prastav*, 54.

> culture and faith. The British brutely anihiliated [*sic*] the revolties and opened these area for missionary conversion.[7]

India was now increasingly projected as "Hindu"—such linkages were assumed even if not always articulated.

Strengthening of the Organisational Structure

In the course of boosting its activities, the VHP also began strengthening its organisational structure. At the expense of a slight digression, a brief description here of the organisational structure of the VHP would be useful. The Board of Trustees *(Nyasi Mandal)* and the Governing Council *(Prabandh Samiti)* have been established as the two main deliberative and executive bodies, with members appointed for life. The Board of Trustees, according to the VHP constitution, has a maximum of 101 members — 71 from India and 30 from abroad. It is structured as a deliberative and advisory body whose members, without holding any functional post within the VHP, attend its programmes and helped the organisation in various ways from time to time. Most of the members of the Board of Trustees are not members of the RSS.

At the apex of the VHP organisational hierarchy is a president, followed by a general secretary and three joint-general secretaries. This leadership panel heads the VHP in India and overseas. At the all-India level there are secretaries and joint-secretaries, all of whom are members of the Governing Council. There are departments or divisions, such as those for publications, accounts, external affairs, Sanskrit-promotion, celebration of festivals *(parva samanvya)*, temple-protection, and the religious leaders division *(dharmacharya vibhag)*—each looked after by a joint-secretary. At present there are eighteen such departments functioning.

The VHP organise its work into five geographical *anchals* (zones). The five zones are: Uttaranchal (North), Pashchimanchal (West), Madhyanchal (Central), Poorvanchal (East) and Dakshinanchal (South). These zones are divided into *kshetras* (regions), regions are further divided into *prants* (provinces), provinces are divided into *vibhags* (blocks), blocks are divided into *zilas* (districts), districts are

[7] D. S. Chauhan (Secretary, V. G. P. Ghorawal), "Regaining of Past Glory of Vananchal," *Vanvasi Kalyan Kendra*, 53.

divided into *prakhands*, and prakhands are further divided into *upkhands*. Each upkhand has a population of approximately two thousand, and a prakhand of about one hundred thousand.

The geographical division of the country into units by the VHP, as described above, is starkly different from the official administrative division. The map of India was redrawn to create twenty-two regional provinces. The task of this distinct mapping was not a difficult one because the existing RSS organisational network provided a ready model to be emulated, and the VHP borrowed its organisational set-up from the RSS. There are differences in smaller units of work, such as those at the district and village level, and the terminologies used to describe the various levels are distinct. For example, the VHP's smallest unit is called an "upkhand," while the RSS's smallest unit is known as the "shakha"; but broadly, the mapping style is the same.

The prakhand is the main unit of activity in the VHP organisation. Its meetings are held once every month, but the number of meetings in a month may increase if the matter at hand is of an urgent nature—as happened during the Ayodhya agitation in the early 1990s. It was considered necessary to form a small unit of activity, namely the prakhand, "to enable even common people to devote their time for social work after satisfactorily fulfilling their family and domestic obligations and responsibilities."[8] The total number of prakhands demarcated on the map in 1995 was 7,137, but only 4,560 of them were functioning.[9] In 1989–90, however, the number of prakhands declared by the VHP was 6,988, but only 2,355 of these were working.[10] The prakhand meetings usually discuss politicised religious issues, for example, the various agitational programmes to be undertaken—such as that of the Ramjanmabhoomi (RJB) and demands concerning various other temples—the "infiltration" of Bangladeshi Muslims into India, the issue of minority "appeasement" by the state, religious conversions by Christian

8 Nana Bhagwat, "Organisation is Strength," *Hindu Vishva*, silver jubilee issue, 1989–1990, 24, English edition.

9 Raghunandan Prasad Sharma, *Satat sadhna yatra ke tees varsh 1964–1994* (Thirty years of devoted meditation) (New Delhi: Vishva Hindu Parishad Publication, n.d. but in print in 1995), 8.

10 Nana Bhagwat, "Organisation is strength," *Hindu Vishva*, silver jubilee issue, 1989–1990, 24.

missionaries and Muslims, corruption in public offices, the VHP's principles and objectives, principles of the Hindu nation, and westernisation of society.

The table below gives a clear idea of the VHP organisational grid.

Table 1: Organisational Structure of the Vishva Hindu Parishad

Anchal or Zone	Kshetra or Region	Prant or Province
Uttaranchal	1. Chandigarh	-Jammu and Kashmir, Punjab and Himachal Pradesh
	2. Indraprastha	-Haryana, Rajasthan and Indraprastha (Delhi area)
Madhyanchal	1. Lucknow	-Eastern Uttar Pradesh and Western Uttar Pradesh
	2. Bhopal	-Mahakoshal and Madhya Bharat
Poorvanchal	1. Patna	-Bihar and Orissa
	2. Calcutta	-Assam and West Bengal
Dakshinanchal	1. Madras	-Tamil Nadu and Kerala
	2. Bangalore	-Andhra Pradesh and Karnataka
Pashchimanchal	1. Mumbai	-Mumbai and Gujarat
	2. Pune	-Maharashtra and Vidharbh

Source: Nana Bhagwat, "Organisation is Strength," *Hindu Vishva*, silver jubilee issue, 1989–90, 23.

Ekatmata Yatra

Coming back to its programmes, the VHP organised an ekatmata yagna yatra programme to be held for a month, from 16 November 1983 to 16 December 1983.[11] This event marks a watershed in the history of the VHP, in the sense that this was the first organised,

[11] The VHP planned three main yatras:
one, from Kathmandu in Nepal to Rameswaram in Tamil Nadu;
two, from Gangasagar in coastal West Bengal, to Somnath in Gujarat;
three, from Haradwar in Uttar Pradesh to Kanyakumari, the southernmost point of India. Besides these, a number of small yatras were taken out, covering the countryside. In the course of these yatras, 1.5 million 50 cc plastic bottles of Ganges water were sold by the VHP. See Sumit Mitra, "Road to Revival," *India Today*, 30 November 1983, 82.

countrywide mass programme it undertook. With these month-long processions criss-crossing the country, the VHP launched itself into large-scale activism—and I shall call this political activism—by organising a programme that aimed to be a mass movement. A lot of planning, organisational skills and resources went into the yatras that aimed to meet the so-called danger from internal and external divisive forces.[12] The smallest of all organisational units of the VHP was activated into an orchestrated common action.

From this point onwards, the VHP shed its nature of a random worker and tried its hand at mass-level political activism. So far, within India it had intermittently worked in certain regions and occasionally organised religious sammelans and conventions, ostensibly to protect Hindu dharma. It had tried to stop tribals and Dalits (those placed outside the classical Hindu caste hierarchy), who sought social equality, from converting to Islam and Christianity. Now the VHP attempted to take on a new role for itself, that of a political organiser and political leader of the Hindus. Though it never ventured into electoral politics directly, it did try to influence voting trends by campaigning energetically for the BJP from the late 1980s.

The VHP yatras received cooperation from district and state administration and were able to pass uninterrupted through most towns and districts. The VHP leaders—namely, Harmohan Lal, Ashok Singhal and a few others—had met the president of India, Giani Zail Singh, before the start of the yatras, and had briefed him on their aim, the route they would take and their schedule.[13] According to Giriraj Kishore, a senior VHP leader, Bahraich in Uttar Pradesh was under curfew but the district magistrate lifted the curfew for six hours for the yatra to pass uninterrupted through the town. During this period a well-publicised programme was held and the district magistrate accompanied by his wife attended it and performed the *poojas* (prayers).[14] In the VHP programme at Imphal (Manipur), the deputy chief minister of the state was the chief guest.[15]

The then prime minister, Indira Gandhi, did not reply to three letters from the VHP, inviting her to their central rally in New Delhi

[12] See reports on yatras, *Times of India*, 13, 17 November 1983.

[13] A photograph of VHP leaders meeting the then president of India, Giani Zail Singh, published in *Ekatmata Yajna 1983* (New Delhi: Vishva Hindu Parishad Publication, 1984), between pages 12–13.

[14] Giriraj Kishore, "Report on Ekatmata Yajna," *Ekatmata Yajna 1983*, 13–14.

[15] Ibid.

on 17 November, but she did not personally issue any statement discouraging the rally either. The organisers of the processions interpreted her silence as *mounam sanmatilakshanam*, implying that silence is a sign of consent.[16] It is alleged that the yatras had the tacit support of Mrs Gandhi, but she was advised not to greet the yatra when it arrived in New Delhi, to maintain the secular values of the Congress Party and the Indian state.[17] The case, however, was that Mrs Gandhi had begun cosseting Hindu sentiments, which had much to do with the weakening of the Congress Party organisation.

The yatra programme attempted to involve as many Hindus as possible and with this purpose tried to reach out to towns and also the villages. Involving the countryside was considered necessary and important for expansion of social reach. The RSS's work, in its own view, "was confined to urban and suburban areas while even today majority of Hindus live in villages; the RSS should, therefore establish themselves immediately in villages."[18] Reaching out to the villages was seen as necessary for expansion of the social base.

It is important to point out that the yatras were organised against the backdrop of the Punjab and Assam militancy that had developed out of movements for political autonomy and, subsequently, secession. In this period—1983 and 1984—the unrest in these regions was in one of its worst phases, witnessing both state repression and regional militant retaliation. During these yatras the saffron-clad sadhus mobilised by the VHP and the RSS had one central theme running through their ardent speeches: "Hinduism is in danger,"[19] to counter which there was a need for "national unity" and "national integration." It is interesting, however, that "national unity" and "integration" were used interchangeably with Hindu unity and integration.[20] The then general secretary of the VHP, Harmohan Lal, admitted in an interview that developments in Assam were behind the idea of these yatras, as was the problem of conversions—

[16] Sumit Mitra, "Road to Revival," *India Today*, 30 November 1983, 84.

[17] Manini Chatterjee, "Saffron Scourge: The VHP's Communal Fascism," *Frontline*, 10 September 1993, 8.

[18] H. A. Bablani, "Hindus must unite for survival," *Organiser*, 20 November 1983, 12.

[19] Sumit Mitra, "Road to Revival," *India Today*, 30 November 1983, 84.

[20] See reports on yatras: *Hindustan Times* 2, 3, 15, 16, 18, 25 November 1983; *Times of India* 13, 15, 17 November 1983; *Organiser* 13, 27 November 1983 and 8 January 1984.

especially after the Meenakshipuram episode.[21] He pointed out that a need was felt within the organisation that a special programme must be launched to "tell the Harijans that they are welcome and if those who have left Hindu society and wish to return, they can."[22] This was a significant step, considering that it was also the time of a swift Dalit upsurge and the rise of Kanshi Ram as a strong Dalit leader[23] in North India. Kanshi Ram's presence might have meant that the Dalit vote would move away from mainstream political parties—primarily, the Congress and the BJP. Harmohan Lal also talked about the Punjab problem, making it a point to mention that the Sikhs had been participating in these yatras.[24] Balasaheb Deoras, who was then heading the RSS, declared in a message to RSS workers in Punjab in December the same year that the Sikhs are part of Hindu society, and that in their history the Sikhs had to spend most of their time fighting the Muslims (Deoras 1997: 143–44). The yatras aimed to popularise the idea of a united Hindu society in the wake of regional movements for autonomy and secession. This heavily devotionalised yatra programme was an attempt to call for a strong and centralised Indian state, and check socio-political discontent through organised religious fervour.

A further partition of the Indian state was a fear that was overplayed during the yatra programme by the VHP. This fear was first hyped and then sought to be assuaged by messages calling for Hindu unity. The expansion of the social base of organisations closely associated with the RSS, and testing the ground as to whether this social support could be translated into electoral support, also seemed to motivate this mass programme. Harmohan Lal admitted that there was no economic content to the yatra programme and said that the most important purpose was to bring people together and make them realise the importance of working together.[25] Once this unity was achieved other problems could be easily tackled.[26]

[21] Harish Khare, "Time for Hindu Renaissance," *Hindustan Times*, 25 November 1983.

[22] Ibid.

[23] Kanshi Ram founded the Bahujan Samaj Party in 1984. It was born out of BAMCEF, an organisation of government employees, led by Kanshi Ram.

[24] Harish Khare, "Time for Hindu Renaissance," *Hindustan Times*, 25 November 1983.

[25] Ibid.

[26] Ibid.

The three Hindu symbols of Bharatmata (portrayed as a Hindu goddess—often as an incarnation of Durga/Kali, the symbol of sakti or power), Gangamata and to some extent Gaumata, were used extensively by the VHP during these yatras.[27] Here it is important to recall that the late nineteenth and early twentieth centuries had witnessed attempts to define the identity of an overarching "Hindu community" through social, literary and intellectual movements, which sought to rally opinion around sacred Hindu religious symbols. Two examples of this would be cow protection, where the cow was taken to be the symbol of Hindu religion, and hence of the "community," and the Ganesha festival (Pandey 1990; Yang 1980; Frietag 1980), popularised as a rallying point of nationalism, primarily in the Marathi-speaking areas.[28] The first comes mainly from the areas comprising the Ganges plain or what is today the Hindi-speaking area, and was not regarded as directly related to a self-conscious nationalist agenda. The second is one where religious symbolism was used to rally Hindus to the specific needs of nationalist politics. While this is not the place to go further into a discussion of these movements, one should note that both these trends of early Hindu mobilisation have a strong presence in the activities and world view of contemporary VHP activists. Thus, Bharatmata, Gangamata and Gaumata became the three mother symbols on which the VHP organised its mass campaign. It used these symbols as symbols of Hindu unity, in other words, national unity. The *Hindu Chetna* says,

[27] Gaumata was the rallying symbol of the cow protection agitation of 1966–67, in which the VHP was one of the leading participants. This agitation, however, did not become a large-scale movement and was restricted in its scope to some parts of North India, like Delhi and some districts of Uttar Pradesh. It is only in 1983–84 that the VHP was able to take these symbols into practically every region of the country, and receive popular support.

[28] In Gyanendra Pandey's (1990: 199) words, "The all-India 'Hindu community' (and, to a large extent, the all-India 'Muslim community' too) was a colonial creation for . . . the social and economic changes brought by colonialism. Indian efforts to defend indigenous religions and culture against western missionary attacks, the 'unifying' drive of the colonial state—which was marked at the level of administrative structure and attempted political control ('Muslims' must not be antagonized, 'Hindu' sensibilities must not be touched), and the very history of movements like that of the 19th century, tended to promote the idea of all-India 'Hindu community' and an all-India 'Muslim community' which was supposedly ranged against one another for much of the time."

> Bharatmata and its symbols—Gangamata and Gaumata have the eternal essence of bringing together each and every Bharatiya. These three have the ability to unite Hindu society, uplifting it from caste, sect and language.[29]

Used in mythicised forms they proved potential symbols of mobilisation. According to Ashok Singhal,

> Wherever the chariots went they enthused the masses with respect and devotion towards their country, their motherland and their mother Ganga .... Hindu society which was divided for centuries became well organised and united as a single individual.[30]

The selection of symbols and the construction of myths were done meticulously by the VHP. For example, the cow, a ubiquitous feature of India, helped to a certain extent, to situate the VHP in the remote village domain and held the potential for generating an anti-minority fervour. The aim was that the symbols should find ready acceptability among all Hindus, beyond specific regional or caste boundaries. Symbols, myths and perceptions, if restricted in their imaginative reach to certain sections or regions, cannot form the basis for a pan-Hindu/Indian identification. Their remoteness from the everyday world of people would make their acceptance difficult. Therefore, their selection has to be based upon specific ground realities. It has been the effort of all national and other identity-based movements to focus on certain universally held beliefs of their group, and to initiate political mobilisation through publicly visible and easily accessible symbols which embody them. These beliefs and mobilisation around symbols are the basis on which unity of political action is built. The VHP worked in a similarly strategised fashion.

While it is possible to identify such beliefs and symbols, mobilisation across social and geographical space, especially in a country of India's size and complexity, is difficult to organise. Symbols and myths while having a strong influence in certain spatial locations are not as effective in others. For instance, the VHP's attempt at mass activity and handling of religious symbols was not as successful in South India as it was in the North. In subsequent years also, its religious campaigns for political mobilisation were more successful in North India.

[29] "Dwitiya Ekatmata Yatra" (The second ekatmata yatra), *Hindu Chetna*, 16 July 1995, 7.

[30] Ashok Singhal, "Ekatmata yagagni sada prajjwalit rahe" (May the ekatmata yajna fire be forever bright), *Ekatmata Yajna 1983*, 9.

The yatras invited severe criticism from the Congress and left parties, on the grounds that they were organised under the inspiration of the RSS to exploit the religious sentiments of the people and create communal disturbance.[31] It cannot be denied that the yatras as attempts to "awaken Hindus" throughout the country[32] were a complete Hindu-centric affair and their messages were based on a selective and communal reading of events. This made the minorities insecure and unable to identify with their purpose. Responding to the criticism, Chinmayananda, founder president of the VHP, said that those who opposed the yatras "have no respect for national unity and suffer from alienation from the country."[33] He, thus, clubbed the VHP "Hindu" and the "Indian" together to strengthen the narrow perception that defiance of the former means detachment from the latter.

The yatras used Hindu symbols for mobilisation, and they began and ended at major Hindu pilgrimage centres. The leaders who attended the ceremonies were members of the VHP, RSS and the BJP, and the three main yatras assembled at the RSS headquarters in Nagpur, on 29 November 1983. A large number of sadhus of varied sects were also involved in this campaign to reach out to devotees of every possible sect, and thus to fuse, in public perception, the ideology of the VHP with widely held religious beliefs. Their speeches were replete with sectarian, communal and abstract interpretation of the political situation, without pinpointing the exact nature of the problems talked about. The attempt was to get the people thus approached to identify with the ideology and programmes of the organisation. For instance, in the words of Ashok Singhal, who was the joint-general secretary of VHP at that time, "The Hindus today, are being subjected to numerous insults and humiliations in their own homeland."[34] According to him,

> The aim of the ekatmata yatra is social harmony and brotherhood. . . . It is because of social discord and poverty that foreign powers such as Islam and Christianity with their monetary strength are conspiring to divide Hindu society. [35]

[31] See *Hindu*, 3 November 1983; and *Hindustan Times*, 16 November 1983.

[32] "Dwitiya Ekatmata Yatra," *Hindu Chetna*, 16 July 1995, 7.

[33] "Ganga and Bharat Mata are symbols of National Unity," *Organiser*, 13–19 November 1983, 1.

[34] Ashok Singhal in *Organiser*, 8 January 1984, 4.

[35] Ashok Singhal, "Ekatmata Yatra," *Ekatmata Yajna 1983*, 9.

Hindu self-protection against Islam and Christianity—both of which were dubbed "foreign powers"—was constantly harped upon.

The yatras were met with a tremendous devotional response in the course of their processional routes, in both towns and villages. Response was reported to be overwhelming in the case of women, whose religious devotion led them to participate in religious ceremonies of the processions in large numbers. Encouraged by the throbbing response to its ekatmata yatra programme the VHP, from the following year onwards, launched its Ramjanmabhoomi liberation campaign. It looked as if the RSS's goal of Hindu nationalism was after all beginning to gain clarity within the VHP.

The "Bond" with Rama

The VHP-RSS leaders, amidst much fanfare on Ramnaumi day (31 March 1984), resolved to take up the issue of Babri Masjid–Ramjanmabhoomi and wrest control of the Babri mosque site for the construction of a Rama temple.[36] The Dharma Sansad, in a meeting on 7 and 8 April 1984 at New Delhi, resolved to "liberate" the Ramjanmabhoomi.[37] It was widely known that the issue was communally sensitive. It had generated serious communal tension in the past, but it matched well the sectarian goal of Hindu nationalism.

At this time the Punjab crisis was at its height. Soon after the army intervention at the Golden Temple (Amritsar) in June 1984, Mrs Gandhi openly declared in a speech at Garhwal that Hindu dharma was under attack and made an appeal to save Hindu *sanskriti* (culture) from Sikh and Muslim attack (Kothari 1988: 247). Her government's flirtation with Hindu chauvinist themes, not generally associated with the Congress Party, seemed a definite way of consolidating and expanding its social base at a time when the Congress-I faced an erosion of mass support and a fractured party organisation (Vanaik 1985: 78–79). This has been called an "astonishing development of the early 1980s," and something which many who are familiar with the Congress during Nehru's lifetime, or in Mrs Gandhi's earlier years as prime minister, would find "difficult to believe" (Manor 1988: 80). She began to display an antagonistic attitude towards Sheikh Abdullah's National Conference in Kashmir and towards Sikh militants in Punjab (who were earlier encouraged by

[36] Reported in *Organiser*, 29 April 1984, 10.

[37] Ashok Singhal, quoted in Manini Chatterjee, "Saffron Scourge: The VHP's Communal Fascism," *Frontline*, 10 September 1993, 8.

Congress to divide the opposition Akalis). This appears to have won over to the Congress-I, in the Kashmir and Delhi elections of 1983, Hindu voters who traditionally voted for the Bharatiya Jana Sangh (Andersen and Damle 1987: 231; Manor 1988: 80).

The RSS supported military action against the Sikh militants at the Golden Temple (Andersen and Damle 1987: 232). The VHP leaders when closely questioned admitted that they admired Gandhi's "toughness" towards Pakistan and her "positive role" in Jammu and Kashmir.[38] The leanings towards Hindu chauvinist and anti-Sikh sentiments continued up to the elections of 1984.

After about a year, the VHP—again on Ramnaumi day—renewed its pledge to "liberate" RJB. The resolution that was passed said,

> Lord Rama was the only source of inspiration not only for the Indians but also for the entire mankind. Several neighbouring countries like Indonesia, Sri Lanka, Indo-China, Mauritius have been influenced by Indian culture through Lord Rama. . . . The Hindu Samaj will deem itself to be still a "slave" until the freedom of this area is achieved.[39]

The construction of a Rama temple at Ayodhya provided the VHP with a potent agenda for mass mobilisation, and for this reason the temple issue became the central focus of the VHP's activity. In this phase, it came to rely heavily on Hindu cultural metaphors to spread its message.

The VHP's most important symbol of mobilisation, which brought it considerable publicity, was Rama, a revered Hindu deity of North India. It would be interesting to probe the question of why the VHP selected Rama over a plethora of other divine beings in Hindu mythology that would also share similar attributes and similar popularity as him, for example, Shiva or Kali/Durga, or even Krishna? Some factors can be shown to have contributed to the VHP's selection of Rama and to indicate that it was not a random choice. The dispute over Rama's so-called birthplace was already a local issue of considerable importance when the VHP took up Rama and the cause of "Ramjanmabhoomi's liberation." Rama is a familiar name in India, and he figures as one of the most important deities within popular Hindu traditions at the local level in North India. Rama and his exploits have been integrated into the myths and legends of people over a large part of India, except perhaps in some areas of the South. He also represents one of the better-known

[38] Sumit Mitra, "Road to Revival," *India Today*, 30 November 1983.
[39] See *Organiser*, 14 April 1985, 25.

ethical ideals of Hindu thought, and the epic, Ramayana, is familiar all over India as an exposition of everyday morality. Local songs, stories and histories are replete with references to the life of Rama, and every region in India has been touched by some episodes of the mythical Ramayana. This is also because every year, in the month of October, episodes from it, depicting the virtuous lives of Rama and his wife Sita, are dramatised in residential localities and playgrounds during the Hindu festival of Dussehera. In these theatrical performances, which are also arenas of community participation, Rama through his godliness defeats the evil forces, represented by the demon king Ravana who attacks the accepted virtues and morals of society. Rama may not be worshipped as the main deity by many people, but he is familiar to all as one of the important Hindu deities. Apart from the orthodox Hindu versions of Valmiki and Tulsidas, the various other living traditions of the Ramayana—both as sanctified religious tradition, as amongst the Buddhists and Jains, and as popular culture among the masses—make Rama a widely known deity.

Another factor which facilitated the VHP's bond with Rama is the tremendous growth of tele-media in India in the mid-eighties, though under state control and supervision. Television sets spread into most middle-class homes and even entered the hutments, where a single set would be watched in a group by a large number of people. This process also spread to many villages, where village councils arranged for television sets in the community halls. In 1987–88 the serialised telecast of the Ramayana on the national television network encouraged the VHP to accelerate its campaign to turn Rama into the supreme moral ideal for the Hindus.[40]

The commentary in the beginning of each televised episode depicted the telecast Ramayana as a synthesis of approximately twenty-two versions of the epic from various regions and sects. The producer claimed this Ramayana to be a self-avowed narration relevant to the needs of modern India and a "symbol of national unity and integration"

[40] The nature and impact of the tele-media, and specifically of the televised Ramayana, have spurred some insightful research (Thapar 1989; Lutgendorf 1997; Rajagopal 2001). Thapar, in her discussion of the local traditions of Ramayana, points towards a prospect of state-sponsored cultural homogenisation, partly through the airing of this particular version on national television. On the other hand, as a commentator removed from contemporary Indian politics, Lutgendorf takes a much more uninvolved view and chooses to focus attention on the televised Ramananda Sagar's Ramayana as another enthralling version of the religious epic. Rajagopal, in his book, tries to establish the correlation between television-mediated politics and the rise of Hindu nationalism, and argues that for both Hindu nationalism and liberalisation the tele-media came in handy to expand beyond their existent narrow confines.

(Lutgendorf 1997: 222). It is said that this televised Ramayana was the most widely watched television programme in India. Many who saw it were first-time television viewers, and many watched it with feelings of great devotion equalling that seen in a temple during actual worship. This telecast went on for 104 Sunday mornings, when unprecedented numbers of Indians sat in their homes or community television rooms between nine and ten o'clock in the morning, expressing their common affiliation to Rama.[41] A meeting of the Board of Trustees of the VHP at this time reiterated its previous resolutions regarding the "solution of the Ramjanmabhoomi Mukti [liberation]."[42] It directed all the VHP units, whether in the country or outside, to mobilise public opinion for the Ramjanmabhoomi agitation, and "to marshal the strength of Hindus to achieve" these goals, and to be "prepared for come what may."[43]

It would be useful to discuss the specific manner in which Rama was used as a symbol for mass mobilisation, and how his image was subtly transformed to suit the larger interests of the VHP. In some pictures, the VHP depicted Rama as a calm and composed individual with a smile on his face (as on the cover of the *Hindu Vishva* of October 1991). This was primarily to project the impression that a Hindu and the Hindu community per se are generous, good-natured and tolerant. The VHP, however, through stickers, cut-outs, magazine covers and calendars also made a tremendous effort to publicise Rama as a strong warrior, fully armed, standing unmoved and determined before a surging tide, with a stoic expression on his attractive face, his open long hair flying against the wind. Rama was presented by the VHP as a *rashtrapurusha* and also a *maryadapurshottam.*[44] The calmness

[41] It would be worthwhile to remember the insights provided by Benedict Anderson in his work (1991).

[42] For details see appendix III.

[43] Ibid.

[44] "Rashtrapurusha" means man of the nation. "Purshottam" means the perfect man, one who is not given to digression or provocation, who is restrained in temperament and displays equanimity of behaviour; and "maryadapurshottam" means the actions and thoughts of the perfect man which uphold the "honour" of his position. One is reminded of the special issue of *Kalyan* (1930) on the Ramayana, edited by Hanuman Prasad Poddar and Jwala Prasad Kanodiya, which contains an article called "Maryadapurshottam Rama" by Rao Bahadur Vaidya, 33–35. This article makes a comparison between Aurangzeb and Rama to bring out the latter's so-called goodness of character. It says that Aurangzeb never kept his word, he tricked Shivaji and took him and his sons into captivity, he vandalised and destroyed the holy places of Hindus, and his rule was the complete reverse of *Ramrajya* (rule of Rama). The article then says that looking at this comparison, the readers will have some idea of how and why Shri Rama was a "maryadapurshottam" (p 35).

or *shanta rasa* with which he is traditionally associated came to be replaced by aggression or *ugra bhava* (Kapur 1993: 85). Rama was transformed from a tranquil, tender figure to an interventionist warrior (Kapur 1992: 48). Rama's anger signified, according to the VHP, that a Hindu had the potential to take the offensive if it came to "protecting" his rights and interests.

The depictions of the various moods of Rama and other gods and goddesses not only define their various aspects, but also enable the devotees to cultivate corresponding traits and attitudes within themselves (Datta 1993: 50). As such, the VHP tried to popularise a belligerent image of Rama which symbolised working for, and devotion to, a Hindu *rashtra* (nation). The VHP suggested to those it considered outside the precincts of Hindu society that a Hindu is as virtuous and invincible as Rama, and at the same time told the Hindus that they had to be like Rama, generous and good-natured as well as unconquerable when it came to defending their community rights. These two themes were simultaneously worked on by the VHP.

The traditional depiction of Rama in lithographs has been accompanied by a mood of tranquility and serenity. Even in Tulsidas's Ramacharita Manasa, which is more popular as a sacred text than Valmiki's Ramayana, it is calmness and tranquility which are associated with Rama—he rarely assumes an angry disposition. Why is it then, contrary to Rama's usual mythical attributes, that an aggressive picture of his is publicised by the VHP? In reply to this question an activist of the VHP said that this was done to arouse a burning fervour *(josh)* in the Hindus.[45] The consistent calls by the VHP for "virility," for the protection of the motherland, fitted perfectly its choice of Rama as a rashtrapurusha who could protect the holy and vulnerable Bharatmata from the "sinister" Muslims, just as he saved his wife Sita from Ravana. Every Hindu was called upon to be like Rama and protect Bharatmata. The VHP itself admitted that Rama's name is not only a symbol of devotion, but also of power, that it was the most potent and reliable way of galvanising and unifying the Hindus.[46] The VHP leadership claimed that the one who moves towards Rama prospers in life, and the one who opposes Rama would lose all during his lifetime; therefore it would be because the VHP chose to

[45] Raghunandan Prasad Sharma in an informal conversation with the author at New Delhi on 30 January 1997.

[46] Kailash Chandra Kotiya, "Ram shila se Ram mandir tak" (From Rama's brick to Rama's temple), *Hindu Vishva*, January 1990, 7. This article was first published on 5 November 1989 in *Rajasthan Patrika*.

adopt Rama as its model that it is moving ahead.[47] Thus, Rama came to occupy an exalted status above all other divine entities for the VHP. Moreover, he came to be projected as a historical figure, whose actions (especially the slaying of Ravana) brought not only "south India, but the entire geographical expanse between Madagascar and Australia, within the influence of Aryavarta [the land of the Aryans]."[48]

This sort of elevation of one divine entity over the rest is not something unheard of. From the medieval era of Indian history there have been many instances within "Hinduism" of elevating a particular divine being over the rest of the pantheon, for instance, the special place given to Krishna by Meera, to Radha and Krishna by Chaitanya, and to Kali by Sri Ramakrishna. The difference, however, is that this elevation was never forced on those who were unwilling to accept it, and also, it did not have an agenda that was political, and went against the minorities. The VHP accepted the multiplicity of divine entities worshipped by the Hindus, but its overarching conception of a Hindu identity was built around the cult of Rama. And, it should be added that this conception was overarchingly political, and had an exclusive agenda directed against the religious minorities built in it. The VHP succeeded in drawing national attention to, and consequently, popular support for, its position regarding Rama and Ramjanmabhoomi.[49]

It has been pointed out that Hindu nationalism, specifically the nationalism espoused by the RSS, cannot be classified "straightforwardly as a fascist movement" (Jaffrelot 1996: 63). One of the reasons stated is that the movement has lacked "the obsession with the supreme leader" and that "it does not rely on the central figure of the leader" (Jaffrelot 1996: 62, 64). However, interestingly, in the absence of such a supreme central leader around whom the movement could revolve, the direction, especially since the mid-1980s, has been to push forth the figure of Rama as a supreme leader and an exemplary personality to be emulated. The VHP-RSS leaders tried to centre the movement around Rama.

[47] Nrittya Gopal Das, a prominent VHP sadhu, in a personal interview at Ayodhya on 19 February 1996.

[48] "Ram ki Aitihasikta" (The Historicity of Rama), *Vandemataram*, 19–25 October 1993, 8.

[49] Subsequently, when the VHP and its allied organisations tried to raise controversy over the disputed temples/mosques at Mathura's *Krishnajanma Sthan* (Krishna's birthplace) or the Vishwanath temple at Varanasi, no such support was forthcoming—even from states like Uttar Pradesh, which had been swept by popular fervour for the Ayodhya cause.

Insistence by the VHP on supposedly Rama-like traits in a Hindu was developed in accordance with its mass campaign for the "restoration" of the Babri mosque site. As the campaign picked up, this insistence grew and became unprecedentedly clamorous during the last few months of 1992. .Hanuman, the monkey god and mythical devotee of Rama, also became an important projected symbol for mass emulation.

Birth of the Bajrang Dal

While talking of Hanuman, I must take a detour to mention something about the Bajrang Dal, launched by the VHP in the mid-eighties. To organise popular support, the VHP branched into a subsidiary organisation, the Bajrang Dal (the name means army of monkeys). Programmatic success and extension of social support also necessitated the formation of such a mass organisation. The formation of the Bajrang Dal was symbolic of the transformation which the VHP was going through—from a small entity with a limited following to a mass-based organisation with an extended social base. The little-known organisation of the sixties and seventies was turning into a vociferous broad-based entity. This also indicated an increasing politicisation of the VHP's Hinduisation agenda. A young energetic cadre with muscle power was needed to put in the necessary amount of spadework for ideological dissemination and mobilisation of the masses. If Christian missionaries in the interior tribal areas had to be countered effectively and popular mobilisations had to be attempted for Ramjanmabhoomi or cow protection or "national integration," a lot of energy and committed workers were needed. A body of activists which could be prepared for leadership at the state and local levels was also required as a future strength of the organisation. Hence the youth wing, Bajrang Dal, came into existence.

The launching of the Bajrang Dal pointed towards another major change in the VHP: preparing a leadership from its own brotherhood rather than borrowing leadership from state institutions and religious bodies as in the early phase of its formation. Training in samskaras and discipline of this young membership was deemed important, necessitating reliance on the RSS shakha structure—especially for *baudhik* (intellectual) and physical training. The emphasis during such mass-based political action lay on personal contact through building of social relations within the residential town. The aim of maintaining an obvious presence in small localities was to generate among their residents an understanding that Hindutva constitutes a live and breathing movement.

The youth wing of the VHP had as its stated objectives *seva* (service), *suraksha* (defence) and samskara (training in tradition and cultural practices), and through these was promptly able to establish stable personal contact at the local plane. It is rightly pointed out that the neighbourhood—though dependent on its particular location in social space—can provide not only an ideological arena for the production and reproduction of world views, but also of well-indoctrinated workers for the Hindutva cause (Deshpande 1995: 3224).

The local-level activism involving the Bajrang Dal took different forms, ranging from a visible presence and participation in public rituals like Durga pooja and Dussehera, to socio-religious policing.[50] Its aggressive participation in the Ayodhya dispute as a subsidiary of the VHP brought it forward as a militant organisation. Also, the cow-protection movement that the VHP took on its agenda for 1996 had as its enforcer the Bajrang Dal. Its membership, in the nature of loose affiliation rather than a formally structured cadre, is primarily drawn from the lower-middle class faced with the typical problem of educated youth lacking stable employment, in a regime of growth without employment.

In the national press, the Bajrang Dal became synonymous with force, coercion and aggression. Its activities mostly involved use of physical force and physical groundwork. In fact, soon after it gained a formal shape, it displayed mobistic and lumpenistic tendencies that embodied the anger of its support base against their social conditions. This matched well with its burning conviction for Hindu cultural superiority and Hindu nationalism.

The senior VHP leaders, to implement their programmes at the local level, called upon the Bajrang Dal's ranks for physical labour. It was encouraged by the VHP to take part in local-level politics (district corporations and municipalities), and thus attempts were made to build an experienced second line of leadership. The Bajrang Dal's nature and its activities received much publicity during the *shilanyas* (laying of the foundation stone) ceremony at Ayodhya and the demolition of the Babri mosque in 1992, when its ranks moved ahead, aggressively proclaiming

[50] For example, keeping a protective eye on Hindu girls of the neighbourhood, informing on Bangladeshi Muslim boundary-crossers, protection of local cattle from slaughterhouses, relief work during natural disasters and accidents, "defence" and "protection" of temples, and the building and strengthening of Hindu values in Hindu youth. Harish Sharma in a personal interview at Baroda on 27 December 1995.

> *Jo Rama ke kam na aye woh bekar javani hai.* [A youth who cannot be put to the service of Rama is worthless.]

Vinay Katiyar, the former head of the Bajrang Dal, once remarked,

> Might is the only law I understand. Nothing else matters to me. In India it is a war-like situation as between Rama and Ravana.[51]

Ramjanmabhoomi and Politics

Coming back to the main discussion after a detour to the Bajrang Dal, I should mention that the Congress Party under Rajiv Gandhi appealed to Hindu religious sentiments in the 1984 elections. Anti-Sikh sentiments after the assassination of Mrs Gandhi were played upon. It is generally believed that the Congress succeeded in drawing towards itself the vote of a substantial number of RSS-VHP activists, though there is no conclusive evidence to substantiate this.

The Congress government, once in office, continued with its attitude to pander to Hindu communal interests. On 1 February 1986, the Faizabad District Court ordered the opening of the locks of the Babri mosque and permitted Hindus to offer prayers on the site. This decision had the support of the upper echelons of the central government and had the result of transforming the Ramjanmabhoomi–Babri Masjid issue into a controversy. A national Babri Masjid Co-ordination Committee (BMCC) was formed by some Muslim public figures who tried to mobilise opinion for restoration of the site as a mosque. However, Muslim mobilisation efforts fell far short of the VHP's attempts to generate public action in its favour.

The VHP, however, displayed displeasure at the Congress-I government's ambiguous stand on its Hindutva. The Congress-I's attempts at gaining support of Muslim fundamentalists and its balancing act to please the two communities—as displayed during the Shah Bano case in 1986—annoyed the VHP immensely. Along with the Shiv Sena in Maharashtra it stridently voiced its views on the Shah Bano issue (Engineer 1995: 82). The VHP thereafter began pressurising the government to gain control of the Mathura and Varanasi mosque sites as well. It was said that,

51 Vinay Katiyar, "It is a war like situation," interview published in *Frontline*, 24 April 1992, 9–12.

> The Hindus in India have put you [Rajiv Gandhi] in power, only Hindu majority will keep secularism alive in India, so please do not insult Hindu religious sentiments. . . . In the interest of lasting Hindu-Muslim unity and in the interest of your Government, please hand over the three religious places to Hindu *samaj* and please ban cow slaughter through an ordinance.[52]

The VHP, it seems, felt that it should get its due back from the Rajiv government, since it believed that the Hindus had brought him to power, and its demands on the government were made as "the" representative of the Hindus who had played a role in these elections. It was a reminder to Rajiv Gandhi that the Hindus had voted for him and now he should not shy away from protecting their interests.

Rajiv Gandhi's moves did much to communally vitiate politics and social relations. In addition, communally provocative statements by various organisations, including the Babri Masjid Action Committee, further exacerbated the situation. Communal violence spread through Ahmedabad and Meerut in April and May 1987. In 1987, commenting upon the prevailing communal situation in the country, the VHP leadership declared that,

> It is a matter of great concern that the Government had been tolerating the anti-national and inflammatory speeches and activities of communal Muslim leaders and not taking action against them, in accordance with the provisions of the law of the land. . . . The Board further urges the Government to take stringent legal and penal action against all such persons and elements because, the Board warns the Government, that the patriotic and brave sons of the soil shall not watch the anti-national, communal and separatist activities of such elements as mute spectators any further because the interest and service of our Motherland come first and foremost before us and we don't consider any sacrifice too great for that.[53]

The VHP leadership put the blame for the riots squarely on the Muslims, which was unsurprising, though the Hindu communal leadership (including the VHP) was no less responsible for the violence.

The Ramjanmabhoomi agitations gave an outright political character to the VHP, because it was through these agitations, or in their context, that the VHP started questioning and later challenging

[52] Dau Dayal Khanna, "Hon. Prime Minister Rajivji, Are You Listening," *Masurashram Patrika*, February 1987, 7.

[53] Resolution passed by the Board of Trustees of the VHP in a meeting at Patna on 24 April 1987, in Sharma, *Vishva Hindu Parishad Ke Prastav*, 71.

state policy on secularism and positive discrimination for Schedûled Castes, i.e., reservations. It also tried to redefine the very ethos of politics, couching it in the language of Ramrajya (kingdom of Rama, also utopia), Hindutva and Hindu rashtra. Ashok Singhal declared that the Hindus had taken a pledge that they would even give up their lives to build the Rama temple at Ayodhya.[54]

Towards the end of 1989, the VHP organised Rama *shila* (foundation stone) prayers all over the country. What is interesting is that these shila ceremonies were organised on the election eve of 1989, with the stated purpose of collection of bricks for the proposed Rama temple at Ayodhya. The Congress government at the centre, also with an eye on the elections, and reading the VHP's programme as comprising a popular movement, permitted the shilanyas of the temple. Sadhvi Rithambhara, a prominent member of the VHP, mobilised support for this *kar seva* (manual work, in service of a cause) through a taped speech released in 1989. This tape was widely circulated. The contents of the speech were markedly flavoured with an aggressive and sectarian tone. The Muslim social presence was identified as iemon" in "milk," and it was stated that they were bent on curdling it. The speech used communal stereotypes about Muslims not accepting family planning and thus increasing their number in geometric progression, having special rights, running separate religious schools, and so on. These stereotypes were juxtaposed with what, according to her, the Hindus did not possess, i.e., freedom of religious expression, security for religious processions, temples, religious beliefs and free expression of opinions. By doing this she further added to the damaging communal polarisation.

These shila *pujans* (prayers) were preceded in various towns by shila processions which became a source of widespread communal tension and riots in October and November 1989. Northern and western India, especially towns in Bihar, Gujarat, Madhya Pradesh and Rajasthan, witnessed bloody communal carnage. The VHP, in a belligerent mood, deliberately led shila processions, accompanied by much communal banter and provocative sloganeering, through predominantly Muslim residential areas. This led to serious communal riots. Violence began from the very day the shila collection began, and on those very routes through which the processions passed. It subsequently spread to the adjoining areas.

[54] "Agami Prayag ke mahakumbha par . . . Sri Ramjanmabhoomi par mandir nirman ki tithi ghoshit hogi" (In the coming mahakumbh fair at Prayag the date of the construction of the Rama temple at Ayodhya would be declared), *Hindu Chetna*, November 1988, 35.

The VHP took an aggressive and uncompromising stand from the very beginning of the processions. It was evident that the potential for social damage in its slogans and the sensitive routes it had chosen for its processions were going to raise trouble. It announced that if the government did not give it protection it would make its "own arrangements."[55] Khargone, Mhow and Ratlam in Madhya Pradesh were rocked by violence during the shila processions, and so were Palanpur, Vadavali and Cambay in Gujarat. Communal tension also led to violence in Jaipur. The VHP declined the plea of the administration to shift the venue of the Ram shila function from the communally sensitive Bapunagar area to a relatively calmer place in Ahmedabad, and declared that if any curb was imposed, notwithstanding riots, "we will fight it out."[56] In violation of all democratic and constitutional norms, the VHP's shila processions continued—and so did the riots. In Bihar the most seriously affected districts were Bhagalpur, Darbhanga, Gaya and Sitamarhi. In Bhagalpur the gruesomeness of the killing and destruction sprees led to army intervention to help ease the situation. On 1 November 1989, the death toll had reached 152 in Bhagalpur.[57] The Bihar government banned all rallies and processions on 3 November in view of the escalating communal violence in the state. However, despite the ban and continuing violence, organisation of Ram shila processions was reported in all parts of the state.[58]

The shila processions of the VHP came in for much criticism from the left parties and the secular opinion, who demanded checks on them to ensure communal harmony. However, the central government decided not to ban them, on the grounds that the police force was inadequate and that a ban would lead to more confrontation.[59] The VHP for its part threatened to launch a *satyagrah* (a mass agitation) if the shilanyas ceremony was obstructed.[60] Bajrang Dal workers were entrusted with the work of assisting and defending the shilanyas ceremony held at Ayodhya by the VHP on 9 November 1989 amidst heavy police and paramilitary presence. While towns in

[55] "Good response to Ram shila poojan," *Hindu*, 2 October 1989.

[56] "VHP refuses to shift Ram shila function venue in Ahmedabad," *Hindu*, 18 October 1989.

[57] "Bhagalpur violence spreads; toll 152," *Hindustan Times*, 1 November 1989.

[58] "Army called out in Sasaram as 6 die in riots," *Hindu*, 8 November 1989.

[59] "No ban on Ram shila rallies: PM—Bhagalpur situation reviewed," *Hindustan Times*, 27 October 1989.

[60] "VHP threatens to launch satyagrah,"*Hindustan Times*, 4 November 1989.

Bihar and Rajasthan were torn by communal riots, the shilanyas at Ayodhya took place. According to the VHP, the brick consecration ceremony (shila pujan) took place at 297,705 places and an estimated 110 million people participated.[61]

Not only did Rajiv Gandhi's government not stop the Ayodhya event, he began his own election campaign from Faizabad (not far from Ayodhya) with a call to establish Ramrajya. His address was received with loud cries of *Ramchandraji ki jai, Jai Bajrang Bali* and *Har Har Mahadev* (These can be translated as "Hail Lord Rama," "Hail Lord Hanuman," and "Hail Lord Shiva").[62] The services of Arun Govil, who acted as Rama in the television serial *Ramayana,* were taken to campaign for the Congress-I. This was obviously an attempt to counter the BJP and consolidate the Congress Party's support among the Hindu electorate.

With the shilanyas at Ayodhya performed, the VHP went forward with its demands and announced that it would begin construction of the Rama temple on 30 October 1990. The VHP's writings of this period are replete with militant utterances to evoke the "national" sentiments of the "Hindu society" to build a Rama temple at the site where the Babri mosque stood. "Paramhamsa" Ramchandra Das, a prominent sadhu of the VHP, declared,

> A Hindu is one in whose heart the flame of Hinduness is burning and who is ready to die for the nation's *dharma.*[63]

It was emphasised that,

> The history of Sri Ramjanma Bhoomi struggle is replete with sacrifices and martyrdom.[64]

Ashok Singhal said in one of the meetings of the Marg Darshak Mandal in July 1992,

[61] Manini Chatterjee, "Saffron Scourge: The VHP's Communal Fascism," *Frontline*, 10 September 1993, 8.

[62] P. K. Roy, "U.P. for the prime slots," *Frontline*, November 1989, 11.

[63] Message from "Paramhamsa" Ramchandra Das, *Hindu Vishva*, January 1989, iv.

[64] Editorial, "Sri Ramjanma Bhoomi," *Hindu Vishva*, March–April 1989, 3.

> The task of rebuilding the temple is not an easy one, thereby the people should be prepared to make any kind of sacrifice which might be required. (Sharma 1992: 3)

Swami Satyamitranand in the same meeting said,

> If the Central government tries to stop the construction of Rama temple, the Rama devotees would not let it stay in office. (Sharma 1992: 6)

There were also some militant declarations by Paramhamsa Ramchandra Das, such as:

> Once the date of rebuilding of the temple is decided upon the so called Babri mosque would be ripped apart and thrown away. (in Sharma 1992: 7)

The ideas of "dying" and "sacrifice" for the nation and its dharma were evoked on other occasions as well. For example, defending the act of *sati* (self-immolation by widowed Hindu women) by a young widow in Rajasthan in 1987 as a "glorious act of supreme sacrifice," the editorial of *Masurashram Patrika* says,

> The Hindus have suffered setbacks because very few of us are prepared to die for Hinduism. The more men and women come forward to make that supreme sacrifice, the more strong Hinduism will be.[65]

It was said that,

> the land of Bharat is Sita personified. China and Pakistan tried to abduct this land in the same way as Ravana abducted Sita. This land, this country is ours. We had our right over it and shall also have it in future.[66]

The ideas of dying and sacrificing for Hindu nationhood, and of Hindu rights, came to occupy a significant place in the utterances, writings and video films of the VHP during this particular phase.

The mass campaigns of the VHP brought it closer to the BJP than ever before, propelling the latter to adopt the Ramjanmabhoomi issue as a part of its political agenda in 1989. Thereafter, the two became overt political allies. The VHP actively campaigned for the BJP and

[65] Editorial, "Maligning Hinduism," *Masurashram Patrika*, October 1987, 1–2.
[66] Editorial, "Yeh sota desh jagana hai" (This sleeping country has to be awakened), *Hindu Vishva*, October 1991, 4.

took upon itself the monumental task of mobilisation for Hindu nationalism. Before this phase the two outfits had apparently carried on their work in their own respective spheres, without interfering in each other's activities. Ostensibly, the VHP had not forged strong political ties with any political party before the late 1980s. B. L. Sharma, a senior leader of the group, made it clear at this point that they intended to create a Hindu vote bank which would electorally support those who agreed with their demands.[67] In an interview, Singhal declared that the VHP would take the help of those who were willing to help it, be it Shiv Sena or Congress or Janata Dal or Lok Dal, and expressed his satisfaction that the BJP had come out openly in favour of the Hindus over the Ramjanmabhoomi issue.[68] The VHP also busied itself in implementing strategies of "mass mobilisation and *hinduisation*" which had been proposed by the Dharma Sansad in its convention in 1989.[69]

For the BJP leadership, the emotive Ramjanmabhoomi dispute was an effective mobilisational issue to build for itself a mass base. It also provided the BJP with a bulwark to challenge the Congress-I and emerge as a national alternative to it. The RSS under its next sarsanghchalak, Balasaheb Deoras, came to regard active electoral politics an important vehicle for the dissemination of the idea of Hindu nationalism. Unlike his predecessors who had shunned active politics and restrained the RSS and the VHP (Malik and Singh 1994: 161–63; Jaffrelot 1996: 73, 115, 347), Deoras believed in employing religio-cultural symbols for political mobilisation (Malik and Singh 1994: 163). The VHP, within this changed orientation, seemed competent for the job of building a mass-based political movement grounded in religious demands. This was a scenario where religion became à strong instrument for political power and identity politics, which eventually became the basis of material advancement for sections associated with the VHP and related organisations.

The VHP, besides spreading its message through printed pamphlets, leaflets, booklets, newsletters and newspapers, began making extensive use of electronic technology in its ideological work from the mid-eighties. This use of electronic media and of modern means of communication by the VHP displayed an astute ability to exploit a medium, potent in its social effect, at a time when the electronic

[67] B. L. Sharma in *India Today*, 30 November 1988.

[68] Ashok Singhal in an interview in *Hindu Vishva*, March–April 1989, 34.

[69] See appendix IV for details.

network was spreading far and wide in the country. The speeches of its leaders were recorded, its public programmes and meetings, such as those of the Dharma Sansad, were videotaped to be circulated in homes and localities. The VHP's employment of Hindu symbols and the work of its subsidiaries became much more effective when popularised through the electronic media. It seems that this was something which the VHP learnt from the telecast of the *Ramayana* on state television. The build-up in the Ramjanmabhoomi campaign was accompanied by a rise in the use of video and audio devices. The scale of dissemination of an ideological message through audio tapes and videotapes as done by the VHP is unprecedented in India. This was possible partly because of the VHP's support abroad, which made the latest technology and the knowledge to operate it easily accessible, as well as the finances needed to procure it.

Chapter 4

A Non-Electoral Actor in Indian Politics

The VHP, for its part, could espouse the cause of Hindu nationalism confidently. The Hindu rightist legacies which were internal to the Congress (coexisting with its largely secular commitments), and had been crucial in shaping the independence movement, provided the VHP with precedents for building its Hindu nationalist propaganda by grounding it exclusively in Hindu religious imagery and mythology. It is not that the VHP needed these, but they helped it in its propaganda. The Congress did its best to adhere to secular principles and to be sensitive to the interests of minorities, despite strains between its leaders. The tension between Nehru and Sardar Patel (1875–1950) over the question of Indian Muslims made some Congress members look to Patel rather than to Nehru to uphold the idea that the Indian state, if not representing a Hindu nation, should at least reflect the views of the Hindu majority (Graham 1988: 178). After a spate of communal violence in East and West Bengal in 1949–50 this tension grew, and Nehru came close to suggesting that Patel did not share his concern about the insecurity of the Indian Muslims (Graham 1988: 179). Patel in a letter to Nehru said, "I quite realise that in the matter of giving a sense of security to the minority the responsibility of the majority is paramount, but, at the same time, we have to allow for the irritant effect of fears of the majority on the question of loyalty of the minority community or a section thereof. I do not think it will be possible for us to ignore that altogether" (Das 1974, 9: 478–79).

Patel doubted the loyalty of Muslims who had stayed back in India after the Partition and felt that though they had opted for India they had a tendency to disloyalty, especially with relation to Pakistan. To him Muslims in India were hostages to be held to ensure the fair treatment of Hindus in Pakistan (Gopal 1979, 2: 15, 16, 92).

Moreover, as the historical evidence indicates, reliance on religio-cultural symbols to rally mass support by some leaders within, or closely associated with, the Congress was a part of the Indian freedom struggle.

Some Congress leaders—for example, Tilak and Malaviya—did not hesitate to employ Hindu symbols for local and provincial support, and thus crucially shaped and mediated the complexities of cultural identity formations. The secular credentials of most of the leaders were never in doubt, nor can the larger secular character of the independence movement be denied; however, recourse was taken to Hindu cultural myths and symbols for anti-colonial mobilisation. The prioritisation of socio-cultural symbols, as a means of heightening anti-imperialist fervour by a flourishing group of leaders within the Congress, led it towards forms of mobilisation which appealed to Hindus while doing the damage of alienating Muslims from the national mainstream (Hasan 1981: 199–223; Vanaik 1992: 46–47). Several notables attached to the Congress were engaged in activities such as *gau raksha*, *shuddhi sabhas* and *Devnagari prachar*,[1] whose potential for schism was immense.

As members of the mercantile elite—bankers and traders—became active in the Congress at the regional level, they not only provided much-needed monetary support to the party, but also helped to strengthen forces of Hindu cultural revivalism in northern India (Bayly 1973: 349–88). Their participation in religious sabhas and contributions to religious endowments made them a socially prestigious category, which helped the Congress in local Hindu mobilisation. However, it would be incorrect to interpret the freedom movement in its entirety as reflecting the Hindu communal voice. There was a definitive variant in the movement which was religiously Hindu, without necessarily being communal, though many times it was. The Congress was pulled in opposite directions, by left-leaning forces on the one side and by Hindu revivalists on the other. It thus represented both socialist and rightist trends, and the constant struggle between these sections made it an ideologically eclectic and therefore a socially pervasive body. The right wing of the Congress, however, played an important role in providing inspiration to the post-Independence Hindu nationalist groups such as the BJP and VHP.

Throughout the 1960s, many of those who voted self-consciously as Hindus stayed with the Congress rather than any of the Hindu nationalist groups, regarding it as championing their interests despite its avowed policy of secularism (Graham 1993: 225). As a leader of

[1] *Gau raksha* can be defined as cow protection, *shuddhi sabha* as a gathering for the conversion of non-Hindus to Hinduism, and *Devnagari prachar* as the popularisation of Hindi in the Devnagari script.

the Hindu Mahasabha lamented, "indifference was shown by the Hindus" to the calls of the Hindu Mahasabha, and the Hindus accepted the "territorial definition of patriotism" put forth by the Congress, rejecting the "clarion call of the Hindu Mahasabha as unpatriotic" (Prakash 1966: 4). This phenomenon, which surfaced at the time of the 1967 general elections, continued in varying degrees until about the mid-1980s. Though considerably enfeebled at times, it witnessed in its trajectory the cosseting of Hindu sentiments both by Mrs Gandhi and her successor Rajiv Gandhi. This legitimised the use of religion for political leverage. The manipulation of religious sentiments to weaken opposition forces by none other than the Congress Party rendered less questionable such a manipulation by other political groups. Moreover, it is believed that the RSS leadership tacitly buttressed several political moves of Congress-I under Mrs Gandhi's leadership. Allegedly, there was support within the RSS for Mrs Gandhi's decision to send the army to Punjab and Kashmir, to maintain civil peace and suppress militant opposition to the Indian state. Such an action went well with the RSS's idea of a strong and unified state.

The RSS's support to the Congress-I was a further source of encouragement to the VHP. The VHP, though not a political party, used religious icons and symbolism, and helped the BJP in political mobilisation. The BJP relied heavily on urban Hindu votes, and its social base started broadening after it allied closely with the VHP on the Ramjanmabhoomi issue. As with its predecessor, the Jana Sangh, the BJP's strongest support, towards the late 1980s, came from the territories of Madhya Pradesh, Uttar Pradesh, Rajasthan, Himachal Pradesh and Delhi. In Gujarat, too, it eroded Congress-I's support base.[2]

The point which needs to be emphasised is that as the secular, socialist and developmental nationalism of the Congress Party began to lose vigour, not least by the type of politics it itself undertook, the space left vacant began to be occupied by the RSS-VHP's blueprint of nationalism. In other words, as the ideological instruments of the Congress started losing their appeal, alternative ideologies were provided by various other groups such as the RSS and VHP by the use of those very strategies.

[2] See appendix V for details.

Hindutva and Political Mechanics: Late 1980s to Early 1990s

The RSS, joined later by the VHP, had been for many years working at a nationalist alternative which they felt was more responsive to the interests of the majority community in India—an alternative almost resembling a theocracy. By working ceaselessly in the social arena, the VHP tried to popularise the Sangh Parivar's perspective on Hindu nationalism, as against the Nehruvian model of secular nationalism. The VHP made itself present amongst the masses in the most simple and impressional ways. The space surrounding individuals in their daily prosaic activity formed the locale of activity of the VHP. Its programmes contributed immensely to politically sensitising the masses as "Hindus," and "non-Hindus."

In this scenario, the Ramjanmabhoomi issue attracted the urban, upper-caste, middle-class professional Hindu away from the Congress and towards the BJP. The novelty of the BJP, and a middle-class sentiment that it ought to be given a chance to rule, also dictated the swing of votes towards the party. The Muslims and Dalits moved towards the newly formed Jan Morcha of V. P. Singh (who had resigned as the finance minister from the Congress) and also towards the Bahujan Samaj Party of Kanshi Ram. Regional parties also saw a severe anti-Congress swing and moved closer to Jan Morcha in a bid to defeat the Congress regional units, which in most states were ruling or formed the main opposition. Strengthening of regional politics on the one hand, and the mobilisation of socially and educationally backward sections in an anti-Congress alliance on the other, saw the Congress with a heavily dented support base.

The year 1989 saw a noteworthy social polarisation that became clearly visible in the Lok Sabha elections at the end of that year. The Brahmin, Thakur, Baniya, Dalit and Muslim grand alliance that had evolved in support of Rajiv Gandhi in 1984 crumbled by the late 1980s—a development facilitated by several factors. Apart from the highly centralised manner of functioning, the government did not fare differently from the previous regime as far as the influence of sycophants and coterie politics were concerned. Factional fights suppressed by "high command" dictates and the culture of sycophancy flourished within the Congress. Policy failures such as the IPKF fiasco in Sri Lanka, corruption scandals such as the Swedish Bofors gun and German submarine deals, and the compromise with both Hindu and Muslim religious fundamentalism affected the government to its detriment. Anti-Sikh riots after Indira Gandhi's assassination, and the Congress government's inability to take a hard stand against the perpetrators of the anti-Sikh pogrom, had to an extent already tarnished its image. These factors brought together the opposition forces in an alliance against the Congress and led to the formation of a non-Congress coalition under the prime ministership of V. P. Singh, supported by the BJP from outside.

The BJP, first under L. K. Advani's and then under M. M. Joshi's leadership, developed a close rapport with the VHP, and supported the proposed plan of temple construction at Ayodhya openly and unflinchingly. Advani, at a party workers' meeting, declared that he would not ask the VHP to abandon its plans, adding that the construction would commence as scheduled and that the BJP activists should participate in the construction.[3] Support to the VHP on the temple construction programme was considered more important than support to the National Front government that looked keen to implement the Mandal Commission report.[4]

The BJP's defence of the VHP emboldened the latter while becoming a major source of embarrassment for the government of which the BJP was a partner. Advani, while preparing for his Somnath-to-Ayodhya *rathyatra* (literally, chariot-march), maintained that the Ramjanmabhoomi issue was not communal, but was one of nationalism versus "minorityism."[5] The rathyatra was to be undertaken across nine states—Gujarat, Maharashtra, Andhra Pradesh, Madhya Pradesh, Rajasthan, Haryana, Delhi, Bihar and Uttar Pradesh—and would culminate at Ayodhya on 30 October 1990, the proposed day for temple construction by the VHP. The aim of the rathyatra was to publicise the Ramjanmabhoomi issue and also to take some air out of the government's decision to implement the Mandal Commission report.

Advani's rathyatra or, in the words of a political analyst, *raktyatra* (journey of blood) (A. A. Engineer 1995: 93), once again led to severe communal tension across North and West India. The following places,

[3] "Ram temple of more import than NF: BJP," *Times of India* (Bombay), 2 September 1990.

[4] Kalyan Singh, the then leader of the BJP legislative wing in Uttar Pradesh, declared in Faizabad that the temple would be constructed at all costs and his party would withdraw support to the NF government if necessary. Ibid.

[5] "Ayodhya rathyatra will go on: Advani," *Times of India* (Bombay), 17 September 1990.

in particular, experienced major communal rioting and tension: Aligarh, Gonda and Faizabad in Uttar Pradesh; Raipur and Dhar in Madhya Pradesh; Udaipur and Chittorgarh in Rajasthan; Hyderabad in Andhra Pradesh; and Delhi. Advani, for his part, denied that his rathyatra had increased communal tension in the country, and claimed that it had rather helped in defusing communal tension.[6] The Ayodhya-bound Advani was arrested by the Laloo Prasad Yadav government in Bihar, and the BJP withdrew political support from the National Front government at the centre. Much later, Advani declared in Parliament that Ayodhya was not the only reason, but it was certainly the last straw in bringing the V. P. Singh government down (Malik and Singh 1994: 88). Besides the temple-mosque controversy, the issue of reservations of jobs for the Backward Castes in the central government seemed to irk the BJP. It had led to serious strains between the BJP and the National Front, making it increasingly difficult for the former to continue supporting the government.

There was another major outbreak of riots towards the end of 1990, in the aftermath of the 30 October 1990 karseva organised by the VHP to begin construction of the Rama temple. On 30 October the Babri mosque became the target of a mobistic crowd. It was attacked with "crowbars and iron angles,"[7] which was the "culmination of a three-hour siege by thousands of frenzied devotees."[8] The active cooperation of the police made it possible for the devotees to enter the sealed town of Faizabad. In fact, one of the VHP leaders admitted that the karseva became possible because "the Provincial Armed Constabulary (PAC) personnel turned themselves into karsevaks."[9] Gujarat, Uttar Pradesh and Andhra Pradesh saw some gruesome rioting. Godhra, Baroda, Ahmedabad, Bijnor, Hyderabad and some other cities had to be put under curfew to bring the violence under control. The partisan role of the police made matters worse. I would like to quote A. A. Engineer to describe the state of this communal violence:

> The intensity and spread of violence was such that it shook the nation and it can be said without exaggeration that after 1947 such violence had

[6] "Advani issues warning," *The Hindustan Times*, 11 October 1990.

[7] "11 killed as mob attacks masjid; kar seva foiled," *Economic Times* (Delhi), 31 October 1990.

[8] Ibid.

[9] Ibid.

> not been witnessed in the country. It was not only the scale and intensity but also the cruelties committed during that wave of communal violence that were unprecedented. Women and children were killed either by stabbing or burning. In many cases the limbs of these children and women were cut before killing them. Some of them were first stabbed, then burned while still alive. (A. A. Engineer 1995: 98)

The entire VHP–Bajrang Dal force had geared itself to claim the site for the construction of a Rama temple, and the consequences were there for everyone to see. The BJP, on its part, fully backed the VHP's agenda. Advani and Singhal, soon after the former's release in November, came together at Ayodhya to address rallies and public meetings. Advani declared that by taking up the temple issue he was performing his duty to strengthen nationalism.[10]

A political analyst points out that the BJP leaders saw the Hindutva-Ramjanmabhoomi movement both as part of a long-term Hindu self-assertion which would change basic political paradigms, and as a short-term springboard to political power within the existing paradigm.[11] The BJP did indeed see the Ramjanmabhoomi issue as politically lucrative in the near future. In its national executive meeting in June 1989, the BJP had passed a resolution that the "sentiments of the people must be respected" and that the Ram *janmasthan* (birthplace) should be handed to the Hindus.[12] Before the mid-term poll of May 1991, the BJP reiterated its commitment to build the Ram *mandir* (temple) (BJP 1991:5).

Ayodhya became the centre of activity of the VHP, and its attention was diverted from its interests overseas and the tribal North-east to North India. This move would subsequently expand its support base and bring it more publicity. The VHP's programmes became more offensive, increasingly rolling out both oral and physical violence with every move on the Ramjanmabhoomi issue. Congregations, conferences and prayer meetings gave way to loud yatras, militant processions, vociferous conversion ceremonies, and incidents of violence and vandalism—particularly directed towards the Muslims.

The Ayodhya campaign drew culturally conservative and right-wing support towards the VHP, coming from vast sections of the

[10] "Advani storms Ayodhya," *Hindu Chetna*, 21 November 1990, 16.

[11] Praful Bidwai, "BJP's growing Incoherence: Between the sadhu and the moneybag," *Times of India* (New Delhi), 9 February 1994.

[12] *Resolutions Adopted at the National Executive Meeting—BJP*. 9, 10, 11 June1989 at Palampur (H.P.), 17.

upper bureaucracy, state clerical employees, industrialists, commercial and trading classes, rural landed interests and urban upper-caste middle-class professionals. However, this support came more from northern and western India than other areas.

This was also the juncture at which the RSS started playing a larger role in VHP activities, gradually taking organisational matters into its own hands. Ashok Singhal, an RSS pracharak who had been deputed to work in the position of the VHP's joint-general secretary, had become its general secretary in 1986. Later, Singhal remarked in one of his speeches,

> It is our responsibility to serve society by leading an austere life. At this moment of time, it is the Sangh activists who are ascetics in the real sense. If there hadn't been trained RSS *swayamsevaks*, we would not have been where we are now. "Service" is the key word of our culture and Sangh's *swayamsevaks* are symbols of "service." Today in all spheres of activity such workers are needed.[13]

On being asked how the RSS supplemented the efforts of VHP, Rajendra Singh remarked,

> We gave VHP our excellent workers to help it in its commendable work of organising and awakening Hindu society and instilling a sense of discipline and oneness in it. Otherwise how could the VHP get trained workers in its early years? The sadhus and sants had become a part of VHP but they could not do everything on their own. They had to be escorted everywhere. There had to be someone with them to accompany them wherever they went. The RSS helped the VHP in all its activities.[14]

Involvement of Sadhus

Also at this time, the VHP began recruiting sadhus of various ashrams and *akharas* (monastic orders) in a big way for the expansion of its social base. The participation of religious leaders in the VHP activities gave the organisation a strong mobilisational force essential for rallying support throughout India and outside. Reverence for

[13] Ashok Singhal, "Chal-prapanch aur zor zabardasti se ahindu banaye gaye logon ko VHP punha hindu banayegi" (The VHP would reconvert those who were made non-Hindus by fraud and force), *Hindu Chetna*, 16 April 1995, 5.

[14] Rajendra Singh, former sarsanghchalak of the RSS, in a personal interview at Allahabad on 5 November 1995.

religious leaders who live a life of renunciation springs from the belief that renunciation and celibacy are sources of extraordinary power, with a capacity to attain a higher purpose; ordinary humans, engrossed in the efforts of the family and society, supposedly cannot realise this state. This belief becomes instrumental in rallying sadhus for expansion of the social base amongst Hindus. The VHP, as a body advocating Hindu nationalism, politically mobilised the sadhus in a unique move which sought to legitimise their participation on non-religious platforms. Reciprocally, the involvement of sadhus in its mass campaigns enhanced the VHP's social legitimacy, which in turn gave a boost to its activities.

During the earlier phase of the VHP, sadhus were expected to perform a two-fold task: one, provide guidance to Hindus in religio-spiritual matters, and two, as VHP representatives, spread the message of Hinduism in India as well as outside. Their role in the secular realm, that of politics, if not completely ruled out, was in no way emphasised. They were not expected to engage themselves in mundane "this-worldly" activities, having renounced the world at some point in their lifetime, and it was surmised that they would follow a strict moral code. Thus, in 1972, the VHP deplored the growing tendency to level indiscriminate criticism against "religious leaders and *mahatamas*"[15] on the basis of a few instances of "misbehaviour here and there"[16]; however, it also called upon the religious leaders to be careful in their "behaviour and activities so that there could be no reason for any criticism."[17]

The VHP, however, from the mid-1980s converted this detached status of the sadhus into one of active and even militant involvement in temporal affairs. This was done with the aim of involving the sadhus in the work of mobilising support. The VHP encouraged sadhus to engage in political activity, and tried to create an environment where it sought to place their authority beyond doubt. Their involvement in the secular realm of politics and governance was projected by the VHP as beyond challenge, and their word as final. Accordingly, the VHP "propagated the fiction" that the sadhus within its Marg Darshak Mandal took all the decisions concerning its activities (Van Dyke 1997: 3150). For example, the sadhus expressed their opinion on matters

15 Sharma, *Vishva Hindu Parishad Ke Prastav*, 86.

16 Ibid.

17 Ibid.

like that of Kashmir, where they demanded that "to suppress terrorism the security forces should not be encumbered by any juridical or executive restrictions and should be given full liberty."[18] The sadhus accepted the VHP's Ramjanmabhoomi liberation movement and made occasional remarks appreciating "the sensitivity and sincerity of the VHP to the country's basic problems."[19] This, while giving the VHP activists strong moral support, was bound to have a forceful impact on a society where religion is central to its self-conception.

The number of ascetics in 1981 in VHP's Marg Darshak Mandal was forty-one. This had gone up to a hundred and sixty in 1992.[20] Through the efforts of the VHP the sadhus and sants, besides performing their sacred role, came to form a distinct political category —which was unprecedented in independent India. The dreams that Bharat would become the *jagat guru* (world leader) once more, and regain its "glorious past," represent an attempt to elevate the ascetic force to a decisive political level, at least ostensibly if not actually. This also reflects a clinging to a constructed past as a remedy for the insecurities of the present. The linkage is interesting to note— aspirations to a utopian future are linked to a constructed past through the musings and actions of the present. Omprakash Dubey, a lifelong trustee of the VHP who set up VHP units in Zambia (Africa) says, "The VHP dreams of a traditional Bharat. It dreams of jagat guru Bharat. Spiritual gurus used to be above kings in the hierarchy. In Bharat not the ruler but the renouncer was worshipped. We honoured those who had renounced the world."[21]

The Dharma Sansad, in its preliminary meeting at Allahabad in January 1989, discussed ways and means for mass-awakening what it called "Hinduisation." Detailed proposals were laid down for the sadhus as well as other members of the VHP, to guide them in the task of mobilisation and Hinduisation.[22] Ashok Singhal, in the Dharma Sansad conference at Allahabad which followed a few

[18] Report, "Deshbhar ke 20 hazar sant october mas main mandir nirman ke liye samarthan jutane sainkaron sant-yatron ke roop main niklegain" (Twenty thousand ascetics from all over India would move in the form of yatras to garner support for temple construction in the month of October), *Hindu Chetna*, 1 May 1994, 4.

[19] Ibid., 5.

[20] Sharma, *Satat sadhana yatra ke tees varsh*, 6.

[21] Omprakash Dubey in a personal interview at Allahabad on 31 October 1995. Interestingly, Rama and Krishna, major icons of the VHP, were both kings.

[22] Refer to appendix IV.

months later, called upon the sadhus and said that Hindu society is "desperately" waiting for them "to solve its several problems."[23] He went on to say that,

> History is witness to the fact that whenever such a crisis has come on the country *sadhus* such as Vishwamitra, Bhardwaj, Valmiki, Agastya etc in Sri Rama's time through their organised efforts protected the identity of the nation. Similarly, during Sri Krishna's time Vyasa, Jamini, Maitreye, Asti etc brought about a colossal change through their efforts. During Shivaji's time great saints like Samarth Ramdas protected dharma. Today, society expects a similar intervention from *mahapurusha* like you who are bearers of the *rishi parampara*—legacies and tradition of sages.[24]

It seems that the VHP wanted to emulate the tradition of *rajgurus*—Brahmin advisors to the king, to whose advice the king was morally bound. In the same conference *Hindu Vishva* reported that the swamis and dharmacharyas realised that there was a need for their intervention in the country's politics. Some mahatamas were so agonised by the prevailing political situation of the country that they even offered to contest elections in the coming years.[25]

Sadhus have been urged to give "dictates"[26] to the youth, both men and women, to join the Bajrang Dal and Durga Vahini, and to make the "Hindu movement"[27] more effective through their participation. The VHP had brought these sadhus together as the Dharma Sansad, which was placed above democratically elected state institutions.

A leading VHP member told me,

> The Dharma Sansad is the dharma guru of the Hindus. We have kept its role as it was performed traditionally. Tradition has it that though during his coronation the king used to proclaim himself above law, he could not go against the wishes of the dharma guru, the *kul* [clan] guru—which means that he could be punished if he violated the principles of dharma. We, the people of the VHP, are working under the *chhattra-chaya* [shelter]

[23] "Prayag main Dharma Sansad adhiveshan" (The Dharma Sansad conference at Prayag), *Hindu Vishva*, March–April 1989, 16.

[24] Ibid., 16–17.

[25] "Teesra Dharma Sansad adhiveshan" (The third Dharma Sansad conference), *Hindu Vishva*, March–April 1989, 9.

[26] Ashok Singhal quoted in "Sants firm on action plan to build temple," *Times of India* (Ahmedabad), 4 April 1994.

[27] Ibid.

> of the Dharma Sansad. We want that whenever we commit any mistake, it should correct us.[28]

The sadhus who are affiliated with the VHP explained their involvement in "worldly" affairs thus,

> When we saw that the administration had become indifferent towards religion and was making our religious and spiritual quest impossible, we reached a conclusion that our knowledge of *dharma* was of little use if we remained detached from national affairs. Therefore, we decided to study political affairs and accordingly guide society.[29]

The sants pledged that they would not let "Bharat disintegrate like the Soviet Union,"[30] and warned the central government against "Islamisation of Ayodhya" on rumours about the government's intention to rebuild the demolished Babri mosque.[31] Interestingly, the sadhus, while justifying their intervention in matters of politics, opposed state intervention in religious matters, specifically the Ramjanmabhoomi issue after the demolition of the mosque. On the question of building of the Rama temple at Ayodhya on the site where Babri mosque once stood, the sadhus affiliated to the VHP demanded that the government should leave the matter in the hands of the Ramjanmabhoomi Nyas (formed by the VHP), because, in the words of one of its members, Swami Haridas Giri, the state had "no right to intervene in matters of religion."[32]

The VHP's use of the sadhus during the late 1980s and early 1990s during the Ramjanmabhoomi campaigns turned out to yield "impressive results for the Bharatiya Janata Party" (Van Dyke 1997: 3150), as was expected by the VHP. The sadhus' potential for mobilisation was much flaunted by both the sadhu and non-sadhu

[28] Girija Singh in a personal interview at Allahabad on 14 November 1993.

[29] Editorial, *Hindu Chetna*, 1–15 August 1993, 5.

[30] Ibid.

[31] Report, "Sri Ramjanma Bhoomi Nyas manch ko Shri Narsimha Rao ki chunoti manzoor" (Sri Ramjanma Bhoomi Nyas accepts Mr. Narasimha Rao's challenge), *Hindu Chetna*, 1 August 1994, 4; and "Shankaracharya Nyas ke faslon ka virodh nahin karenge" (The Shankarachrayas will not oppose the verdict of the Trust), *Hindu Chetna*, 1 August 1994, 9.

[32] Report, "Shankaracharya Nyas ke faslon ka virodh nahin karenge" (The Shankarachrayas will not oppose the verdict of the Trust), *Hindu Chetna*, 1 August 1994, 9.

leadership of the VHP, and it was said that India is "once again turning into a land of temples, saints and ascetics."[33] The potential of the sadhus as crowd-pullers is often mentioned in VHP writings and speeches. The VHP seems eager to utilise this ability of the religious leaders in its various programmes, in order to give the organisation a mass character. The *Hindu Chetna* states that

> thousands of devotees travel on their own initiative and expense as far as Chitrakoot, Badrinath, Vrindavan and Ayodhya to listen to sadhus like Murari Bapu and Asaram Bapu; is there such magnetic force in any national leader or politician? Even today there are sants like Satya Sai Baba in Bharat who is visited by 10 to 15 thousand devotees from all over the world every day at Puttaparti. They come for his *darshan* [to pay respects] on their own initiative without being summoned. Does any political leader possess such a charisma?[34]

Describing the mobilisational capability of the religious leaders, Sant Ramsharan Das of Banar-s suggests the following strategy for the Hinduisation of Indian politics:

> There are dozens of dharmacharyas with Hindu society and each has a vote bank of approximately twenty-five lakhs (or 2.5 million). For example, there is Gujarat's sant Sri Murari Bapu, Rajasthan's Sri Ramsukh Dasji Maharaj, U.P.'s [Uttar Pradesh's] sant Sri Devrah Baba, RSS's Sri Deorasji, Ayodhya's Sri Nrittya Gopal Dasji Maharaj, etc. Besides them there are hundreds of dharmacharyas who wield a vote bank of at least one lakh. The Hindu society has about ten lakh strong team of sadhus. If each mobilises a hundred people, the politics of this country would take a new turn and get hinduised.[35]

The sadhus associated with the VHP are not opposed to violence while working towards their aims. It is said that "if need be we shall use violence to stop" Christian missionaries from converting Hindus.[36] Violence is rampant in their speeches also, as was found during the course of interviews for this book. It is also stressed that

[33] Editorial, *Hindu Chetna*, 16 November 1995, 5.

[34] Ibid.

[35] Ramsharan Das, "Pachchis crore ke Hindu vote bank dwara rajniti ka hindukaran"(The Hinduisation of politics through a vote bank of twenty-five crores or 250 million), *Hindu Vishva*, May 1989, 22.

[36] Shirish Dharmadhikari, "Arunachal rajya isaiyon ki chapet main" (The state of Arunachal in the clutches of Christians), *Hindu Chetna*, May 1989, 17.

whenever the government worked without the guidance of dharmacharyas, India had to bear immense pain and suffering.[37] The sadhus of Haradwar and Rishikesh declared that during elections in the future they would appeal to the masses to give the mandate to leaders such as Kalyan Singh, who "wiped the blot of bondage"[38] from Ayodhya and made the "dreams of the ascetics come true."[39] Kalyan Singh, when he was very much a part of the BJP, himself said that the kind of guidance given by sadhus in the Ramjanmabhoomi "liberation movement" would be written in letters of "gold in the pages of history."[40] Thus, the sacred is utilised to legitimise the political quest. The VHP attempts to tightly bind the Hindus, so that they may provide ideological support to its nationalism. The support given by the religious leaders to achieve this goal is very valuable.

It is interesting to note that from the mid-1980s the VHP attempted to consolidate Hindus as a political community, and entrench them as a perpetual political majority in India, to the detriment of democratic values. This was done mainly with the support of the backward-looking sections within the urban middle classes, and an increasing dependence on the sadhus and the RSS. A Hindu political community was now conceived as including the tribals and those outside the ranking of the four varnas. In the first two decades after its formation the VHP followed its original charter, involving itself in Hindu unification at home and overseas, and opposing the work of Christian missionaries in India. Thereafter, it took to direct political issues, trying to influence state policies through political mobilisations. Its campaigns on what it calls the Ramjanmabhoomi at Ayodhya, the Krishnajanmabhoomi at Mathura, the Kashi-Vishwanath temple at Varanasi, as well as the periodic "call to the Hindus" by the Dharma Sansads to vote for a "Hindu party," helped the BJP expand its support base in northern and western India. Moreover, issues such as cow slaughter and conversions came in handy for the BJP to garner votes during elections.

[37] Acharya Ramnath Suman, "Shasan dware ho raha apne dharma guruon ka apman" (The insulting attitude of the government towards our religious leaders), *Hindu Chetna*, 1–15 August 1993, 17.

[38] Kalyan Singh, "Ayodhya main santon ke aashirwad . . ." (The blessings of ascetics in Ayodhya . . .), *Hindu Chetna*, 1 March 1993, 11.

[39] Ibid.

[40] Ibid.

The VHP and Democratic Politics

In this context, it is interesting to note that the VHP and its activists have a distinct understanding of democracy, even if it is largely untheorised by them. Democracy is seen as rule by the numerically strongest community defined in terms of religion, and therefore as being compatible with Hindu majoritarianism. This conception is based on an exclusion of religious minorities, mainly Muslims and Christians, from the cultural majority it seeks to define and represent. It is asserted by the VHP that since democracy means governance not only by the majority, but also in the interests of the majority, democratic rule should make the Hindus rather than any other group its central focus. It is claimed that because of the Hindu majority, the state should preferably be self-consciously Hindu, or that the government should at least give primacy to the demands of the Hindus as a political community. It was stated in a resolution passed in one of the VHP's meetings that

> the time has come when the government and other political parties should review their policy of appeasement and should not let the country's unity and security be exposed to danger of any sort. The interests and honour of the majority community should be safeguarded in every way and no activity which hurts their sentiments should be allowed.[41]

It is believed within the VHP that it is only when Hindus control power and determine policy that India will realise its historical potential. It is further argued that a government which is insensitive to Hindu demands as voiced by the VHP is an undemocratic government.[42]

The following statement of a senior leader of the VHP would give some clues to the VHP's understanding of democracy:

> It is the paramount duty of the Hindu society to defeat all the political forces that have become dangerous for the very existence of Hinduism, Hindu society and the country. If Hinduism and Hindusthan are to be protected, these forces must be defeated with all the might. The masses should vote for the BJP, which stood like a rock for the reconstruction of

[41] "Muslime Tushtikaran Ko Koka Jaye" (resolution passed at Bhopal on 4 May 1986 by the Board of Trustees of the VHP), in Sharma, *Vishva Hindu Parishad Ke Prastav*, 70.

[42] "Stop this anti-Hindu stance: Dedicate Ayodhya, Mathura and Kashi temples to Hindus," *Hindu Chetna*, 21 January 1991, 1, English edition.

> Shri Ram Temple. . . . People should go for polling in a well organised manner chanting "Jai Sri Rama" peacefully and loudly and create history in the democratic process and usher in an era of peace, Dharma, *Nyaya* [justice] and safety for the Hindu society and others.[43]

Immediately after the 1991 general elections the *Hindu Chetna*, one of the VHP's fortnightly magazines, stated,

> It [the BJP] has proved itself to be an effective instrument for change and democratic revolution with an alternative ideology rooted in the ethos of the land, with a sober and mature leadership, with selfless and disciplined working cadre spread all over the country.[44]

According to Rajendra Singh, former sarsanghchalak of the RSS,

> The present age is the age of democracy where the masses actually can do anything they wish to. (Therefore) in this age, to make India great (*mahan*) those individuals have to be brought forward who are imbued with the ideals of *Hindutva*. The people should bring only those in power who are driven by the urge to protect Hindu *dharma* and its principles.[45]

To place the VHP's views on democracy in perspective a few words about democratic rule are important. Democracy, most straightforwardly, stands for rule of the people—a system where everyone has a right to vote and thus decide what kind of governance within a democratic framework they want. Since everyone cannot be directly involved in governance and policy making, they elect representatives who govern on their behalf. So, democracy is a rule of all through their representatives, elected at regular intervals in elections supposed to be free and fair, where any kind of coercion of the voters is not permissible. In other words, in a democracy people possess an unfettered franchise to select their government. They have freedom to express their opinions, and take decisions which might change the set of rulers or the government. To be democratic this representation of the people has to be universal—

[43] On the occasion of the 1991 general elections. "A new dawn beckoning the country: BJP wave all over," *Hindu Chetna*, 21 May 1991, 1, 8, English edition.

[44] "Back to square one: Snub to pseudosecularists, boost to nationalist forces," *Hindu Chetna*, 25 June 1991, 2, English edition.

[45] Rajendra Singh at the closing ceremony of the VHP's second ekatmata yatra in October 1995 at Nagpur. Excerpts of his speech produced in Sharma (1996: 20).

each citizen has a right to express her or his will in selecting individuals, whether belonging to a political party or contesting independently, who will represent the citizen in the government. However, since differences exist in ideas, beliefs and principles, a set of ideas getting the largest amount of mass support becomes the ruling set of ideas. This means that the government is formed by those who get the largest number of votes in elections. Hence, policy is decided by majority opinion and, once made, is applicable to all without consideration of majority or minority. Every citizen is equal by law and in legal rights and claims, but has also to abide by law and governmental policy. Discrimination against those who do not belong to the ruling majority is not a norm in a democracy. All are equal. And as an extra precaution, minority rights are granted to minorities, whether political or ethnic. Democracy is about individuals and their opinions—individual opinion expressed through the ballot is given primacy—and not the opinions of a group or community, however defined. Another point that needs to be emphasised is that a democracy has certain procedural requirements which need to be followed by whoever forms the government. This means that a democratic state has certain procedures—rules, guidelines and so on—established by law, which cannot in any case be bypassed, notwithstanding the character of a majority.

The VHP's conception of permanent majority goes against this basic principle of democracy, both in theory and practice, and possesses fascist elements. Democratic rule presupposes the possibility of continuous alteration of political majority and the ruling group; the majority and minority are not fixed entities, but may go through periodic alterations as decided by the polity. In theory, the act of fixing the government on the basis of Hindu majority means the effective disenfranchisement of individuals who by the incident of their birth belong to numerically smaller ethnic or religious groups. A permanent Hindu government also pushes out from state decisions individuals who, for different reasons, do not believe in the VHP's ideology. These groups and individuals who do not agree with VHP politics, or actively oppose it, would be condemned to a permanent exclusion from the government. Further, they would find it hard to express anti-government views for the fear of inviting the government's retaliation.

In practice, all of the VHP's decisions are taken in the name of the Dharma Sansad. The VHP gets its mandate from this body of sadhus; members are appointed by the VHP on the basis of their agreement with VHP's line of thinking. The Dharma Sansad, a purely theocratic body, supposed to possess divine sanction, sits, deliberates and takes decisions on a regular basis—decisions which are implemented or meant to be implemented by the VHP. Such an organisation subverts the idea of democratic functioning. It is not an elected, but a nominated body— its members being nominated by the VHP—and the Hindus are supposed to heed its decisions because of its putative divine ordainment. The formation of the Dharma Sansad is itself not morally or legally wrong, or anti-democratic; everybody possesses a right to form associations and institutions like the Dharma Sansad. However, if such an institution challenges the authority of the state institutions that are procedurally created—the parliament and the supreme court, for example—and works parallel to them, it goes against the established democratic norms. The Dharma Sansad of the VHP does just that. It considers itself above state institutions, which was amply demonstrated during the demolition of the Babri Masjid and the subsequent VHP activities. It considers its word as the final word. The masjid was demolished in violation of established rules and procedures of democratic functioning. The VHP did not let the Ayodhya dispute be tackled by the legislature and the courts of law—the institutions of state—but in utter disregard for democratic norms, struck on its own, claiming the support of Hindus. The VHP mirrors what Golwalkar had to say about sadhus and sants, which is,

> The political rulers were never the standard-bearers of our society. They were never taken as the props of our national life. Saints and sages, who had risen above the mundane temptations of pelf and power and had dedicated themselves wholly for establishing a happy, virtuous and integrated state of society, were its constant torch-bearers. They represented the *dharmasatta* [power derived from possession of spiritual knowledge]. The king was only an ardent follower of that higher moral authority. (Golwalkar 1996:65)

According to a former VHP member, Sakshi Maharaj,

> The sadhu has always ruled society. We *sanyasis* [ascetics] have come forward today to purify politics, just as Lord Shiva stepped forward to drink the poison which sprang from the churning of the cosmic ocean.[46]

In a similar vein Ashok Singhal says,

[46] In Ranjit Hoskote, "The Ascetic Armed," *(Sunday) Times of India* (New Delhi), 8 August 1993, 1.

> *Sants* are our guiding lights. We walk behind them. We share a reciprocal relation with them. Outsiders cannot understand this. That's why they keep saying and writing whatever they please.[47]

It must be pointed out that in all present-day political parties of India, democratic functioning is deficient. However, since democratic structures and procedures—of deliberation, discussion, one person–one post, decisions by voting etc.—are present in these parties, their working cannot become completely arbitrary. This means that the aspirations of a wide cross-section can more or less be fulfilled. However, in the functioning of the VHP, democratic structures and procedures are hard to find. One source of its mandate is the Dharma Sansad and the other, and more important, is the RSS. The agendas of both these organisations have to be implemented by the VHP. This implies that the VHP provides a perfect plan for a theocratic state. And, in an enthusiasm for issues such as Ramjanmabhoomi, Krishnajanmabhoomi and conversions, the real social and material issues of *roti, kapda aur makan* (food, clothing and shelter), so very important for a democratic polity, are pushed into the background. These crucial issues of people's struggles have always constituted an important agenda of Indian democracy and all parties have felt it imperative to build it into their programmes. Even a completely power-drunken government of Indira Gandhi, driven by an authoritarian and centralising agenda, raised the issue of *garibi hatao* (eradication of poverty) during the 1971 elections. The JP movement and the huge railway strike in the 1970s drew on these basic mass issues. At that time, the VHP's and Sangh's propaganda on conversions and cow slaughter did not get much response, and they were compelled to join the aforementioned movements.

Today, however, the VHP is setting the agenda of Indian politics, and Rama, Krishna etc. have become the central issues of governance, overshadowing all popular struggles centred round livelihood. This is happening even when the real demands of food, cloth, clean drinking water, shelter and basic education have not been fulfilled.

[47] In Raghunandan Prasad Sharma, *Marg Darshak Mandal ki vibhinn baithakain chhati Dharma Sansad ke aayojan par* (The various meetings of the Marg Darshak Mandal on the occasion of the 6th Dharma Sansad) (New Delhi: Vishva Hindu Parishad Publication, n.d.), 67.

The VHP's conception of democracy as compatible with practices violating established procedures of the democratic Indian state are fascistic symptoms. This does not mean that the Indian State has become fascist, but the VHP has been making use of the atmosphere to accelerate the demise of Indian democracy.

Ideological Consolidation

This was the period when great emphasis was placed on conducting all VHP work in Hindi. Earlier, the minutes of VHP meetings and other paperwork were written in English. From the mid-1980s, however, this changed, and considerable stress was laid on the use of Hindi in both formal meetings and informal social mixing.[48] Members were advised to use Hindi in social communication and specifically discouraged from using English as a means of interaction.[49] A sanitised, Sanskritised Hindi from which Persian/ Urdu terms were expunged was sought to be popularised. This began with the coming of Ashok Singhal to the VHP organisation, and displayed a marked change from the first phase in the functioning of the VHP. During my fieldwork it so happened that an activist began conversing with me in English, but another, who insisted that the former should speak in Hindi, the "national language," immediately interrupted him. On another occasion I was asked to say the Sanskrit "dhanyawaad" instead of the Arabic-derived "shukriya" while I was expressing thanks for tea during an informal meeting with an activist.

The VHP tried to devise ways to expand its mass base by insisting on the "vastness" of Hindu dharma as Hindutva, and thus assimilating various previously excluded groups into this broad definition. The VHP reiterated its arguments of the vastness of Hindu dharma and its "all-pervasive" character, which were attempts to popularise its

[48] As I was informed by Raghunandan Prasad Sharma at New Delhi on 30 January 1997. Sharma has worked in the Official Language Department of the Home Ministry. He was also involved with a body called the Kendriya Sachivalaya Hindi Parishad (Central Secretariat Hindi Association), whose objective was to see that all the work of the Government of India which was being conducted in English should be done in Hindi. Sharma is in charge of the publications department of the VHP at present. He has authored and edited several booklets for the VHP.

[49] Ibid.

ideology of identifying the Indian as Hindu and Hindutva as nationalism, and thereby generate support for itself. It has also emphasised time and again that Hindu dharma is "a way of life," i.e., a distinct code of communication and conduct peculiar to the Hindus, rather than a religion. The "way of life" aspect of the Hindu dharma was denoted by the term "Hindutva," which was borrowed by the VHP from V. D. Savarkar. The contemporary VHP closely identifies with Savarkar's idea that the word "Hindu" denotes much more than merely a religion. Savarkar felt that the inability to arrive at an exhaustive definition of the term "Hindu" lay in the popular error of identifying the word almost entirely with its religious aspect (Savarkar 1949: i–ii). It was important, according to Savarkar, to coin terms such as "Hindutva" and "Hinduness" to express "the totality of the cultural, historical and above all the national aspects along with the religious one, which mark out the Hindu people as a whole" (Savarkar 1949: iv). According to him, Hinduism formed only one part of the broad concept of Hindutva, which implies a way of life, Hindu traditions, customs etc. In other words, he saw Hindutva as embracing all departments of thought and activity of the whole being of the Hindu race. Hindutva was for him an all-pervasive concept (Savarkar 1949: 4). Accordingly, in the larger understanding of the VHP,

> The followers of any religion which originated in Bharat like *Sanatan Dharma* [orthodox Hinduism], Jainism, Sikhism, Buddhism etc., though they may be residing elsewhere in the world, are Hindus. Because they share certain values and beliefs in common like immortality of the soul, *punarjanma* [rebirth], *sarvadpanth sambhav* [equality of all sects], *ahimsa* [non-violence] etc.[50]

Taking the discussion further, it must be said that besides defining the Buddhists, Jains and Sikhs as Hindus, the VHP attempted to bring certain other sections within the Hindu fold in a move that can be called "inclusive." Those who were once pushed out of the caste hierarchy by the priestly caste—the *atisudras*, and the various tribal

[50] A. Shankaran, "Bharat in Danger," *Masurashram Patrika*, November 1986, 8. This monthly, in the English language, was started by Brahmachari Dattamurti (1901–1966), one of the founders of the Vishva Hindu Parishad, and an active member until his death in March 1966. His ashram, called "Masurashram" after his guru Masurkar maharaj, was in Bombay and is still being run by his disciples. The *Masurashram Patrika* is printed and managed by the ashram.

groupings which lay on the periphery of the caste system—were declared by the VHP to be Hindus in a major move to reshape orthodox Brahminism. The aim was not only to redefine Hindu identity, but also the very notion of Hinduism (as Hindutva), in order to include those who were traditionally regarded as outside the pale of Hindu dharma or simply *adharmik*. The VHP sought to include in its Hindu society all non-Hindus who were born within India's boundaries and were not Muslim or Christian. It wanted to check the exodus of this section to Islam and Christianity. Many of those ostracised from Hindu society converted to escape social and economic oppression at the hands of caste Hindus. The VHP of the present offers an alternative explanation for conversions:

> The tribals and outcastes were very much part of the Hindu society till the Christian missionaries came and made them break away from the rest of the Hindu society. The section of Hindu society residing in forests and remote villages was labelled by the Christian missionaries as "tribals." The tribals were told lies that they were the original inhabitants of India and the rest of the people came to the country as invaders. To divide and weaken the Hindu society, the Christian missionaries misled the tribal population that it is exploited and oppressed by the Hindus. Differences were also created between the Harijans and the upper caste Hindus. This task of a handful of Christian missionaries is now undertaken by the Muslims.[51]

Another VHP member said in a similar vein that the Muslims and Christians are making all efforts to create serious differences amongst Hindus.[52] About the development of untouchability in India, a senior member of the VHP said,

> Untouchability developed in India during *gulami* [imprisionment], that is, when India was ruled by the Muslims and the British. The Hindus to protect themselves from the foreign invaders locked themselves in their homes. They buried their money and raised the boundary walls of their houses to hide their women folk. The *gurukuls*[53] were shut down and children kept indoors. Thus, contact with the outer world broke down

[51] Kailash Chandra, "Soya Bharat Chete" (Bharat should wake up), *Hindu Vishva*, January 1990, 13–14.

[52] Arvind Brahmabhatt, in a personal interview, at Baroda in December 1995.

[53] A gurukul was a residential school which imparted knowledge of sacred Brahminical texts in pre-modern India.

> and children became *samskar shunya* [negligent of true knowledge and a sense of duty towards their motherland]. Even the books were kept aside during the foreign attacks. There was no exchange of knowledge during thousand years of foreign attacks. The Hindus because of this closed environment became alienated from each other. Each one of them began considering oneself the best. A superiority complex formed in each Hindu and this led to the practice of untouchability. [54]

A different account of the origin of untouchability, but which still links it to Muslims, went in the following way:

> When Muslims were on their conversion drive some Brahmin intellectuals refused to convert to Islam. As a consequence of their refusal to adopt Islam, the Muslims made them do such jobs as the cleaning of toilets. They cleaned shit but they did not give up Hinduism. Because they were engaged in a *mahtvapurna* [essential] work they began to be called *mehtars*. The term *mehtar* acquired a negative connotation over the years. However, all mehtars [Sudras] are Brahmins or upper-ranking Kshatriyas. [55]

The above accounts project an attempt by the VHP to conceal the unpleasantness attached to Hindu society by way of untouchability and oppression of the lower castes by the privileged castes. It attributes the wrongs of Hindu society and the maladies prevailing therein to those who seem to it the most easily available "villains" of history, and passes the blame to the Muslims and the Christians. Research into the ancient history of the Indian subcontinent, however, has revealed that harsh rules of conduct which forbade bodily contact with, and even the sight of, the Sudra on certain ceremonial occasions began to appear towards the end of the Vedic period, which dates to c 600 BC. There is evidence of growing contempt for manual labour towards the close of the Vedic period, especially for certain kinds of work, such as that dealing with corpses, and for the people engaged in it, such as Chandalas. Increasing restrictions came to be imposed upon the Sudras not only on ceremonial occasions, but gradually in daily life as well. The rules regarding defilement by touch became more elaborate as time passed (Dutt 1931: 179; Sharma 1980: 84–85).

It is on the question of untouchability and discrimination based on caste hierarchy that the change in the VHP's position is very clearly

[54] Gurujan Singh in a personal interview at Allahabad on 14 November 1993.
[55] Raghunandan Prasad Sharma in a personal interview at Delhi on 15 October 1995.

visible. Right up until the early 1980s, it emphasised the reform of Hindu social practices such as untouchability, caste discrimination and women's oppression. These social practices were held responsible for the weakness and degeneration of Hinduism, and therefore were held to be exploited by Christian missionaries and Muslims. It was assumed that it was the responsibility of the upper castes to take the initiative in addressing these shortcomings and eliminating them, because as a socially and economically privileged class they were better equipped to do so. It can also be argued that, though looking for change, some of the earlier leaders followed a "Gandhian" line on the basic acceptability of some form of occupational-cum-social division, provided no one was exploited. However, in the contemporary phase of the VHP's activities, the primary objective has been to politically unify the Hindus as a self-conscious organisation the world over. For this purpose it has been found necessary to suppress the lines of division in the caste hierarchy, and see all Hindus as part of a larger political formation. From this has followed the peculiar "theorising," which presents caste and gender discrimination as a direct result of, and a strategy of resistance against, the rule of the "other"—both Muslim and British. It is not as if this conception of caste and gender discrimination did not exist in pre-1980s Hindu thought, but rather, it now became the only understanding of this issue, and the discourse of social reform was almost completely forgotten. The political and organisational fallout of this change was that the Muslim, and to a lesser extent the Christian missionary, could be (and was) made the direct political enemy. This was done through mass mobilisation on those issues where this antagonistic relation is most apparent—for example the Ramjanmabhoomi issue.

On the question of women's position in the family and society, a similar argument is forwarded by the activists and leaders of not only the VHP, but all other related organisations such as the Bajrang Dal, Durga Vahini and Rashtra Sevika Samiti. It is said that the rape and plunder of the country consequent to the Muslim invasion(s) is the most important, if not the only, cause for the low status of women within Hinduism.[56] In fact, it is on the question of women that the VHP, along with the other Hindu organisations, has been able to

[56] My formal and informal conversations with the VHP activists revealed that this is universally believed within the organisation.

consolidate its ideological and political position within a large section of Hindus; it is therefore a favourite topic of discussion in most of their political writings and speeches. The educational backwardness, low legal status and oppression of women, as well as sexual discrimination against them, are all related to the need for defending Hindu society during a long period of religious attack and cultural siege during the last thousand years of Muslim rule. Even the contemporary situation, where women face massive discrimination and oppression, is linked to the presence of the Muslim in India, and the need for protecting women's dignity and the honour of the Hindu family. The issues relating to women's position in society, being a supra-class problem, are addressed with fewer complications than questions of caste; especially in a context where self-conscious lower-caste assertion has become an important facet of Indian politics.

The upper-caste but non-Brahmin trader-professional class constitutes a substantial part of the membership of the VHP, but the Brahminical notion of Hinduism is steadfastly held by this particular class. The strengthening of extreme conservatism in the VHP has occurred in a subtle manner and in a new garb. Certain Brahminical notions were either swept away or provided with a facade, in order to strengthen certain other ideas which were equally conservative. The VHP's conservative stance on social issues and fear of any kind of socio-economic restructuring is reflected in the character of the organisation, and in turn[57] draws to it the support of the urban trader-professional-bureaucrat section. It is interesting how the question of threat to these particular sections within the middle class gets transformed into a threat to Hinduism and Hindu society as portrayed by the VHP.

On the question of caste, the VHP world-view is tuned in favour of accelerating religious mobilisation in a manner that does not deny caste, but downgrades it in ontological significance.[58] However, the aim of this downgrading of caste is to promote a transcendent unity of

[57] The policy of reservation of seats in education and jobs is opposed by VHP leadership every now and then, as was evident from interviews with Girija Singh and Deoki Nandan Agarwal at Allahabad on 14 and 15 November 1993, respectively; from Sharma, *Vishva Hindu Parishad Ke Prastav*, 78, 148; and Muktananda Saraswati (n.d.: 48).

[58] Nowhere in the VHP publications or in interviews is the caste structure consciously contested, but there are moves to bring the various social levels closer together for a united Hindu nation.

the Hindus. In order to insulate the caste structure from internal friction the myth of the *virat purusha*, or primeval man, is propagated. This myth states that the four varnas were created out of the body of the virat purusha: priests (Brahmins) were created from the mouth, rulers or warrior kings (Kshatriyas) from the hands, the common people (Vaishyas) from the thighs and menial workers (Sudras) from the feet. A unity of these varnas is advocated by the VHP because, following the above illustration of the virat purusha, there exists an organic unity between the varnas—their source being single, and it is believed that conflict would result in disorder. There is also a sense of urgency that this idea about the lack of any conflict in the different parts of the same body has to be continuously propagated, otherwise conflict might result between the various levels of the Hindu social hierarchy.[59]

As noted earlier, classes which were once considered outside the pale of Hindu dharma, and as "pollutants," are now being accepted, though verbally, as integral sections of "Hindu society." At the same time, an attempt is being made to re-establish the authority of Sanskrit and that of the Dharmashastras, such as the Manusmriti and the Vedas, in society. The implication is that though equality is a widely discussed issue, attempts at eliminating social tensions have been marginal, and some sections are still considered to be more equal and "purer" than the others.

At this stage the leadership of the VHP—until now managed by the political elite and religious leaders—gradually passed into the hands of traders, small industrialists and service professionals. This phase witnessed the VHP making attempts to become a mass organisation and actually make significant inroads into the middle classes. From an elite organisation that did not have much of a popular base, the VHP increasingly worked towards the expansion of its social base through a change in its programmes, the involvement of youth in its activities and working at the local level. Raising its involvement in activities such as temple construction and management, *bhajan* and *kirtan* (Hindu devotional songs) functions, local festivals and cow protection, brought it immediate local contacts and publicity.

The VHP also took upon itself the task of defining the Hindu and the Hindu's leadership, in a move that remains to be successfully

[59] The VHP draws its perspective from *Integral Approach* (New Delhi: Suruchi Prakashan, 1991), 40.

challenged in today's politics in India. It considers itself the representative body of the Hindus and does not see any competition from any quarter with regard to its self-defined role as their leader. The fieldwork for this study revealed that all the VHP activists who were met (formally interviewed or not) nurture without exception a bitter anti-Muslim sentiment, so much so that they seem to take as the core of Hindu identity nothing but an anti-Muslim feeling. It is unquestioningly believed by the VHP activists of the present day that if one is a religious Hindu, one is also bound to be opposed to the Muslim community. An anti-Muslim sentiment becomes axiomatic in identity claims and the quest for a Hindu rashtra. Moreover, it is also important to point out at this juncture that much of the support for the VHP comes from sections whose consciousness over the decades has been embedded in a vendetta against Muslims due to certain historical factors, one of the most visible of which is the 1947 Partition. In the VHP activities these sections derive legitimacy for their own beliefs, and thus can redress what according to them is a historical wrong, and of which their families were victims. The VHP on its part seeks a receptivity to its message in these groups, so as to secure a firm social base for fulfilling its larger claims. The two thus provide each other a base to grow on and derive sustenance.

Chapter 5

Demolishing the Babri Masjid

Launching an "Army" of Durgas

A very interesting development within the VHP in the early 1990s was the birth of Durga Vahini, a result of the realisation of women's importance to the Hindu national project. To take this project forward an effective organised front of women assumed importance. Durga Vahini, an organisation of women between the ages of fifteen and thirty-five years, was formed with a view to organising women and involving them in the task of consolidating the Hindu political community. Interestingly, all members of Durga Vahini were closely related as sisters, wives, mothers or daughters to members of the VHP and RSS. There were even some *sadhvis* (women ascetics), vocal on social and political issues, whose potential to mobilise women was recognised, and who came to provide effective leadership to the Hindutva movement—for example, Sadhvi Rithambhara and Uma Bharati. Women, both as agents and subjects of mobilisation, played a significant role in the VHP-sponsored events such as the shilanyas, karseva, the demolition of the Babri mosque, and the organised vandalism against the film *Fire*.

Women in the Hindutva discourse, rather than being regarded as a category in their own right, are seen to possess the potential to take ahead the goal of Hindu rashtra. Their role in the Hindu nationalist movement is considered important not only because they provide support in numbers, but also because their participation seems to legitimise anti-Muslim sentiment. Further, they are regarded as builders of a "Hinduised" future generation. As such, their politicisation as a distinct category geared towards their own emancipation is suppressed; however, their politicisation as agents of Hindu nationalism is celebrated and encouraged. Thus, there is no objection to the extension of their personal sphere into platforms for Hindu national awakening. They became effective tools to demonise groups existing on the socio-economic margins and categorised as the condemnable "other."

Membership of the two women's wings of the VHP—Durga Vahini and Mahila Vibhag—was devised strictly of women who were drawn from the urban middle and lower-middle classes of professional or trader backgrounds. A large section of the membership was, and still is, of women not engaged in professional careers, but involved in full-time household activities. Those in leadership positions are confident, vocal, economically well endowed, and well-educated middle-class women. Together with leading the women's wings, they attend the VHP meetings and, as such, perform the role of intermediaries. Their role is to carry the VHP-RSS perspective on socio-political issues to the local women's units, and in turn report back to the parent organisations on the responses of units.

While the objectives of Durga Vahini were defined as seva, suraksha and samskara (similar to those of the Bajrang Dal), that of Mahila Vibhag, supposed to be more politically mature because of its members' seniority in years, was to raise "social and national consciousness in women."[1] A member in charge of the activities of the Durga Vahini unit of South Gujarat told me,

> In present times people are forgetting the principles of seva, suraksha and samskaras and we need to reinstil these values in them. This can be done only through women.[2]

What is insisted upon is that a Hindu woman should be *samskarsheel* or of a "good moral character." The Durga Vahini leadership emphasised that,

> If a woman in a mother's role is not samskarsheel (of a good moral character and who adheres to the values of Hindu dharma) no section of society can be virtuous. Good character of a woman is very essential for the well-being of society.[3]

A leading activist of Durga Vahini said,

[1] Shanti Devbala, all India joint secretary of Mahila Vibhag of the VHP, in a personal interview at Lucknow on 14 February 1996.

[2] Bina Sharma, South Gujarat mahila pramukh of Durga Vahini, in a personal interview at Baroda on 21 September 1995.

[3] Dr Malti in a personal interview at Delhi on 3 March 1996.

> What we say is that as a woman, wherever and in whichever role you are, you can get organised and improve society. We don't advise that a woman should leave her home or become a sadhvi. We don't insist upon such a thing. What we say is that if a woman in a mother's role is not samskarsheel no society or section can be virtuous.[4]

Regarding the mobilisational work of Durga Vahini, one of its members remarked,

> Our way of spreading our message is by keeping in regular touch with women. We keep meeting people in localities and neighbourhoods. We go to places where there are *kirtans* and *kathas* [small-scale religious meetings]. If someone invites us for a religious gathering we attend it and talk to people over there. At times we go in groups and at other times individually.[5]

So, like the Bajrang Dal, here also the neighbourhood is the main locale of mobilisation of support, and within this neighbourhood it is the sphere of religious devotion that becomes Durga Vahini's focus of attention. Religious gatherings, kathas and kirtans are considered to occupy a domain where effortless contact with women of a particular social background becomes possible. Most women who are part of these gatherings belong to middle- or lower-middle-class families, with strong religious proclivities. They accept the roles of mothers, wives, and grandmothers as natural to being a woman. Hence, they seem particularly vulnerable and receptive to Durga Vahini's message of Hindu religious nationalism.

In the regular meetings and workshops of Durga Vahini stress is laid on self-protection and self-help as defence from sexual harassment and other forms of assault. Training is imparted to girls in martial arts and other self-defence techniques for this purpose. This, however, does not mean that the patriarchal socio-cultural set-up is questioned or that a movement is built against the various forms of gender oppression and discrimination. The activities of Durga Vahini and Mahila Vibhag do not generate any kind of larger social emancipatory efforts for women as a distinct political class. In fact, the leaders of these organisations are very clear on the issue, and hold that theirs is not an attempt to build any kind of "women's

4 Ibid.

5 Sushma Rana, a member of Durga Vahini and a school teacher in Delhi, in a personal interview at Delhi on 3 March 1996.

liberation" movement. Such a movement in the West or in India is looked down upon as something not suited to Indian cultural values.

The reason for creating two separate wings for women is explained by a senior member of Mahila Vibhag:

> This division between Durga Vahini and Mahila Vibhag is not very rigid because to most of the places where women go, girls, or their daughters, accompany them. In fact, in our Bharatiya culture, young girls are never sent anywhere unaccompanied. Yet, Durga Vahini was separated from Mahila Vibhag because it was felt that the problems of girls are different from those of women above thirty-five years. Also, there is a need to create a second line of defence. If young women do not come in a movement a significant change in society cannot occur.[6]

Regarding the aim of the VHP's senior women's wing, Mahila Vibhag, one of its leaders said,

> We have to awaken women. We do not want women's liberation but *nari shakti*. We want that as a mother or as a wife a woman should have power —nari shakti. One of our goals is to make women all over the country a part of VHP, and keeping this goal in view we want that in a population of 2,500, ,one unit of ours should function and that its members should meet once in every 7–15 days.[7]

The goal does not seem to seek any change in the social structure or a departure from the existing gender relations, but to strengthen Hindutva through women. With this end in view, both young and middle-aged women are mobilised. The same leader adds,

> Around 1,000 to 3,000 of our units are functioning all over the country. In these meetings, besides discussions on dharma, there are discussions about the problems facing society. Most of the social problems concern women. These problems begin before a girl is born—such as female foeticide and infanticide. In Bihar and Rajasthan these problems still exist.[8]

Though maladies like female foeticide, infanticide and dowry are recognised as social problems specific to women, there are no strategised ways to tackle these. As issues of discussion and action

[6] Ibid.

[7] Shanti Devbala, all India joint secretary of the Mahila Vibhag of the VHP, in a personal interview at Lucknow on 14 February 1996.

[8] Ibid.

they are overshadowed by more "pressing" problems confronting the nation—like those of "infiltration" by Bangladeshis, conversions to Islam, the growth of the Muslim population in the country, the coming of anti-Hindu governments to power, and the anomalies of the Congress Party—all of which are sensationalised with a heavy communal flavour. According to one of the women leaders, the members of the women's wings are told about religious conversions and infiltration of Muslims into India in their meetings to make the members aware of the everyday social and political occurrences.[9] These issues dominate the sessions of the women's wings of the VHP, while the socio-cultural and economic problems confronting women are overlooked and become marginalised.

The aim of Durga Vahini and Mahila Vibhag is to generate in a woman an overall awareness of those social and political events that are held by the VHP to have important implications for its Hindu nation. The purpose of these discussions is to make women perform their domestic role suitably well, because it is believed that only when they are aware of these issues can they build similar awareness in their children.

Women are expected to be good mothers and wives, and their domestic role is given much importance. Their assertion of womanhood is intelligible only within the conventional patriarchal framework and a familial environment, breaking away from which is discouraged. This, however, does not imply that the women's domestic role makes them mere passive onlookers as far as public extension of Hindutva is concerned. Their domestic role extends into a public role as activists of the Hindu nation. The familiar "feminine" quietude is shunned in favour of an active role within the household and outside. Family and nation are the two important commitments that are held to necessitate adherence. The participation of women in good numbers during the karseva, shilanyas, the demolition of the mosque at Ayodhya, and in incidents of violence against Muslims shows that women of the Hindutva movement have not been innocent bystanders of violent sectarian activities. According to the historian Tanika Sarkar,

> In a bitterly ironic inversion of women's former invisibility in the domain of public violence, large numbers of women have been extremely active and visible, not only in the rallies and campaigns but even in the actual episodes of violent attacks against Muslims. (Sarkar 1995: 189–90)

[9] Ibid.

The contribution to the building of a Hindu nation, besides mobilisation activities, finds expression in active participation in violence—directed, for instance, against the Muslims. Flavia Agnes, a lawyer and an activist, writes, "The shakti of the modern Durga was not directed against violence within the home and community but was directed externally towards the Muslims—both men and women" (Agnes 1995: 141). Violence, verbal or active, is not directed against gender injustices, but focussed against the so-called cultural enemies of Hindutva.

Inspiration from Golwalkar

Apart from clarity over mobilisation affairs with regard to women, the VHP, by the late 1980s and early 1990s, had also come to acquire a distinct thinking on the ideological front. A uniform conception of the "Hindu" had also come to crystallise within the VHP as a notion of a Hindu political community. This was carried forward in a clear agenda of action for Hindu nationalism. M. S. Golwalkar, through his speeches and writings, became a great inspirational source for the VHP in its advocacy of Hindu nationalism. One of the secretaries of the VHP, Mandakini Dani, wrote during the silver jubilee ceremonies of the VHP, "Sri Guruji was not only one of the main founding trustees of the VHP, but also the original source for its establishment. On the occasion of the Silver Jubilee year of the Parishad, it is immensely essential for us to be acquainted with the path indicated by him for us to follow."[10] Golwalkar is described as the main inspiration behind the formation of the VHP, and is considered to have taken the pioneering steps towards awakening Hindu society.[11] The *Hindu Vishva* in one of its editorials mentions that "the great *mantra* of Guruji—*garv se kaho ham Hindu hain* (assert proudly that we are Hindus)—breathed life into and awakened the Hindus."[12]

In fact, as the interviews for this study affirmed, the VHP's core understanding of Hindu nationalism is drawn from Golwalkar, who believed that Hindus formed an ancient nationhood. He expressed his dissatisfaction with political leaders of the freedom struggle like

[10] Mandakini Dani, "Sri Guruji on problems facing the Hindus," *Hindu Vishva*, silver jubilee issue, 1990, 25, English edition.

[11] "Pranams to Pujya Guruji," *Hindu Chetna*, 21 February 1991, 6.

[12] Editorial, *Hindu Vishva*, September 1991, 4.

Nehru over the question of Indian nationalism—that they called India "a nation in the making," and said that India is "not yet formed as a nation" (Golwalkar 1966: 141). He wrote that the leadership of the freedom struggle "forgot that here was already a full-fledged ancient nation of the Hindus" and, on the contrary, "tried to create an entirely new nationality" on the basis of "the common danger of a foreign rule" which he felt could not happen (Golwalkar 1966: 141–42).

Golwalkar's notion of nationalism not only disregarded the role of minority communities of India but contained the potential for their complete extermination. He did not consider the entire citizenry of India as constituting the nation; for him Hindus alone formed the nation (Gangadharan 1970: 87). According to him the various minority communities which were living in the country "were here either as guests, the Jews and Parsis, or as invaders, the Muslims and Christians" (Golwalkar 1966: 142). They could not be called "the children of the soil merely because, by an accident, they happened to reside in a common territory under the rule of a common enemy" (Golwalkar 1966: 142). He went on to say that the Congress attempted to forge "a united front of all those who lived here" to confront the British rule which was also in line with the Congress' s "notion of nationalism" (Golwalkar 1966: 146). "There was no difficulty about the Hindus. They naturally love this country as their sacred motherland" (Golwalkar 1966: 146), but as for the others: "the Jews were ignored as they were very few," the Parsis largely "merged in the mainstream of Hindu life here," the Christians kept themselves "aloof from the freedom struggle" because there was a "natural co-ordination between the local Christians, the Christian Missions and British Government," and the Muslims had come here "as invaders and their antagonism was not merely political but was so deep-rooted that whatever we believed in, the Muslim was wholly hostile to it"(Golwalkar 1966: 147–48). Of a Muslim, he wrote, "If we worship in the temple, he would desecrate it. If we carry on bhajans and car festivals, that would irritate him. If we worship cow, he would like to eat it. If we glorify women as a symbol of sacred motherhood, he would like to molest her. He was tooth and nail opposed to our way of life in all aspects—religious, cultural, social etc."(Golwalkar 1966: 148).

Golwalkar held that only Hindus genuinely qualified to form the Indian nation. His deep-seated anti-Semitism forms the core of the VHP world-view also. The principle of "territorial nationalism" which he believed was the work of the Congress leadership was, according to him, entirely misconceived. He also wrote that among the Hindus

> those only are nationalist patriots, who, with the aspiration to glorify the Hindu race and Nation next to their heart, are prompted into activity and strive to achieve that goal. All others are either traitors and enemies to the National cause, or, to take a charitable view, idiots. (Golwalkar 1939: 44)

The VHP and the RSS

The publications of the VHP talk reverently about the RSS, but do not usually discuss the kind of relation which exists between the two organisations. The VHP writings are neither explicit about its affiliation with the RSS nor do they have anything to say about the RSS patronising the VHP since the time it was formed. The general trend until the mid-1980s was to avoid questions about the VHP's associations with the RSS. The erstwhile Maharana of Udaipur, Bhagwat Singh, former president of VHP, was insistent that the Parishad had nothing to do with the RSS (Goyal 1983: 33). The earlier hesitation to acknowledge any relationship with the RSS, however, was eased considerably with the development of events in the early 1990s. Association with the RSS no longer remained an embarrassing issue. References to the RSS are still avoided publicly in speeches by the VHP leaders, but in interviews for this study members were willing enough to talk about the VHP's relations with the RSS. Girija Singh, a member of the VHP, admitted that

> the VHP is a part of the RSS. But, despite being a part of the RSS, it is independent in its working. For instance, in a human body the work of the hands is not done by the eyes, the work of the ears is not done by the nose, the work of the nose is not performed by the eyes, and so on; they have separate functions and each performs its own function. Similarly, the VHP is autonomous, i.e., independent in its functioning but at the same time it is a part of the RSS.[13]

Deoki Nandan Agarwal, as a non-RSS member of the VHP, was more candid about the VHP-RSS ties:

[13] Girija Singh, vice president of the Uttar Pradesh unit of the VHP, in a personal interview at Allahabad on 11 November 1993.

> The entire functioning of the VHP—decision making and implementing —is in the hands of the RSS members who are in the VHP as organisational secretaries. The Governing Council and the Board of Trustees of the VHP are more or less ratifying bodies. They ratify the proposals of the RSS sangathan mantris [organisational secretaries].[14]

Vijay Parnami, in describing the relationship, said that the RSS is the body which runs organisations such as the VHP and the BJP. Moreover, those in the VHP of a non-RSS background are drawn towards the RSS in the course of time.[15] When questioned about the relation of the VHP with the BJP he said that the VHP as a separate organisation has an independent thinking of its own, distinct from other Hindutva bodies.[16]

Surya Dev Tripathi, an RSS member who looks after the work of the VHP in Delhi, forthrightly says that the VHP was formed as an RSS front for ideological dissemination:

> If one has to spread one's ideology in every walk of life one has to open several fronts. That was the basic idea. That is why RSS opened fronts in many directions such as the Mazdoor Sangh for the labour movement, Vidhyarthi Parishad for students and Jana Sangh in politics etc. One body cannot tackle everything. The basic idea was to spread the organisation in various directions. It had to be multifaceted. This is how VHP came up. The RSS did not organise temples, sadhus and shankaracharyas. Somebody had to do that work. The Hindu society was divided into fragments—the Arya Samaj, Sanatana Dharma, Buddhism, Jainism, Sikhism etc. were all distinct from each other. A broad platform was required to bring these together. For example, Sikhism is not an independent religion but an offshoot of Hinduism. Similarly, Jains are our own people. Our broad idea is to bring all these faiths within the Hindu fold again so that all feel that they are Hindus. This is the aim of the VHP.[17]

A. B. Saran, who heads the VHP unit of Allahabad at present, said in an interview that

[14] Deoki Nandan Agarwal, former vice president of the VHP, in a personal interview at Allahabad on 15 November 1993.

[15] Vijay Parnami, an RSS member who is also active in the VHP, in a personal interview at Baroda on 21 September 1995.

[16] Ibid.

[17] Surya Dev Tripathi, general secretary of the VHP's Indraprastha (Delhi) unit, in a personal interview at Delhi on 22 April 1996.

> In 1948, the RSS was made an untouchable as a result of a grim conspiracy by the Congress Party. The RSS was deliberately linked to Gandhiji's assassination and banned. Godse was in no way a part of the RSS but he was linked to it and a ban was imposed on it by the Congress. From that day onwards the RSS became an untouchable. People hesitated to go near the Sangh and they still do. They would not hesitate to join other Hindu organisations but it is not so when it comes to the Sangh. The Sangh was forced to become an untouchable.[18]

When asked if he meant that there was a need to form a body that could attract Hindus, he replied,

> Yes, this is a fact. People usually hesitate to involve themselves in the RSS but many of them have got associated with the VHP.[19]

The RSS leadership neither accepts nor completely rejects the fact that it has had a major role in the formation and functioning of the VHP; rather, the relationship between the two bodies is downplayed to some extent. Rajendra Singh, the former sarsanghchalak of the RSS, on this question, remarked,

> The RSS has not floated any organisation. Its aim is to create good swayamsevaks who are responsible Hindu citizens. It is they who, accepting the challenges of the situation, float various organisations.[20]

This position of the RSS is reiterated in another publication of theirs, which says,

> Many and varied have been the organisations formed by the swayamsevaks. . . . However all these bodies are entirely independent, complete with their own distinct constitutions, office bearers and policies and programmes. (*RSS: Spearheading Indian Renaissance,* 45)

Ashok Singhal, who heads the VHP and who has been an RSS member since 1942, on being asked about the relationship between the two organisations said that the RSS is engaged only in "character-

[18] A. B. Saran in a personal interview at Allahabad on 30 October 1995.

[19] Ibid.

[20] Rajendra Singh, in an interview in *Organiser*, 10 November 1985, 8. At the time of this interview Singh had not yet become the sarsanghchalak of the RSS, but was its general secretary.

building through shakhas."[21] However, he also pointed out, "There are lakhs of swayamsevaks who guide and help thousands of organisations (one of them being the VHP) to function."[22] When asked what the need for an organisation like the VHP was, when the RSS was already working for the spread of Hindutva, Singhal replied,

> Sangh is like a university. A sole university is not the only requirement, it cannot fulfil all tasks. Not all are able to go to universities, therefore, to spread the ideas and principles of the RSS in society various types of organisations were required and formed. The VHP is one of them. It works in the socio-religious sphere. The swayamsevaks initiated several organisations and are working zealously in these organisations.[23]

It cannot be denied that the RSS has considerable control over the functioning of the VHP, but the latter has a distinct personality of its own. It was after the uproar over the Meenakshipuram conversions in 1981 that the RSS swayamsevaks began working for the VHP in large numbers, in order to help it build a mass movement (Andersen and Damle 1987: 238–39). The RSS activists who began work as VHP members had spent a considerable period of time being trained in RSS shakhas. They brought with them to the VHP the RSS's sense of discipline, organisation, and experience in mass mobilisation. They were the most active in doing sundry jobs for the VHP and spreading its message across the world through their wide organisational network.

Demolition of the Babri Mosque

The VHP-RSS combine, working with this spirit of exclusive nationalism, decided to perform a "symbolic karseva"[24] at Ayodhya on 6 December 1992. By "symbolic" they meant the offering of prayers with bhajan and kirtan performances amidst chanting of *slokas* (sacred Sanskrit couplets). On 5 December 1992, the VHP's Marg Darshak Mandal sanctioned the beginning of karseva for the

[21] Ashok Singhal in a personal interview at New Delhi on 4 February 1997.
[22] Ibid.
[23] Ibid.
[24] "Advani to take part in symbolic karseva," *Telegraph*, 30 November 1992.

Rama temple on the following day. However, it made it clear that there would be no construction on any part of the 2.77-acre disputed area around the Ramjanmabhoomi.[25] This announcement was made to nearly 200,000 karsevaks present at the site, though the sadhus did not give any details of what the karseva would involve doing.[26] Assuring that there would be no violence on 6 December, Paramhamsa Ramchandra Das, the chairman of the VHP's Ramjanmabhoomi Nyasa (Trust), asserted that the RSS-VHP-BJP cadres were a "disciplined lot"[27] and would not indulge in any confrontation. However, in an operation that lasted about six hours, a mob of karsevaks pulled down the mosque in what can be called a brisk action, while the police and the paramilitary forces looked on.[28] The Babri mosque was demolished on 6 December 1992 by violent Hindu mobs mobilised by the VHP, RSS, Bajrang Dal and Shiv Sena, while the central and U.P. governments witnessed the action helplessly. In the words of Achin Vanaik, "The post-July run-up to the demolition of the Babri mosque on 6 December 1992 is a story of retreat after ignominious retreat by the government." (Vanaik 1997: 50). The Indian state once again revealed its "soft" side by shrinking back and failing to check Hindu communalism. Many like Vanaik felt that it went along with the dominant Hindu middle-class opinion in North India on the demolition question.

Devastating communal violence across the country followed the demolition. The states of Maharashtra, Gujarat and Uttar Pradesh were the worst affected. On 9 December 1992 the number of deaths in communal riots crossed five hundred.[29]

25 Sajeda Momin, "Only symbolic kar seva at Ayodhya: Sants decide not to begin construction," *Telegraph*, 6 December 1992.

26 Ibid.

27 Monimoy Dasgupta, "We do not expect violence, says sadhu," *Telegraph*, 6 December 1992.

28 Mohan Sahay and Ishan Joshi, "Mob on a rampage as police looks on," *Statesman*, 7 December 1992.

29 "Bandh evokes mixed response: Violence toll crosses 500," *Indian Express*, 9 December 1992.

TABLE 2: Deaths in Communal Riots, 6–9 December 1992

Maharashtra	151
Gujarat	117
Uttar Pradesh	55
Madhya Pradesh	48
Karnataka	40
Assam	29
Rajasthan	28
Andhra Pradesh	19
Bihar	10
West Bengal	8
Kerala.	6
Tamil Nadu	2
Orissa	1

Source: "Bandh evokes mixed response: Violence toll croses 500," *Indian Express*, 9 December 1992.

By 10 December the death toll had crossed 950.[30] On that day, the central government headed by P. V. Narasimha Rao issued a notification under the Unlawful Activities (Prevention) Act 1967, banning the VHP, RSS, Bajrang Dal and two Muslim fundamentalist groups by the names of "Jamait-e-Islami-Hind" and the "Islamic Sevak Sangh."[31] The ban on the RSS and the Bajrang Dal was, however, revoked by the Justice P. K. Bahri tribunal on 4 June 1993, as it felt that the charges against these two bodies had not been substantiated by the central government.[32]

Nrittya Gopal Das, a sadhu and a high-profile member of the Ramjanmabhoomi Nyas of the VHP, when asked about the 6 December demolition, said,

> *Yeh Bharat ke upar lagay huay kalank ka mitna hai* [It is the wiping off of the blot that had been smeared on India]. Despite the attainment of independence by India in 1947 this blot continued to exist. Babur came to India, converted Hindus to Islam and destroyed temples. That structure [Babri mosque] was a blot on India's face. Its destruction was a second independence for us. The first independence was incomplete. Therefore, a

[30] "Shoot-at-sight in Calcutta; toll mounts to 950," *Economic Times*, 11 December 1992.

[31] "Govt bans RSS, VHP, ISS and two others," *Hindustan Times*, 11 December 1992.

[32] "Ban on RSS, Bajrang Dal lifted," *Pioneer*, 5 June 1993.

> second independence was needed. The government has passed the Places of Worship Act, but till [*sic*] structures exist on the Hindu sacred sites of Varanasi and Mathura, etc., Hindus would not be able to rest in peace.[33]

For the VHP, history moves around the centrality of "the Hindu." The Hindu becomes the pivot around which history revolves. Issues that become focal points are Hindu glory, Hindu honour, Hindu bloodshed and Hindu onslaught. Indian history becomes a very linear pattern of classical Hindu splendour and glory, medieval decline due to Muslim misrule, and the modern Christian takeover of administration—which, although it rescued Hindus from Muslim rule, is itself unfavourable for Hindu sanskriti. This notion of Indian history is not new, but originates from the historiography which acquired currency in the late nineteenth century among the Indological scholars from Europe and the early nationalists. They held that the Hindu classical age had been followed by decay and anarchy during the rule of the Muslims.

Phalahari Baba, a sadhu who is not a VHP member but who was a member of the trust formed subsequently by the Congress-I to build the Ramjanmabhoomi temple, had the following to say about the demolition of the Babri mosque:

> There is a limit to patience and the patience of the Hindus was exhausted. Therefore, the 6 December event took place. However, the manner in which the mosque was brought down cannot be defended. It led to riots and generated anger. The mosque-temple issue could have been tackled in a civilised way. The government with a court order could have built the temple, which is actually the correct approach to the problem.[34]

It is interesting to see what Phalahari had further to say about the Ramjanmabhoomi–Babri mosque issue,

[33] Nrittya Gopal Das, *mahant* (head of a Hindu religious order or sect) of Chhoti Chavani (literally: small cantonment), Ayodhya, in a personal interview on 20 November 1993 at Ayodhya.

[34] Phalahari Baba, in an interview at Ayodhya on 20 November 1993. Phalahari, a prominent sadhu of Ayodhya, belongs to the Ramalaya Trust (which became non-functional after its very formation), formed on the initiative of the Congress-I government as a countermove to the activities of the VHP.

> Q: Do you think that the Babri mosque was a blot (*kalank*) on the history of India?
> A: It is not so. If it had been so our entire history would have been a kalank.
>
> Q: On the question of construction of the temple would you support the VHP?
> A: The temple should be built, there is no doubt about it. However, the job of construction should be handed to those who can do it; it should be handed to the Hindu society. The Hindus should take up this responsibility. The sadhus and sants should not involve themselves in this construction business. A sadhu should remain immersed in his spiritual quest. He should not get involved in worldly affairs. He renounces the world for spiritual success and he should not abandon this quest.[35]

About the VHP, Phalahari remarked,

> The VHP has come into politics. What the VHP has worked at is to bring the sadhu and sants into politics and they have become more of politicians than men of religion.[36]

A two-year ban was imposed on the VHP for its role in the demolition of the Babri mosque, but the Indian state did not actually put an end to its activities. The VHP continued to work in a low-key manner, shunning publicity. In some places it assumed the name of Hindu Sangam. The nonchalant attitude of the VHP ranks during the ban was evident. According to them the central government's ban was only nominal.[37] In fact, on 25 January 1993 the VHP went ahead to form the Ramjanmabhoomi Nyas Manch —a trust to guide the construction of the proposed Rama temple on the *garbha griha*, the spot where Rama is supposed to have been born and where the mosque once stood. Despite their disagreement over who was going to build

[35] Ibid. It is worth noting that Phalahari advocates the non-involvement of sadhus in worldly affairs, but is himself involved in the politics of Ramjanmabhoomi–Babri mosque, though he is opposed to the VHP.
[36] Ibid.
[37] Harish and Bina Sharma, Bajrang Dal and Durga Vahini members respectively, in personal interviews at Baroda on 27 December 1995. The VHP office in Baroda had a lock on its main entrance, but the back door remained open for activists to freely move in and out and to hold meetings, with the lone police constable keeping guard on the main entrance lest the VHP office "starts functioning." There was a similar situation at the VHP headquarters in Ramakrishnapuram in New Delhi.

the temple, the shankaracharyas (who backed Narasimha Rao's move to form an "apolitical trust" to construct the Rama temple) and the Sangh group were one over the issue that a mosque should not come up in or around the area of the proposed Rama temple.[38] After the charged atmosphere of the late 1980s and early 1990s, the locals of Ayodhya-Faizabad had become somewhat indifferent to the tirades between the central government and the VHP. According to Ram Swarup, owner of a sweets shop in Ayodhya,

> Now that the mosque is no more, we know that the temple would eventually come up. So, why should we waste our energy on the issue? [39]

Amongst some non-VHP sadhus of Ayodhya, the opinion that the Rama temple should be built on the site of the former mosque is quite strong. Ram Subhag Das, an old sadhu of Ayodhya, is one of the sadhus who placed the Rama-Sita idols inside the Babri mosque in 1949. Though not a member of the VHP, he feels in much the same way that the Rama temple should be built under all circumstances.[40] There seems to be a general understanding among the people of Ayodhya that the Rama temple will come up at the controversial site now that the Babri mosque no longer exists. The VHP's temple construction work is indeed going on in a consistent and innovative way, without any kind of state intervention. In 1996, during my meeting with VHP members at Lucknow, a local VHP member casually mentioned,

> Construction of a building means construction of its doors, windows, walls, pillars etc.—and this work of ours is going on consistently in a commendable manner. Marble and sandstone for the temple is being cut

[38] Minu Jain, "Domes of Contention," *Sunday*, 18–24 October 1994, 24.

[39] Sharat Chandra, "All Quiet on the Ayodhya Front," *India Today*, 4–10 September 1994, 22.

[40] Unrecorded conversation with Ramsubhag Das at Ayodhya on 20 February 1996. Ramsubhag Das manages two temples in Ayodhya, one of which is believed to be the place where Rama lived and carried on his rule. Ramsubhag Das did not join the VHP because of his resolve to stay away from the media and public gaze, much in accordance with his *sadhutva*. He told me that he does not speak from any platform and does not address public meetings or religious gatherings, in keeping with his promise to his guru to lead a quiet ascetic life.

> and carved at Ayodhya as well as at those villages where these stones are being procured. For the convenience of the workers, the VHP has decided to get some stones carved at those very places where the stones are found.[41]

The disputed site and the surrounding land are at present in the possession of the central government that stands as the receiver of 2.77 acres of land. This land, according to the Supreme Court ruling of October 1994, cannot be transferred to any individual or organisation until the Ayodhya dispute cases are finally settled by the Lucknow Bench of the Allahabad High Court. According to Deoki Nandan Agarwal, a retired judge of the Allahabad High Court, who is actively involved in the Ayodhya litigation despite being more than eighty years of age,

> The VHP had decided that it would start construction on the area which surrounds the 2.77 acres of disputed land, i.e., the area lying between the shilanyas site and the boundary wall of the old structure. This would have taken 2–3 years, by which time the judgement of the High Court cases (on the transfer of land) would have come. However, the construction could not even begin on the adjoining land because the entire area is in, [the] possession of the government of India. Therefore, what is happening is that workmen in their homes are doing the carving and cutting of stones, to be used in the temple. The stone is being supplied to them in their homes. This whole work would take about two or two-and-a-half years to be completed, by which time we hope that the suit would be decided.[42]

Stones are being designed both at Sirohi (Rajasthan), where the stone is found, and at Ayodhya. Sculptors from Rajasthan and Gujarat are carving stones for pillars in the VHP's Temple Construction Workshop (Mandir Nirman Karyashala). This workshop has become a sightseeing spot, with a local VHP member performing the role of a guide to "enlighten" visitors and devotees about the "history" of Ayodhya and of Ramjanmabhoomi. A wooden miniature of the temple, modelled on the Somnath temple of Gujarat, is displayed in a glass case at the workshop's entrance.

41 Harijeevan, secretary of the VHP, Lucknow unit, in a personal interview at Lucknow on 14 February 1996.

42 Deoki Nandan Agarwal in a personal interview at Allahabad on 3 February 1996.

Mid-1990s

Moving towards the 1996 elections, the VHP's Hindutva idiom once again became caustic. It planned some more yatras as the elections drew closer. Uma Bharati's speeches, flavoured with a charged and explosive vocabulary, were recorded and subsequently circulated during October 1995, on the occasion of the VHP's second round of ekatmata yatras. The language used by Uma Bharati in her speeches can only be compared to the language employed by Rithambhara during the height of the Ayodhya movement. The expressions and vocabulary employed here, woven in the idiom of militancy, were damagingly communal. It is interesting to note that such an idiom was not used in the first twenty years following the VHP's formation. In the live recordings of her speech Bharati, amidst huge applause, says,

> Crores of illegal Bangladeshi immigrants are streaming into this country every day, but a woman like Taslima Nasreen[43] is not being allowed to come [to India] because instead of "talaq, talaq, talaq"[44] she will teach how to give "tit for tat" and say "tadaq, tadaq, tadaq!" [tries to replicate the sound of slaps]

She continues,

> A Hindu refugee can come in this country and take shelter because a child has a legitimate right to its mother's lap, but someone who has kicked the womb of Bharatmata after calling it impure and then left the country,[45] should be kicked in the same way and thrown out of the country.

Amidst clapping in the background from the audience she continues even more aggressively, that "The cow is killed in this country because

[43] Bangladeshi writer who had to seek refuge overseas when her novel *Lajja* infuriated Muslim orthodox opinion in Bangladesh.

[44] The term "talaq" signifies divorce, i.e., the annulment of marriage. However, there are differences within Islamic opinion, and even between families, as to whether uttering the term thrice in the same instance leads to divorce. Some hold that the term has to be repeated over a particular period—say three days, three weeks, or even three months—before a married couple finally divorces. Some believe that the term has to be repeated before the same witnesses who solemnised the marriage. These differences depend on the interpretation of personal law, the social situation and the religious beliefs of the families involved.

[45] Referring to the Muslims and the Muslim League's demand for Pakistan in 1947.

she is a Hindu's mother and she will continue to be killed till the time a Hindu regards her as a mother." She goes on to say that if "Muslims have the freedom to practise their religion by slaughtering cows, then Hindus should have the freedom to kill the slaughterers of cows." One is reminded of Sarkar's words about the VHP's women activists and their role in violence against the Muslims (Sarkar 1995: 189–90). This violence is not only manifest as participation in programmes directed against the Muslims, but also as vitriolic pronouncements against them.

Exploration of the language of mobilisation employed by the VHP forms an interesting area of enquiry. The language used by it might differ from place to place. Differences in this language of mobilisation across various regions are related significantly to the socio-political milieu. Not only is the content of the speeches and statements area-specific but also the pitch and aggressiveness. For example, the language of mobilisation for the Ramjanmabhoomi agitation in the North-Indian urban towns had the aggressiveness and virulence corresponding with the highly contested political environment in these areas. But in the tribal areas of North-east and central India this aggressiveness was absent; the VHP's programmes were more in the nature of social activism and they continue to be so. In addition, the rhetoric for cow protection was louder in the Uttar Pradesh towns of Allahabad, Lucknow and others—here it was more effective and had greater potential for communal polarisation than, for instance, in the East or the South.

The organisation's language of mobilisation can also be seen to have changed over time, especially since the mid-1980s, when it entered active political life and took upon itself the task of organising and uniting Hindu society within India on a political level. This change also led to a diversion from the earlier centrality of concern with the Indian diaspora.

The period from 1981 to 1986 forms the interface in this process of transition from a religious-reformist language of mobilisation to an openly militant and loud genre, a change which saw the VHP adopting an overt interventionist stance in political power contests from the late 1980s. This transition can be attributed to a variety of interrelated factors, the more important of which have already been discussed, but in a different context. It would be useful here to briefly recall those points for the purpose of elucidating the argument. The expansion of the RSS's active presence in the VHP from the mid-

1980s partly accounts for this change, where the former, as part of its larger strategy, pressed a more aggressive agenda upon the latter, reserving for itself its traditional low-profile façade in keeping with its original image.

The composition of the VHP was also transformed over the years, and this was instrumental in bringing about changes in the character of the organisation. Earlier, the VHP's membership comprised right-wingers and conservatives who belonged to the political mainstream (many of whom were close to the Indian National Congress at some point in their political careers), some activists of the RSS, Indians residing overseas, and leaders of various religious sects. Unlike the early years, mass membership became an important feature of the organisation in the late 1980s—so much so that subsidiary organisations, like the Bajrang Dal, were born, and soon came to wield considerable mass influence of their own. The organisational stress of the VHP shifted from issues of reconversion and partial social reform to political consolidation of the Hindus. The leadership, as also the membership, became largely identified with a single political party, the BJP. This also provided the opportunity for members of the VHP to directly enter electoral politics as BJP contestants, for instance, Vinay Katiyar and Uma Bharati. By the late 1980s the VHP leadership had come to consist mainly of traders or service professionals, and its membership had by now expanded to include sections from the OBCs as well as some SCs. Support in the countryside, though limited, had grown. On account of this ideological tightening and change in social composition, the VHP's language of mobilisation changed from mild socio-religious criticisms of the established order to a vitriolic and politically potent attack on the entire social and political ideology of the Indian state and its Constitution.

The socio-political milieu also witnessed changes, and the VHP's mobilisation strategies directed against the social and political "other" —where the political other was the Congress Party and the social other invariably the "anti-national" Muslim—found a ready acceptance among sizeable sections of the population. The VHP's language of mobilisation drew on the prevailing prejudices and tried to mould them to suit its political project of uniting Hindus against the Muslims and their deemed protector, the Congress-I.

The growing discontent with the Congress made further space for Hindutva politics. Despite partial growth in various sectors of the national economy—like industry, health and education—progress achieved was grossly inadequate in addressing, in any meaningful way, the issues of poverty, unemployment, illiteracy and the growing differences of wealth. The structural adjustment programme adopted during the early 1990s coincided with the rise of Hindutva militancy. The state decided to go on an economic liberalisation drive to offset the debt burden it had come under through heavy borrowings from the World Bank and the International Monetary Fund.

Economic growth and food grain abundance in the country went hand in hand with growing unemployment and glaring poverty, due to disinvestment and retrenchment drives. The cuts in subsidies by the government meant a cutback in the state's role in the economy, a move that was to increase income inequalities and livelihood insecurities. On the one hand the country's import costs shot up because of the Gulf crises, and on the other, the collapse of the Soviet Union brought about a huge decline in exports. Coupled with these factors was the Congress regime's economic mismanagement that brought about a sharp rise in prices of essential commodities, leading to a reduction in real incomes. These affected the Congress Party's political career.

The VHP's adoption of a populist agenda on issues of poverty and unemployment, and its coming closer to the BJP, encouraged it to use a sharper and more aggressive idiom against its "others." Coupled with this, concepts like democracy, secularism and tolerance came to form an important part of the VHP discourse at this time, as it often evoked them when it talked about Hindu nationalism, statehood and citizenship. The VHP significantly transformed the meanings of these terms as they stand in the liberal-democratic vocabulary to legitimise its anti-democratic and sectarian disposition. It put forward its notion of a Hindu as one who is religiously assertive and at the same time truly secular and tolerant, and of democracy as the rule of this Hindu majority. In fact, the language of (Hindu) majoritarianism deeply penetrated the VHP discourse after 1992, so much so that "Indian" became synonymous with "Hindu."

The VHP's whole demeanour by this time provided substantial grounds for the Hindu national movement to be read as a form of fascism (Sarkar 1993; Basu et al. 1993; Ahmad 1993). The VHP's anti-democratic and militant character became much more pronounced and it came to nurture fascist tendencies. Seetla Singh, the editor of *Janmorcha*, a Hindi daily published from Faizabad, remarked,

> The VHP is a kind of *Hindu League*, something similar to the Muslim League, and it wants to set up a theocratic state in India. The VHP's essence lies in being anti-Muslim and fascist.
>
> What is to be noted is that "Rama"came on their agenda in 1984. Rama was made a weapon by the VHP all of a sudden in 1984 after the ekatmata yagna yatras of 1983. It is a potent political symbol which helps VHP politically.[46]

It is significant that the VHP at this stage became quite active in the fields of primary education and tribal work, and in organising religious gatherings. It continued to display an even more aggressive outlook in its day-to-day work. Any diversions from the portrayal of Rama as a supreme entity brought out aggressive retorts from the VHP and its associate organisations. This reaction, for instance, was unrestrainedly demonstrated at Ayodhya on 14–15 August 1993 when SAHMAT[47] exhibited posters and write-ups on the various interpretations of the Ramayana. In one of these, namely the Dasaratha Jataka, Rama and Sita were depicted as siblings (Thapar 1991: 141–63).[48] The exhibition evoked acts of protest and vandalism from the VHP and Bajrang Dal activists, who saw this depiction as "denigration of Lord Rama"[49] and the "left-secularist's antipathy towards the Hindu religion,"[50] and warned that "we cannot allow this to go unchecked."[51]

Portraying a similar militant outlook, Jaibhan Singh Pawaiyya, the then vice president of the Bajrang Dal, expressing indignation over the crossing of Bangladeshi Muslims to India, declared,

> If they don't leave the country, we will throw them into the Bay of Bengal.[52]

Ashok Singhal, while addressing reporters at Ahmedabad in March 1995, declared that the VHP would not tolerate any *maktabs* and

46 Seetla Singh in a personal interview at Faizabad on 22 November 1993.

47 An acronym for the Safdar Hashmi Memorial Trust, based in New Delhi. This organisation has been actively working for communal harmony and against religious fanaticism.

48 Thapar's research on Rama-*kathas* (stories) have shown varied interpretations of the legend of Rama in different ancient literary cultures.

49 Interview with Vinay Katiyar, chief of the Bajrang Dal (a subsidiary of VHP) in *Frontline*, 10 September 1993, 20–21.

50 Ibid.

51 Vinay Katiyar quoted by Venkitesh Ramakrishnan, "Upstaging Hindutva," *Frontline*, 10 September 1993, 17.

52 Dilip Awasthi, "Ayodhya: Temple Cauldron Bubbles," *India Today*, 31 August 1994, 75, Indian edition.

madrassas (Islamic religious schools) run by the Jamaat-e-Islami or any other organisation because children in these institutions are taught anti-Hindu ideas.[53] He went on to say that

> they must be taught Indian culture which cannot be anything other than Hindu culture. *Hindutva* is Indian nationality and they must respect it. They must say Vande Mataram or they will have to leave India.[54]

Jaibhan Singh Pawaiyya declared that if the government tried to stop Hindu pilgrims from going to Amarnath (in Kashmir), they would not let *taziyas* (processions taken out by the Shi'ite community in reverence for Imam Hussain) be taken out in the entire country.[55]

Sadhvi Rithambhara in a public meeting declared that in the ancient past Hindu women have made enormous sacrifices to protect their dharma. She called upon women

> to wake up and become Durgas so that when time requires they are able to march with full strength to Ayodhya and slay demons like Mahishasur.[56]

While discussing the case of Mathura and Varanasi, Uma Bharati fervently espoused the "rights" of Hindus in the following words:

> Mathura and Kashi are as important as Ayodhya. The Christians have a right over Vatican and the Muslims have a right over Mecca and Madina. Nobody can challenge this. Similarly, the Hindus have a right over Mathura, Kashi and Ayodhya. The Muslims should come forward on their own and tell the Hindus that "you took Ayodhya on your own but we cordially give you back Mathura and Kashi ourselves."[57]

The importance of building an independent cadre was emphasised. Ashok Singhal remarked that full-time activists were needed to

[53] Express News Service, "Singhal attacks madrassas now," *Indian Express* (Baroda), 25 March 1995.

[54] Ibid.

[55] Jaibhan Singh Pawaiyya, "Bharat main ek bhi gau katne nahin di jayegi" (We won't let a single cow be slaughtered in India), *Hindu Chetna*, 1 February 1996, 8.

[56] In Acharya Giriraj Kishor, "Jab Hindu samaj roopi shiva ka netra khulega . . . " (When the third eye of shiva like Hindu society opens . . .), *Hindu Chetna*, 1 March 1995, 7.

[57] Uma Bharati in a speech at Allahabad on the occasion of VHP's second ekatmata yatra in October 1995.

strengthen the organisation, and they could be drawn from the youth as well as retired seniors.[58] Emphasis was also placed upon sustained social work to activate the smallest unit of the organisational structure. In addition, the VHP seemed almost sure that on the Rama issue it had mass support. The use of Rama as a means of generating support was considered to have achieved its purpose, and though still very important to the VHP, was set aside for the time being to make way for other VHP programmes. In the words of one of its own activists,

> Bhagwan Rama is in everyone's heart. Bhagwan Rama and Ayodhyaji is in everyone's mind. Bhagwan Rama's universality is now being identified with the Rama temple. . . . Everyone who believes in Bhagwan Rama wants to see the Rama temple built as soon as possible.[59]

The VHP also became emboldened and more publicly demonstrative after the demolition of the Babri mosque. This confidence was amply reflected in the statements of its activists during interviews. As regards the shift in the VHP over the decades, a senior leader said,

> Earlier the VHP was only protecting Hindu interests. We had a number of small institutions in northern India: small schools and small circles. We were trying to stop conversions through these institutions. The VHP had restricted itself to reforms and propaganda. But now we are coming out in the open. Now the VHP is coming out to support a political party and to campaign for a party which it thinks would protect Hindu interests.[60]

As to whether the VHP had decided to take a more militant stand on issues than it had ever done in the past, he said,

> Yes, this is the case. We have decided to oppose whenever we see any anti-Hindu acts committed.[61]

On changes in the VHP after 1992, another activist informed,

> Because of the temple issue of 1992 many people became involved with excitement of the temple issue. Despite the ban there had been a broadening

[58] News report on the VHP full-time workers' camp held at Ayodhya, *Hindu Chetna*, 1 January 1995, 4.

[59] Nrittya Gopal Das, a prominent VHP sadhu, in a personal interview at Ayodhya on 19 February 1996.

[60] Chunnibhai Patel, president of the VHP unit of Baroda and Bharuch, in a personal interview at Baroda on 2 December 1995.

[61] Ibid.

> of our social base. Many people who were not part of us definitely became involved with us after 1992. We believe that they [Muslims] had built the mosque at Ayodhya after destroying the Rama temple. A number of Hindus united for the cause of removing the [Babri] mosque. Even after the removal of the mosque, a number of Hindus have become active in the VHP. Earlier it wasn't so, only ten people used to come for meetings but now the number of people attending our meetings has gone up. After 1992, VHP work has not suffered. Despite the severity of the ban we have been working all along.[62]

Replying to a question regarding changes in the VHP after 1992, another senior activist said,

> Before Ayodhya [in 1992] the enthusiasm was tremendous, but certain things are momentary. That time the enthusiasm within people was extraordinary and because of it one could see that people gradually became more receptive to the VHP. So that people become involved with the activities of the VHP several programmes were taken up. In 1984 the first ekatmata yatra was arranged, followed by the Rama shila pujan and then by the Rama *paduka pujan* [prayers offered to slippers]. These programmes were undertaken so that the VHP becomes known to all—right down to the village level.[63]

These programmes were prompted by the need to build a favourable atmosphere and a public mood that would be conducive to political expansion. Also, these programmes acted as an introduction for the VHP as an agent of mass mobilisation.

During the mid-1990s, the Ayodhya unit of the VHP was seen engrossed in the task of preparing prefabricated structures for the Rama temple. This period also saw a spate in the building of Hanuman temples all over the country. The mythical Hanuman as a devotee of Rama and protector of Sita's honour has now, along with Rama, come to have acquired the role of defending the honour of Bharatmata. His two traits of devotion and duty are emphasised by the VHP as exemplary.

[62] Anil Mehrotra in a personal interview at Allahabad on 31 October 1995.

[63] Ramchandra Upadhyay in a personal interview at Allahabad on 2 November 1995.

Chapter 6

Post-Demolition Consolidation

Just before the 1996 elections, the VHP launched two more programmes to publicise Hindutva and garner support for the BJP. The first of these, the ekatmata yatra in 1995, was modelled on the 1983 ekatmata yatra. Through it, the VHP once again tried to build agitation around the Ayodhya, Mathura and Varanasi temples, but somehow did not manage to generate the kind of support that it had during the late 1980s and early 1990s, even in Uttar Pradesh.[1] The second programme, centred on cow protection, was also to generate political support on the eve of the elections. These events had a two-fold purpose: one, to involve the youth cadres and keep their energies engaged; and two, to further consolidate Hindutva as a political platform. The Bajrang Dal declared that it would give a "fitting reply in elections for the ban imposed on the VHP by the government, and the political forces which repeatedly attack hindutva would be uprooted and thrown away."[2] The language employed was quite often belligerent and intimidating. At another place it was said that "Hanuman-devotee Dal activists would take a krantikari [revolutionary] path in order to protect cows,"[3] and the ruling party was called upon to "leave the greed of votes and push back immigrants into their own countries."[4]

These programmes, however, did not find much favour among the central BJP leadership, who were trying to project a more accommodating and moderate image of themselves, with an eye on the elections. The "division of labour" (Noorani 2000) was at work between a "moderate" BJP and an "extremist" VHP. Atal Behari Vajpayee told reporters in March 1995 that he was not in favour of raising the Mathura and Varanasi issues at that stage. According to

[1] N. K. Singh, "Roaring for a confrontation," *India Today,* 15 November 1995, 14.
[2] In *Hindu Chetna*, 1 February 1995, 3.
[3] In *Hindu Chetna*, 1 February 1996, 8.
[4] Ibid.

him, unlike the Babri Masjid, the Gyanvapi mosque in Varanasi was an active mosque where thousands of Muslims offered namaz (prayers), and therefore an Ayodhya-like situation there would be entirely uncalled for.[5] L. K. Advani, president of the BJP, went on record to say that the issue of the Mathura and Varanasi temples was not on the BJP's agenda.[6] Such statements apparently generated tension between the BJP and VHP, because for the latter the agitation for temples did not end with the demolition at Ayodhya. The BJP on the other hand was guided largely by a sense of realpolitik, and did not openly want to associate with the VHP's confrontational approach towards the minorities at this juncture. It was felt that this would not be politically lucrative. When Advani's remarks were pointed out to the VHP president, he said "You cannot predict the agenda of a political party. The BJP has not yet defined its agenda."[7] The VHP, however, did admit later that the BJP had distanced itself, after having made use of the Ramjanmabhoomi movement for its electoral purpose.[8] The VHP's general secretary, Acharya Giriraj Kishore, said in an interview that the VHP had never sought the BJP's support for its temple movement, and the BJP had come on its own to take up the issue. He added that

> They are a political party, they are free to do it (distancing themselves). To achieve political gains or political power, they have to adopt many ways, which we may not like.[9]

Insisting that it would be better if the question (of distancing) were addressed to the BJP, the VHP leader went on to say,

> We are also free to have our own path. It is not necessary that they follow what we say or we follow what they say. After all, we have separate presidents, separate constitution and separate programmes.[10]

[5] Minu Jain, "Family matters," *Sunday*, 19–25 March 1995, 22.

[6] The Times of India News Service, "VHP to work for victory of Hindutva forces: Singhal," *The Times of India* (Baroda), 15 April 1995; Interview with L. K. Advani, *India Today*, 15 April 1995, 63.

[7] Times of India News Service, "VHP to work for victory of Hindutva forces: Singhal," *Times of India* (Baroda), 15 April 1995.

[8] Acharya Giriraj Kishore in an interview to Bishwanath Ghosh, "BJP ditched us for political gains: VHP," *Asian Age* (London), 4 April 1997.

[9] Ibid.

[10] Ibid.

The defeat of the BJP in the November 1993 assembly elections in Himachal Pradesh, Madhya Pradesh and Uttar Pradesh, and its poor performance in Rajasthan, prompted it to take a cautious approach to politics in 1995–96 as far as Hindutva was concerned. This move, however, was a strategic step and not a change of heart. Hindutva was downplayed by the BJP but not abandoned. Later incidents—such as the charge-sheeting of BJP leaders like L. K. Advani in the hawala case—made the BJP take it up again as its main election plank in 1996, though it was quieter on the specific Ayodhya issue.

Challenging Constitutional Principles

Keeping itself busy on the non-electoral front, the VHP felt encouraged to challenge the democratic foundations of the Indian state in the aftermath of 1992. Even earlier, the Indian Constitution had come under the verbal assaults of the VHP, and suggestions were floated that it be amended "to ensure and recognise the rights of the Hindus—the natural sons of Bharat."[11] It was only after the demolition of the Babri mosque, however, that harsh critical voices were heard from within the VHP against principles such as secularism, tolerance and minority rights enshrined therein. The Constitution was also criticised as an instrument of Congress domination over India. In October 1992, the Akhil Bharatiya Sant Samiti of the VHP set up a committee to rework the Indian Constitution, which was headed by a sadhu named Swami Muktananda Saraswati, one of its members. Muktananda Saraswati, in a small tract called *The Present Indian Constitution*, dissects the Constitution and points out the varied "flaws" in it. It is pointed out in the tract that,

> The main cause of communal conflict in India is that the Muslims and Christians have been granted special political rights as communities. Inspired by this, the other communities have also started demanding special rights. This has resulted in the break up of the foundational principles of unity in Bharat. (Saraswati n.d.: 3)

Muktananda Saraswati in this booklet goes on to say,

[11] For instance, minority religious and educational rights are criticised on the pretext that these rights suppress the rights of the Hindus. See R. S. Narayanswami, "Hindu Interests and the Constitution," *Hindu Vishva*, silver jubilee issue, 1989–90, 35–38, English edition.

> British imperialism could not break the Bharat samaj in 200 years the way it has been broken by the constitution in a few years. After independence, the conspiracy to change Bharat into India has been continuously going on. The resolves of the Preamble, have not been defined in the main constitution. The entire constitution is full of articles, which run contrary to the resolves of the Preamble. (Saraswati n.d.: 5–6)

According to Saraswati, naming the country "India," carving out lingual provinces and enacting Articles 30, 370 and 371 of the Constitution have violated the principles of sovereignty and secularism (Saraswati n.d.: 6). He argues that the unity and integrity of Bharat have come under grave danger because citizenship rights are distributed on the basis of minority, majority, Harijan, caste, community and language (Saraswati n.d.: 8). He says that as a safeguard against this danger, citizenship should be linked to nationality, and discrimination should not exist on the basis of the above-mentioned characteristics. Special benefits to citizens should be given only on economic grounds. Calling the Constitution *lok drohi* (anti-people), Saraswati says that the founders of the Constitution seem to have made it without studying the Indian situation (Saraswati n.d.: 7, 10).

The VHP, hence, busied itself in building a campaign against the Constitution among middle-class India; secularism in particular came under heavy assault. While conducting a politics of Hindu majoritarianism the VHP advocated what can be called *Hinduised secularism*. It argued for an Indian state grounded on a Hindu conception of secularism and democracy; Indian democracy was reinterpreted in the Hindutva mould as the rule of a religious majority.

In a plural society like India, following a democratic form of government, there is the possibility of a numerically strong cultural group commanding a political majority. Though discussed earlier, it needs to be reiterated that the rule of an entrenched majority that is defined in terms of religion, and is thus politically immutable, is not what democracy means. A democratic form of government, if it comes to stand for the rule of such an immutable and electorally inalterable group, defeats its very purpose and loses its inherent meaning. The dynamics of democracy presuppose the continuous alteration of the political majority, and hence of the ruling group—though not, of course, of the Indian people as a whole. Crucial to our discussion is the point that even if the political minority is out of government for long stretches of time, it does not exist outside the boundary of the nation or the political community; nor are the majority or minority defined by some pre-political community.

If an ethnically defined political identity with a relatively large geographical and cultural spread can win a parliamentary majority, it becomes next to impossible to dislodge it or to involve other groups in governance. Voters in this context have fixed loyalties towards certain political parties and support them because they are representative of their religious/linguistic/ethnic identity. One must also keep in mind that when such a political majority comes to control the state, there is little possibility of checking it if it decides to trample upon the interests of any group which is excluded from the ruling party. Such a majoritarian form of democracy, that has the inherent danger of effective disenfranchisement of numerically smaller ethnic or religious groups, forms the discourse of the VHP.

The VHP sees Hindu majoritarianism as perfectly compatible with parliamentary democracy in India. In fact, it is assumed that the true nature of parliamentary democracy would be realised in India only if it is working as a Hindu majoritarian system. Within the framework of the majoritarian argument it is difficult to contest the VHP's claims to be an upholder of democracy, which in turn becomes a strong mobilisational force for it. Claims that it stands for democracy bring it support even from those who would otherwise have opposed the VHP on the grounds that it brings religious prejudice into politics. One need only reiterate the point that large sections of Indians have found themselves excluded from the growing economic prosperity of middle-class urban India and the successful Green Revolution farmers. They find themselves not only deprived of economic prosperity, but also feel a lack of political power to be able to influence state policy towards their own benefit. The argument for Hindu majoritarian democracy is posited as an answer to this. While providing an outlet to the frustrations of the lower castes and classes, the VHP is able to maintain the support it receives from the urban middle classes and the rural elite who form the broad spectrum of the upper castes.

The VHP and Secularism

The VHP projects Indian democracy as steered by Nehruvian "pseudo-secularists" (of course, the BJP is exempt from this accusation), and as biased in favour of the Muslims and Christians. According to it, the present system has deprived the Hindus of their basic rights of cultural freedom and religious expression. The VHP isolates and uses certain non-secular governmental actions of the past to generate an anti-minority hysteria among Hindus. For example, it is said that,

> Apprehensions among the Hindus regarding discrimination were caused by several actions of the government including reversal of the Supreme Court order in the Shah Bano case, declaration of Prophet Mohammad's birth-day as a holiday, ban on Rushdie's book, family planning attitude towards Muslims, provocative and anti-Hindu actions of the Mulayam Singh Government in U.P.[12]

It is also argued that failure of the government to be neutral was the cause of the Hindu-Muslim problem:

> There would not have been any disturbances in the case of Mandir-Masjid issue if the Government had been neutral as no real difference exists between Muslims and Hindus on this score. It is to be clearly noted that the upsurge of Hindus in the case of Ramajanma Bhoomi issue is the result of the deep anguish and discontent expressed by them when the government failed to act in accordance with the principles of the Constitution, projecting secularism. This failure of the government is causing insecurity among the Hindus in their own country and their fears are justified.[13]

This argument is further extended to show that the Indian state uses scarce resources to "satisfy" the "non-productive" demands of the Muslims, to appease them—apart from the "massive" funding they receive from the countries in the Gulf. The VHP paints the present-day economic failures of the Indian state in stark communal colours.

> The Board of Trustees and the Governing Council of the VHP opposes the government of India's policy of giving rupees five hundred crores to the minorities for political ends and granting their *ulema* [Muslim clergy] and *moulavis* [Muslim religious leaders] salaries worth crores of rupees. This is done under the government's policy of appeasement of minorities. This work of creating a Muslim vote-bank through their appeasement is an insult to the Hindu society which is intolerable. The central government resources built up through taxing the (majority) Hindu society are spent in giving these salaries to Muslim ulema and moulavis, who already get

[12] "Shri Puttugi Swamy warns about Hindu unrest," *Hindu Chetna*, 21 January 1991, 7, English edition.

[13] Ibid.

> massive financial support from Muslim countries in the Gulf, which is extremely objectionable. It is against the spirit of the constitution and against national interests. Thus, it should be stopped.[14]

The VHP's unhappiness with the present Indian state and democratic governance is closely linked with its attack on the Indian Constitution, primarily on the issue of secularism. Secularism, or as it is often called, "pseudo-secularism," is seen as the central tool by which the Indian state and most political parties subvert the voice of the Hindus and is also seen to be the main cause of the weakness of the Indian nation. It is sometimes described by the VHP as state policy, sometimes as electoral strategy, sometimes as a foundation of the present Constitution, and sometimes as a social malaise afflicting large numbers of the Hindu masses. According to a senior VHP leader,

> In this country secularism is used mainly for winning the Muslim bloc votes . . . for these bloc votes the various political parties except the BJP indulge in Muslim parasti (appeasement) and Hindu virodh (opposition). . . . In countries such as Pakistan and Bangladesh there is no secularism. Look at the state of Hindu minority in these countries. There is not even a single Hindu soldier in these Islamic countries and the Hindus are being thrown out from there. The Muslims want to have secularism in India but want to deny it completely in Islamic countries.[15]

It is stated that the present Constitution of India is of the Indian state and not of the Hindu nation, which is why the Constitution drafters coined the phrase "India is a sovereign state." Instead of the term "nation" they used the term "state" (Sagar 1988: 14). It is straightforwardly pointed out that the Constitution of India is not in tune with the aspirations of the majority and runs against the oneness and indivisibility of the nation. Attacks on secularism become attacks on minority rights. According to a VHP publication, "Secularism has become a basis for discrimination, of Muslim appeasement and of capturing their votes for grabbing power" (Agarwal 1992: 4). The same booklet goes on:

[14] Resolution passed at Bombay on 19 December 1995, in Sharma, *VHP ke prastav*, 76.

[15] B. L. Agarwal in a personal interview at Allahabad on 29 October 1995.

> In the constitution of independent India the so-called minorities have been granted the freedom to profess and propagate their religion in accordance with their capability. This self-injurious policy has been called secularism. In these forty years of independence minorityism or Muslim appeasement has come to mean secularism.
> To become a non-Hindu has become the surest way of obtaining special rights, whereas, to be a Hindu is to be labelled communal and be bereft of special rights. . . . An atmosphere has been created today where it feels that to be a Hindu is committing a crime. (Agarwal 1992: 3)

When asked what secularism means to the VHP, Chunnibhai Patel said,

> "Secularism" is a very vague term. The term is used when it comes to Muslims and Christians but it is used always against the Hindus.
> We believe that all the religions should be equal. Equality does not mean favouring one against the other. There should be no difference in the treatment of one religion and the other. However, when you (the government) want to get votes you forget secularism and give all the benefits to those people from whom you want votes. The government brings in secularism and then breaks it itself. Is giving Urdu a status of [official] language in Uttar Pradesh a policy of secularism?[16]

A senior leader of the VHP remarks,

> People such as Jawaharlal Nehru who represented Hindustan in the West imported an ideology from the West, which was not required here. Ideologies such as secularism and socialism are being imported and imposed on us. Secularism is irrelevant for this country. It is not needed because by tradition we are secular. In the name of secularism what has come to pass is an anti-dharmik feeling. In Hindustan, we have become anti-dharma in the name of secularism. . . . In the name of secularism the rulers of this country have become anti-religion and anti-dharma. Being anti-religion is still understandable but they have become anti-dharma. They say that dharma should not interfere in politics. . . . They want untruth in politics, robbery in politics and corruption in politics.[17]

According to another senior leader of the VHP

> We do not need a certificate to be secular. We are naturally secular. That is why we allowed outsiders to come and prosper in our country. They

[16] Chunnibhai Patel in a personal interview at Baroda on 2 December 1995.
[17] Praveen Togadia in a personal interview at Ahmedabad on 15 December 1995.

> prospered because of us Hindus. However, they misused our goodwill. The Christians and the Muslims do not believe in *sarva dharma samabhava* (equal approach towards all religions). They cannot be explained [*sic*] because they don't listen. Secularism does not mean that you give minorities a superior status. Secular Indians are our greatest enemies. They will bring downfall of the Hindus. They give concessions to minorities. There is no truth in sarva dharma samabhava because the Christians and the Muslims do not believe in it and they just want to convert. In the name of secularism they are communal. They do not respect other religions. This goes against the Hindus. Why are religious conversions taking place when all religions are equal?[18]

The VHP considers a Hindu to be

> secular by virtue of his birth within this community. It is because of the generosity of the Hindus that secularism has prospered in India and not because of the Constitution. It is because of this generosity of Hindus that India afforded a chance to the Muslims and Christians to build their mosques and churches long before Muslim and English rule were consolidated in India. (Agarwal 1992: 6)

A leader of the Bajrang Dal says,

> We are secular. The Hindu dharma has never gone against anyone. History tells us that. The Christians came to Kerala first and settled there. Nobody opposed them and their religion. There was no bad behaviour even with the Jews. We have synagogues in our country. The Parsees have their worshipping places as well. The Parsees were just told that they should not kill cows. Nowhere such a lenient attitude has been found except here. In Muslim rule it has never happened so. The Christians divided the people. The Hindu dharma never taught rivalry with anyone.[19]

The VHP and Hindu Tolerance

Along with the "secular" trait, the VHP makes "tolerance" a central attribute of the Hindus. Secularism and tolerance are interpreted by the VHP almost like cultural traits—ones that only the Hindus are born with. However, it denies these qualities to those who fall outside the boundaries of its Hindutva. A common claim by its activists and leaders

[18] Professor (retired) Javadekar in a personal interview at Baroda on 18 October 1995.
[19] Harish Sharma in a personal interview at Baroda on 27 December 1995.

is that tolerance has historically been a characteristic of the Hindus, that it has worked not only for settlement of differences and disputations internal to the community, but also for establishing relations with the outside world. In other words, what the VHP implies by this account of "Hindu tolerance" is that various social strata remained in their own social sphere but coexisted; and "outsiders" were allowed to live and work in and around Hindu settlements, but had to remain outside the social community of Hindus. The Hindus, it says in a clearly chauvinist tone, as is evident below, were tolerant of the outsiders who came to India and preached their religion, but they in turn misused the "goodwill" of the Hindus. According to a senior VHP activist,

> The Hindus are a very tolerant race. They have never attacked any other country. They have accommodated everyone. But, now we find that these people, these Muslims are maintaining an enmity with the Hindus which is continuing from pre-Partition days.[20]

He continues,

> The Hindus have been practically turned out from Pakistan and Bangladesh, but in our country we have had Muslims as presidents, chief justices, chief ministers and central cabinet ministers.[21]

This mythical tolerance is repeatedly put forth to build a case against the religious minorities and perpetrate violence against them. The "atrocity" and "meanness" attributed to them become the excuse for larger campaigns for the defence of "Hindu unity" and "protection of dharma." It is important to note that the notion of Hindu tolerance built by the VHP is grounded entirely on the "large-heartedness" and "generosity" of the Hindus and not on some moral position, as has been discussed in the earlier paragraphs. It would be useful to keep this point in mind when discussing the ideology of the VHP and its polemics with its opponents. In the present-day context this claim of toleration becomes the central focus on which the VHP and similar Hindutva organisations build their defence against charges of anti-secular politics and anti-democratic intentions. In such a case, where tolerance is held to be one of the main characteristics of Hindu society, events such as those related to

[20] B. L. Agarwal in a personal interview at Allahabad on 29 October 1995.
[21] Ibid.

the Ramjanmabhoomi movement are explained as occasional happenings which are routine in the momentum of history. According to Praveen Togadia, a senior VHP leader,

> I don't believe that tolerance [of Hindus] has abated. What difference has come in tolerance? Babri structure was demolished, there were several riots. But such things keep happening and many people go through these events. For ages people have been attacked, their villages have been burnt down, daughters and sisters have been sold. If you are right you will struggle, otherwise you will sit and cry. In this world except the Jews no one has suffered as many attacks as the Hindus.[22]

Togadia also holds that

> Hindu dharma was tolerant in the past, it is so at present and it would remain so in future. Fundamentalism and Hindu dharma can never be together. If a person is communal, fundamentalist and intolerant he cannot be a Hindu. If there is intolerance it becomes Islam and Christianity. At a philosophical level it becomes Islam or Christianity because that is the difference between them and Hindu dharma.[23]

In situations where violence is involved, confrontation is justified as defence of "Hindu identity" or the "Hindu motherland" or "Hindus' mother," which again does not imply the lessening of Hindu tolerance. On the question of the VHP's cow protection campaigns this activist goes on to say,

> Cows are like mothers to Hindus, so how can we tolerate killing of cows? But this does not mean that Hindu society is intolerant.[24]

According to the VHP, it is not only possible, but rather actively desirable, to tolerate the differences which are embodied in the various sects of Hinduism and within the various regions and castes. What fall outside the pale of tolerance are the lifestyles and intellectual positions which directly question the validity of the self-defined lifestyle and ideology of the Hindu community. In fact, acceptance of these is not considered a valid example of toleration, but rather of weakness and of a lack of concern for the well-being and prosperity of

[22] Praveen Togadia in a personal interview at Ahmedabad on 15 December 1995.
[23] Ibid.
[24] Ibid.

the Hindus. The VHP defines the boundaries of a Hindu's tolerance selectively, so as to include some and exclude others.

The Sikhs, the Buddhists, the Jains, the various tribal groupings and those who were once excluded from the orbit of Hindu society are now taken within its boundaries by the VHP. No threat is seen from the Zoroastrians and the Jews because of their insignificant numerical strength, and because there seem to be no apparent attempts by them to assert themselves as communities. They come within the defined tolerance of the Hindu nation. The Christians, seen by the VHP as a threat to its Hindu society, were treated more with cynicism than with open indignation and placed at the borders of tolerance until recently, when attacks on them gained momentum and viciousness. Now the VHP has shifted them outside the border of Hindu tolerance. The Muslims have always been outside the boundaries of tolerance for the VHP and the Sangh Parivar. Antagonism towards them has never been concealed. This intolerance is not directed so much against their religion as against any political expression by them as citizens of the Indian state.

The VHP through its campaigns and programmes has repeatedly stressed that the specific policy of secularism followed in India is inappropriate and damaging. This, it says, is because in the name of secularism the political parties have all along misused democracy, which has led to the weakening of the nation and under-representation of the Hindu voice in state institutions. To strengthen the nation, the Indian state should be based on Hindu principles and values. Those who do not accept Hindu culture should be barred from having an effective voice in the state institutions, so that democracy is not misused against the interests of the nation. Further, an Indian state based on Hindu principles would not be anti-democratic because Hindus are tolerant by nature and would not oppress any community. In other words, Indian democracy, instead of basing itself on secularism borrowed from the West, should rest on the foundation of Hindu culture, which would ensure a strong Indian nation and an effective voice to the majority of the people in India.

The VHP and the Hindu Community

Extending the discussion further, it must be noted that the VHP's central concern is the rights of the "Hindu community"—as against minority rights—on which it builds its discourse of "threat" to the Hindus as a community. Its concepts of secularism and tolerance are used to strengthen its campaign in this direction. The VHP claims to speak for the rights of the "Hindu community" as an entirety. There is, however, an uncomfortable restraint on the question of the rights of women and the backward sections, and a bigoted headstrongness on the question of minority rights.

The preoccupation with the defence of rights of the "Hindu community" is based on a majoritarian rationale with limited regard for the *culture of rights*: this culture stands for the recognition of differences between individuals and groups; the settlement of differences and disputes through discussion and debate rather than through violence; and tolerance of differences which cannot be settled, rather than seeking resolution through coercion (Bhargava 1994b: 71). The VHP's talk of "rights" is set in a paradigm of Hindu cultural hegemony. Rights have a meaning for it only as far as they politically consolidate the Hindus over the minority religious communities. As such, rights no longer remain rights but become assertions of cultural domination.

Moreover, these "rights" are asserted as group rights—the group takes precedence over the individual. The VHP demands individual subservience to Hindutva, and that individual conduct be totally determined by group ideology. The Hindu community is the overarching entity towering over the individual, who is recognised only as part of the community. The raison d'etre of the individual is that he or she is part of larger collective formations such as the religious community and the nation.[25] A call is given to the individuals to surrender everything to the cause of the Hindu nation. The *Hindu Chetna* says that,

> Whenever our country came under threat, the steersmen of our society defended it with the invincible strength of their organisation. They surrendered their power, wealth and influence to this collective organisation and strengthened it in several ways. With this organisational strength they destroyed the villains and foreign aggressors and managed to avert national crises.... Moreover, the nation was able to protect its ancient culture. The collective power of the *devatas* [Hindu divinities] gave birth to Adishakti. Adishakti was *trinetra* (had three eyes) and *dashbhuja* (had ten arms). The *devatas* prayed to her with full devotion and surrendered their weapons at her feet. She heard their pleas for help and killed the demon Mahishasura.[26]

[25] Here one can draw parallels with Nazism and Fascism.

[26] N. G. Vajhe, "Bhagwati Mahishasurmardini" (The Goddess who killed the demon Mahishasur), *Hindu Chetna*, 16 September 1995, 9.

Giving up everything for the consolidation of the community is considered to be the foremost dharma of the Hindu. Accordingly, the most important role of a Hindu is considered to be that of serving the community, and eventually the Hindu nation. Breaking away from the collective mould by questioning it and revising one's beliefs about value are not very favourably received, although the VHP claims to have a broad definition of Hinduism. Only in so far as they do not challenge the ideology of Hindutva, are differences allowed within the larger Hindu identity.

Chapter 7

Conversions and Reconversions

In the course of its surge forward, the freedom struggle came to have primarily two broad themes: those of secular anti-colonial nationalism and of religio-cultural revival. However, throughout the struggle the former remained the dominant theme. Although gau raksha, shuddhi sabhas, the Ganapati festival and *rakhi* tying[1] also became mobilisation issues for anti-colonial awakening, they could not override the secular strain of Indian nationalism. And in the immediate post-1947 period, those professing this revivalist mobilisation had to be content with forming pressure groups within the Congress under Nehru. However, there were constant endeavours by Hindu nationalist organisations such as the RSS, and their affiliative offshoots such as the VHP, to refashion Indian nationalism on religio-cultural terms—to make Hindu religio-cultural sensibility the core of Indian nationalism.

Today, the secular anti-colonial component is showing signs of weakening. Indian nationalism is increasingly being interpreted along Hindutva lines, so much so that it has once again become the focal point of hegemonic contestations. The issue which arises here is that within this "Hindu nation" the large numbers of Muslims, Christians and others who do not identify as Hindus have to be accounted for; they live within the territories of the nation and are not numerically so small as to be removed from its bounds. Intimidation, coercion and, of course, "reconversion" are therefore the viable ways by which the politics of Hindu nationalism can deal with the non-Hindu groups, as part of a long-term political strategy of conscious Hinduisation. Thus, as the contradictions and tensions within the VHP with regard to the non-Hindu populations continue, so also the woes and insecurities of minority religious communities. It is in this context that I discuss the practice of *paravartan* by the VHP and the anti-Christian violence perpetrated by Hindutva organisations in recent years.

[1] A Hindu customary practice of thread-tying among siblings, with a symbolic vow by brothers to protect their sisters in times of need.

Paravartan or "Reconversion"

The VHP followed in the footsteps of the Arya Samaj and further organised the process of Hinduisation. This practice was in direct confrontation with the tenets of classical Sanatana Dharma that strictly prohibited conversions. The Arya Samaj, however, had taken up conversion activity in the late nineteenth century, euphemising it as *shuddhi karan*[2] when faced with daunting opposition and claims of threats to orthodoxy. Shuddhi was known to Hinduism and was evoked to purify those who had intentionally or unintentionally broken caste taboos. To the Arya Samajists, however, it became instrumental in transforming Hinduism into a converting religion.

The VHP carried this work forward extensively, calling it *paravartan* (transformation or reconversion). Paravartan thus came to imply not only reconversion, but also bringing groups of unsemitised tribals to its fold. The VHP thus legitimised conversions, and transformed Hinduism from a religion whose following was based on birth to a religion based on association and direct absorption through purification. The VHP's legitimisation of conversions was, however, selective; while it tried to legitimise conversion of non-Hindus to Hinduism, it spread loud propaganda against conversions to Islam and Christianity, and called for state intervention to stop the latter.

The VHP's paravartan was accompanied by communal assertions that both the forces of Christianity and Islam had plans "to make Hindus a minority in India in the next thirty years; and, that they want to establish their rule in India and completely destroy Hindu culture."[3] With this understanding, the VHP formulated three major tasks for "propagation of dharma": checking religious conversions (to Islam or Christianity), "reconversion" to Hinduism, and building of strong samskaras.[4] The VHP emphasised a programme for its rank and file that propagated a strong organisation of Hindus at the grass roots. It was a programme of conscious Hinduisation and anti-Semitism:

1. building of a strong Hindu organisation at the village level,
2. a consistent movement for cultural awakening,

[2] *Shuddhi* stands for purification, and implies the purifying of non-Hindus by sacred rituals and ceremonies to admit or readmit them into the Hindu fold.

[3] "Vishva Hindu Parishad—Dharma Prasar Yojana" (Vishva Hindu Parishad—Dharma propagation programme), *Vanvasi Kalyan Kendra*, 112.

[4] Ibid., 111.

3. the expansion of welfare services to the masses,
4. the extensive propagation of social harmony,
5. to warn people of the illusionist propagation by irreligious conspirators and temptations offered by them.[5]

The VHP took up the conversion issue in a major way and tried to build a countrywide movement around it, to further its attack on the minorities and consequently on state institutions. This particular attack was also directed against the Congress Party and Sonia Gandhi, the former Prime Minister Rajiv Gandhi's widow and subsequently the president of the Congress Party. Ashok Singhal in a speech in Badayun (Uttar Pradesh) declared that there would not remain a single non-Hindu in the country; those who had been forcefully converted into non-Hindus would be made Hindus by the VHP. According to him, this is the VHP's aim.[6] He expressed alarm that in 1977 there were no Christians in Arunachal Pradesh, but at present the state has sixty thousand of them.[7] Sonia Gandhi was accused of giving support to the Christian missionaries in India, who, according to him, annually received fourteen billion rupees from abroad to finance their conversion activities.[8] Singhal later stated that the VHP had made a four-year scheme as a step to check the falling number of Hindus, to stop foreign Muslims from coming to India, and to work against missionary activity. Under it, 2,500 Hindus would go into various districts and create around 1.5 million sympathisers, each of whom would contribute two thousand rupees to be used to face the challenge offered by Christian missionaries.[9] The anti-Christian verbal and physical campaigns throughout the country to which the VHP and the Bajrang Dal are linked, and the training of the Bajrang Dal members in the recent past in the use of firearms to fight "anti-nationals," seem part of this scheme as well.

Within this context, conversion or, in VHP terms, "reconversion," became an integral part of the VHP's refashioning of Hinduism as a

[5] Ibid., 112.

[6] Ashok Singhal, "Chal-prapanch aur zor zabardasti se ahindu banaye gaye logon ko VHP punha hindu banayegi" (The VHP would reconvert those who by fraud and force were made non-Hindus), *Hindu Chetna*, 16 April 1995, 5.

[7] Ibid.

[8] Ashok Singhal in *Hindu Chetna*, 1 December 1995, 23; and in *Hindu Chetna*, 1 November 1995, 7.

[9] Ibid.

proselytising religion and also of its endeavours for mass mobilisation and social control. In an attempt to build a widespread movement, far-flung tribal pockets were brought into the orbit of vigorous social activity directed mainly against Christian missionaries. Paravartan became an essential bulwark to check missionary activity; it also acted as a substitute for conversion of Dalits and tribals to Christianity and Islam, and strengthened the VHP's hold over these sections. To make it socially acceptable the VHP describes paravartan as an awakening of glory in "reconverted Hindus (Christians and Muslims) with regards to their Hindu ancestors."[10] It is explained that having become Hindus, they once again start regarding Hindus as "their brothers of faith."[11] In the reconverted families a feeling of respect and devotion to Hindu principles, values, places of worship, Hindu leaders, Hindu scriptures, etc., awakens, because of which it "becomes easier to control communal riots, cow-slaughter and it becomes much easier to protect temples."[12] Hence, the VHP looks at paravartan not only as Hinduisation, but also as an instrument of socio-political regulation and control.

In the 1970s the VHP organised group conversions of Cheeta-Merat Rajput Muslims, spread over the districts of Udaipur, Pali, Bhilwara and Ajmer, in Rajasthan. The best-known mass conversions to Hinduism organised by the VHP have taken place in Gujarat, where around two hundred Mir Muslims were converted to Hinduism by the VHP in 1992–93 on the promise of *swabhiman* (self-respect) and *salamati* (security) (Sikand and Katju 1994). It is claimed that seventy Mir Muslim families fully adopted the Hindu dharma in 1993.[13] What is peculiar about these conversions is that they are group conversions and not individual or family conversions. I was told that it is usually difficult to convert individuals, or one or two families, and that therefore groups are identified and attempts made to "take them back."[14] It is believed that "today the Moray Salaam Muslims have come back to the Hindu fold and tomorrow it would be the entire Muslim community which would take a similar step" because it will realise that "its ancestors were Hindus."[15] I was informed by a VHP

[10] "Vishva Hindu Parishad—Dharma Prasar Yojana" (Vishva Hindu Parishad—Dharma propagation programme), *Vanvasi Kalyan Kendra*, 113.

[11] Ibid.

[12] Ibid.

[13] Arvind Brahmabhatt in a personal interview at Baroda on 28 December 1995.

[14] Ibid.

[15] Ibid.

activist, "We collect Muslims and place certain programmes before them so that they are able to recall who their ancestors were and why did they leave Hindu dharma; we also tell them that now they can come back to Hindu dharma."[16]

The VHP, besides propagating its perspective on Hinduism amongst the above groups, worked amongst tribals—mainly those who had adopted Christianity—whom it sought to Hinduise. It is interesting that vindictive opposition along with replication of roles informed the VHP activities in the tribal areas. On the one hand it vehemently denounced the activities of the Christian missionaries, while on the other it replicated the character of their work in its tribal welfare societies and called upon its activists to emulate the Christians. Ashok Singhal remarked that a Christian gives his everything in the name of his religion and culture, and the Hindus should follow his example.[17] In fact, VHP activists working in tribal areas and carrying on the task of Hinduisation were in some instances called "Hindu missionaries"[18] by their own leadership—vindicating the possible categorisation of the VHP as a "Hindu church" (Jaffrelot 1993: 522).

Emulating this mission work, the VHP claims to run a network of schools, dispensaries and community service-centres in tribal pockets. The following table shows the number of various centres run by the Vanvasi Kalyan Ashram. These centres are spread across Andhra Pradesh, Assam, Bihar, Delhi, Gujarat, Kerala, Karnataka, Maharashtra, Madhya Pradesh, Manipur, Orissa, Punjab, Rajasthan, Tamil Nadu, Tripura and West Bengal, with the highest concentration in Andhra Pradesh, Maharashtra, Rajasthan and Assam.

Table 3: Service-Centres Run by VKA

Tribal villages in India	121,794
Tribal villages where VKA work is going on	18,518
Boys' hostels	125
Girls' hostels	25
Male students	4,158

[16] Ibid.

[17] Ashok Singhal, "Chal-prapanch aur zor zabardasti se ahindu banaye gaye logon ko VHP punha hindu banayegi" (The VHP would reconvert those who by fraud and force were made non-Hindus), *Hindu Chetna*, 16 April 1995, 5.

[18] Ashok Singhal in a report by Ramnath Ojha in *Hindu Chetna*, 16 January 1996, 12.

Female students	158
Bal samskara kendras (Centres for building character among children)	649
Crèches and pre-school centres	1,487
Primary schools	261
Secondary and higher secondary schools	23
Libraries and reading rooms	65
Medical dispensaries	521
Hospitals	7
Centres for agricultural development	33
Industrial training centres	44
Sports centres	1,489
Religious community halls	1,781
Folk art centres	198

Source: Hindu Chetna, 16 March 1996, 6.

The VHP has introduced the practice of bhajan and kirtan in these villages to initiate the tribal populace into Hinduism.[19] It has also taken up distribution of food grains and old clothes amongst tribals, as well as printing and distribution of calendars with pictures of Hindu deities on them. This is done on a scale and manner similar to the Christian missionaries' distribution of food and calendars with pictures of Christ.[20] I was informed by a VHP activist that

> The tribals hang crosses and calendars depicting Jesus Christ on them in their homes under the influence of Christian missionaries, and to counter this we asked some of our members to print some calendars with pictures of Hindu gods and goddesses on them to be distributed amongst tribals.[21]

An activist was of the view that th adhus should have the "devotion of Christian missionaries."[22] The latter have done a lot of work but a "similar zeal is missing in us Hindus."[23]

Rajeshwar, a VHP leader who claims to have conducted paravartan ceremonies since the age of seventeen and has made "reconversion" his life's mission for more than fifty-five years, writes,

> Every Hindu must find out whether the Christians and Muslims coming in contact with him want to become Hindus or not. If they do, then he

[19] Jaishankar Singh Gaekwad in a personal interview at Baroda on 28 December 1995.

[20] Arvind Brahmabhatt in a personal interview at Baroda on 28 December 1995.

[21] Ibid.

[22] Sushma Rana in a personal interview at New Delhi on 11 March 1996.

[23] Ibid.

> should broach the topic with them in more detail. But, if the person in question is difficult, he should be left alone as his case can be taken up later. In a lifetime, one Hindu can easily get five Christians-Muslims into the Hindu fold, and save the other Hindus from going into other religious orders. The non-Hindus of today were a part of our society before going over to Christianity and Islam. Every Hindu with affection and persuasion must try to convert either collectively or individually the Christians and Muslims. . . . All Hindus have to work in this direction, otherwise, in this democratic country the Hindu identity would get wiped off and the many Hindu institutions would get destroyed. (Rajeshwar 1992: 9)[24]

Rajeshwar's book is seen by the VHP as a guide to Hindus on the ways and means of converting non-Hindus to Hinduism. Paravartan is regarded as a *rashtriya karya* (a national duty); it is said that if every single Hindu takes a serious interest in this matter, half of the Christian and Muslim population of India can convert to Hinduism in fifty years, and if all their population has to be brought back to the Hindu fold it would take a century and a half (Rajeshwar 1992: 1–2). He advises those who are carrying out conversions to read chapters thirteen and fourteen of Dayananda's *Sathyartha Prakasha* as, according to him, chapter thirteen has important things to say about Christianity and chapter fourteen about Islam (Rajeshwar 1992: 10). It is zealously declared that the VHP activists should go from village to village, to reconvert Hindus who had left Hindu dharma to embrace Islam and Christianity.[25] The booklet reiterates the VHP's much-too-often-stated propaganda that "through the conspiracy of conversions to Islam and Christianity"[26] the Hindus would be reduced to a "minority in India."[27]

Looking at the VHP's ideological make-up, it seems obvious that the important issues involved in paravartan are not religious, but socio-political. Paravartan becomes not only a power game at the

[24] The author, Rajeshwar, is the former head of the south Delhi unit of the RSS and served for many years as the president of the Delhi unit of the VHP. His book is about paravartan, and gives a detailed account of how it should be undertaken by the Hindus.

[25] Ashok Singhal in a speech at Kanpur in May 1995, published in *Hindu Chetna*, 16 June 1995, 7.

[26] Ashok Singhal, "Hum is punyaboomi ko bhogbhoomi nahin banne denge" (We won't let this sacred/pure land turn into a land of pleasure/consumerism), *Hindu Chetna*, 16 July 1995, 8.

[27] Ibid.

local level, but also a tool at a larger level for political polarisation. Its utility is in keeping Hindutva alive in urban middle-class memory and also in communally polarising masses in the countryside. The VHP's paravartan, however, has not met with much success despite the noise created over it. This is privately admitted. I was told by a senior VHP leader that this is so because society is still not ready for it, and that the task would become easier when society is ready to accept the new converts amidst it.[28] This points to a fundamental difficulty in breaking the existing community bonds and recasting these bonds anew by absorbing non-Hindus into the caste structure that is rigidly based on birth. The drawbacks of paravartan together with the reduced appeal of Rama/Ayodhya and the rising fortunes of the Congress in the tribal belt led the Sangh Parivar to take on the Christian community. The Christian philanthropic work was subject to scathing attacks from the VHP and its ideological partners who accused the Christian community of being "anti-national." The major allegation against the community was that it resorts to conversions.

Anti-Christian Propaganda and Vandalism

The brutal killing of the missionary Graham Staines and his sons on 23 January 1999, and of George Kuzhikandam on 7 June 2000, are only two among several incidents of violence against Christian missionaries. The anti-Christian assaults resemble the Ayodhya-related violence which resulted in the demolition of the Babri mosque in 1992. The train of events leading to the two incidents, one directed against the Christians and the other against the Muslims, converge on two, if not more, important counts. Both represent attempts at delineation of citizenship and nationality on a restricted primordial basis; and both project the anti-democratic work patterns—vandalism, violence, destruction and intimidation—and non-liberal/sectarian ideology of groups within the Sangh network. The hate campaigns and low-intensity violence against the Christians at the behest of the Hindu Jagran Manch and the Bajrang Dal seemed premised on a belief that the social base of Hindutva had to be saved from erosion, and in all possibility extended. What followed was an attack on Christians, together with branding the activities of various

[28] Raghunandan Prasad Sharma in a personal interview at New Delhi on 15 October 1995.

Christian groups as anti-national within the narrow Hindutva interpretation of nationalism. This went further to indicate a realisation within the VHP about the limited political utility of the janmabhoomi question and hence the need for a different emotive issue to solicit mass support. Raking up the Christian conversion issue appeared efficacious in consolidating the Hindutva base among the middle classes at a juncture when this base faced erosion.

The Congress' assembly victories in 1998 under Sonia Gandhi's presidentship of the party, followed by a near formation of the government under the leadership of the Congress in the summer of 1999, give some clues to the strategically planned violence against the Christians. According to the National Minorities Commission of India member Dr James Massey, the dramatic rise in complaints of attacks on the Christian community and encroachment on Church properties indicated "a definite trend."[29] Several such incidents occurred in Punjab as well, where, according to Massey, one "would never have imagined such a problem"—in a state where the Christian community is only 300,000 strong.[30]

The Christians once again became targets of Hindu revival under the VHP, much as they had been in its original agenda of the 1960s and 1970s. Hence, it is misleading to assume that there has been a major reorientation of programme and a paradigmatic shift in the working of the VHP and its frontal organisation, the Bajrang Dal; that their agenda until very recently was to end Muslim "appeasement" and Muslim "anti-national" activities, and of late there has been a shift in their focus from the Muslims to the Christians. The Christian conversion question is not a new issue for the VHP. On the contrary, it represents its original charter and has quite a marked presence in its programmatic history, as discussed earlier. The VHP was formed with the aim of countering Christian influence in the tribal belts of India and protecting migrant Hindus from non-Hindu Protestant/Catholic cultural assimilation. With the recent anti-Christian agenda, the VHP has come back to its original charter of carrying on an aggressive campaign against the Christians.

The politically driven aggressive work mechanics and a penchant for generating mass hysteria, as demonstrated recently in the anti-

[29] Bhavdeep Kang, "Soft Target in Cross Wires," *Outlook*, 22 June 1998, 14.
[30] Ibid.

Christian assaults, are also not recently acquired traits. The uproar over Meenakshipuram in 1981, the rathyatras in 1983–84, the Ramjanmabhoomi issue since 1984, the cow-protection agitation in 1996—all for the "protection of Hinduism" and the "consolidation of the Hindu *rashtra*"—are a few cases that demonstrated the ideological traits of the VHP and Bajrang Dal, and their work processes. The expression of antagonism and distrust against the Christian community is marked by low-intensity violence with its intentions openly flaunted. The relative ease with which Christians are subjected to vandalism and lumpenism reveals a deep-seated vendetta and a calculated perception of their vulnerability. The sustained charitable work of the Christian missions among the Indian tribal communities prompts the ire of the Hindu militant groups and is used as a tool to mobilise the urban middle class.

The Christian community was convinced that the Sangh brotherhood was responsible for these attacks on it, despite all the denials of the latter. Father Allwyn d'Silva, head of the Justice and Peace Commission of the Mumbai Archdiocese, sees the Rashtriya Swayamsevak Sangh as the propelling force behind these attacks on the Christian community, institutions, missionaries and women.[31] According to him, these attacks apparently have been coming to stop conversions, but "the real reason is that Church personnel are working for poorer sections and empowering them," due to which the "upper-caste RSS-VHP feel threatened."[32]

The Christian mission work was openly threatened with violence —a threat which the government did not come forward in condemnation of. The VHP's Rajasthan unit vowed to make Banswara district "Christian free" within three years.[33] Attempts by Christians to protest against violence to which they were subjected were branded "an orchestrated campaign and conspiracy to destabilise the Government" by the then defence minister, George Fernandes.[34]

A Hindu Jagran Manch pamphlet circulated in the Dang district of Gujarat, an area that witnessed some of the worst violence against Christians in the late 1990s, carried the following message:

[31] Bhavdeep Kang, "Soft Target in Cross Wires," *Outlook*, 22 June 1998, 14.
[32] Ibid.
[33] Ibid.
[34] "Protest by Christians a plot to oust Govt: George," *Hindustan Times* (Lucknow), 9 December 1998.

> Conversion activity by Christian Priests is the most dangerous burning problem at present in Dangs district. Innocent and illiterate tribals are converted through cheating, alluring by offering temptations and other deceiving activities, under the pretext of services, these devils are taking advantage of tribal society and exploit them. In the world, wherever these Christian priests have looted its people and have made them helpless. Lie and deceit are their religion. Christian priests teach to steal and to tell lies in the name of religion, converted Christians today after being converted write Hindu in their certificate and proof evidences. They condemn Hindu religion and write Hindu to take advantage in Government Programmes.
>
> Hindus, awake and struggle with these robbers who snatch away your rights by telling lies and teach these people a lesson.[35]

It is interesting to note that the Muslims along with the Hindus were projected as victims of the alleged Christian attacks. It was sometimes openly stated that the Christians had made the Muslims their target of attack as well. For example, a First Information Report was lodged at Ahwa (Gujarat) by a member of the Bajrang Dal, stating that "Christians targeted 2–3 shops of the Muslims, and disturbed the Hindu Jagran Manch rally."[36]

The Bajrang Dal was reported to have been one of those at the forefront of the anti-Christian vandalism. One of its leaders described this violence as a very natural reaction of society (to the activities of Christian missionaries).[37] Revealing that the Bajrang Dal has two thousand balopasana kendras for training in judo, karate, meditation and shooting, he also stated, "Those who want to destroy the Hindus must fear us. We want them to fear us."[38] The Bajrang Dal members were defended as good and nationalistic people by the former BJP president, Kushabhau Thakre, when the group was in the midst of the anti-Christian campaigns.[39]

[35] The Hindu Jagran Manch circulated the pamphlet before 25 December 1998. Its English translation is reproduced from *Violence in Gujarat: Test Case for a Larger Fundamentalist Agenda*, the report of the Citizen's Commission on Persecution of Christians in Gujarat (1999: 43), published by the National Alliance of Women.

[36] The Citizen's Commission, "Special Report on Violence in Gujarat," *Indian Journal of Secularism* 3, no. 2, July–September 1999, 110.

[37] Surendra Jain, all India convenor of the Bajrang Dal, interview published in *Outlook*, 8 February 1999, 20.

[38] Ibid.

[39] In *Outlook*, 8 February 1999, 16.

A pamphlet circulated by the Bajrang Dal in Gujarat spells out its "objectives" as follows:

> To protect the country i.e. mother India.
> To raise a loud voice against people criticising Hindu society.
> To protect religion and culture.
> To work for the protection of Hindu women (sister and daughter).
> To fight against anti-national elements.
> To crusade against cow-slaughter.
> To conduct an awareness campaign against trapping of Hindu girls by Muslims and the anti-national activities of Christian missionaries.
> Bajrang Dal means national power—Hindu power.
> World creator mother Jagdamba, she is Durga mata, she is Bharatmata.
> For. protection of our national interest let us join the Bajrang Dal.
> Our existence has meaning only when the country exists.
> Come youth come out for the country.
> Let us join the Bajrang Dal and pay gratitude to her.[40]

Another pamphlet announcing a Virat Hindu Sammelan (Grand Hindu Conference) on 25 December 1998, circulated by the Hindu Jagran Manch, said,

> The time has come to recognise the real face of the Christian priests, who pretend to serve people, and tell them to "stop". Attacks on our Hindu culture are being carried out through conversion activities. All Hindu men and women are heartily invited to the Hindu Convention to challenge this conversion activity and to show them Hindu power.[41]

During and just after Christmas in 1998 attacks on Christians in Gujarat intensified. The *Hindustan Times* reported, "Churches and missionary schools were attacked, vehicles torched and seven people injured in fresh outbreak of communal violence in Surat and Dangs districts of Gujarat even as the Bajrang Dal and Vishwa Hindu Parishad announced stepping up stir against alleged conversion of Hindus."[42]

[40] This Bajrang Dal–Vishva Hindu Parishad pamphlet, published from Ahmedabad, was circulated before 25 December 1998. Its English translation is reproduced from *Violence in Gujarat: Test Case for a Larger Fundamentalist Agenda* (1999: 45).

[41] This Hindu Jagran Manch pamphlet, published in Gujarat, was circulated before 25 December 1998. Its English translation is reproduced from *Violence in Gujarat: Test Case for a Larger Fundamentalist Agenda* (1999: 47).

[42] "Churches, missionary schools attacked: VHP, Bajrang Dal goons spoil Christmas fun," *Hindustan Times* (Lucknow), 28 December 1998.

Looking at the violence, the chairperson of the National Minorities Commission, Tahir Mehmood, said, "The attacks are going on unabated. It cannot go on like this. We will demand an explanation from the State Government."[43] Clashes between Hindus and Christians were also reported in the tribal-dominated Dangs district.[44] The Gujarat home minister, Haren Pandya, blamed the Christians for the violence, saying that the Hindu Jagran Manch rally was stoned while protesting the conversion of poor Hindu tribals to Christianity.[45] However, he admitted the use of inflammatory speeches by Hindu leaders during the rally that provoked the Christians.[46]

Ashok Singhal denied the involvement of the VHP in the attacks against Christians; on the contrary, he blamed some "militant" sections among Christians for attacking tribal Hindus in Gujarat and fomenting trouble.[47] The laxity of district administration was seen as one of the factors leading to communal flare-ups by a two-member Home Ministry team constituted to report on the violence in Gujarat.[48] Along with the district administration, it saw an active role of the Hindu Jagran Manch and some unsuccessful BJP candidates in the communal violence affecting the state.[49]

Alongside, the VHP and the BJP intensified their campaigns against Sonia Gandhi, targeting her more as a Christian "outsider" than a Congress Party leader. According to a senior VHP leader, "Western forces are not interested in a strong national government in India. They want to bring in a particular individual of a certain party who will be manageable by them. The Church is working towards that end."[50] The central agenda on which the BJP built its election campaign in 1999 was Sonia Gandhi's Italian-Christian birth.

It was reported that among the many booklets and pamphlets that were circulated in Gujarat, one carried suggestions on how to harass

[43] Ibid.

[44] Manas Dasgupta, "Uneasy calm in two Gujarat districts," *Hindu*, 29 December 1998.

[45] Ibid.

[46] Ibid.

[47] "Singhal blames Christians," *Hindu*, 29 December 1998.

[48] "Communal flare-up in Gujarat: Central team blames Jagran Manch, admn." *Hindustan Times* (Lucknow), 1 January 1999.

[49] Ibid.

[50] Bhavdeep Kang, "Method in Madness," *Outlook*, 18 January 1999, 22.

Christian missionaries, to prevent them from proselytising.[51] One of these suggestions was to file false cases in courts against Christian missionaries, so that they are always tied up in contesting these cases.[52]

Ashok Singhal remarked in an interview,

> The followers of Islam and Christianity interpreted the principles propounded by Mohammed and Jesus to suit themselves and made land-grabbing their goal by expanding their numbers. St Paul did it and the caliphs after Mohammad did it. Even today, they are planning to create their own homelands here.[53]

In the same interview he went on to say,

> The Christians don't go to Egypt and Arab countries (to preach). Muslims and Christians don't interfere in each other's territory. Vahan unki daal nahin galti (There they can't have their way). Because they apply the same methods to finish each other off—they just kill the other. Mahavir and the Buddha preached non-violence. But in their religion (Islam and Christianity) there is no place for non-violence. Pahle unko ahimsa ka paath seekhna chahiye (First of all they should learn what non-violence is all about).[54]

According to the United Christian Forum for Human Rights (UCFHR), there occurred thirty-five recorded incidents of anti-Christian attacks between January and June 2000 that were seen by the BJP and the BJP-led government not as as incidents of communal violence, but as "dacoity and loot" by "criminal gangs."[55]

With anti-Semitism at the core of its raison d'etre, the Sangh group, and particularly the VHP, since its inception has gradually worked towards building a consistent movement against both Muslims and Christians, at times quietly and at times with excessive clamour. The growth of the VHP's ideological work in the tribal belt brought it face to face with the Christian missionaries; intimidation became an efficacious instrument to prevent Christian missionaries from

[51] Reported in Parvathi Menon's "An assault on Christians,"*Frontline*, 7 July 2000, 23.

[52] Ibid.

[53] "Quran, Bible should be adapted to our traditions," interview with Ashok Singhal, *Outlook*, 22 February 1999, 16.

[54] Ibid., 17.

[55] Reported in Parvathi Menon, "An assault on Christians,"*Frontline*, 7 July 2000, 22.

working in tribal areas, in an environment of growing political support for Hindutva countrywide. Over the last few decades the resources for the anti-minority campaign have been built so meticulously that at this juncture no large-scale or intense planning is needed to start a spree of physical violence against the minorities. For years the tribal areas were worked upon and efforts made at Hinduisation which could have been used as a springboard to any further activity. The BJP's coming to power at the centre was a major source of encouragement for the Sangh Parivar outfits to target the Christian community both verbally and physically.

Chapter 8

Conclusion

The RSS played a leading role in the formation of the VHP, by mobilising a section of the political and religious leadership of the country, and providing ideological inputs to the new forum in its formative years. The political and religious leadership came together on one platform to build an organisation specifically motivated to consolidate the non-secular, non-modernist and non-communist/socialist opinion against the Congress. It tried to achieve this goal through the revival and propagation of Hindu dharma among the Hindu diaspora and the tribal communities of north-eastern India. It also tried to counteract the Christian missionary work in the tribal belt and build an opinion against it at the local and national levels.

As discussed earlier, the agenda of political activism and Hindu nation-building did not form the central programme of the VHP organisation until about 1983. The VHP's transition to an organisation geared to political consolidation of the Hindus in India began at this time. From a primarily international goal of Hinduising the Hindus abroad its focus became restricted to political concerns in India. It became engaged in building a Hindu nationalist movement based on social exclusivism, an aggressive posture and militant disposition—a change that can be attributed to factors such as the change in the RSS leadership and in the membership of the VHP. These changes in the composition of the leadership and the membership transformed attitudes towards political activism; politics was no longer seen as a realm to be abandoned in favour of social activism. The RSS saw in the VHP the potential to politically unify the various communities and sects, and to evolve a common Hindu cultural programme leading to a unified and cohesive Hindu political nation. In addition, the leadership of the VHP, as also its later membership, did not have the close association with the Congress Party that the earlier membership had. It moved closer to the BJP and openly declared its association with it. Hence, criticism of the state machinery and especially of the Congress-led governments became increasingly strident.

The conversions at Meenakshipuram came as a defining moment in the history of the VHP. This event made the VHP leadership feel that some form of institutionalisation and codification of the Hindu religion was necessary for its protection (though, so far, it has not been able to achieve this). The Meenakshipuram conversions gave rise to the view that the image of Hindu dharma as a dispersed and scattered religion had to be dispelled. The formation of various forums in the early 1980s, such as the Dharma Sansad and the Sanskriti Raksha Yojana, were some determining moves in this direction.

Soon after this came the ekatmata yatra of 1983, which was a mass programme to solicit countrywide support for the VHP's move on Hindu unity. This was also a time when the VHP had started to turn into a politically sensitive forum determined to support a political party which would have a "Hindu" agenda. This phase saw the VHP turning heavily towards mobilisation at a mass level. Anti-Westernism and anti-modernism became its ideological focal points—if not in actual practice then in theoretical discourse. The view that a sustained movement is necessary to bring about social transformation which would ultimately lead to change at the political level came to dominate the VHP organisation in the late 1980s. Henceforth, the VHP focused more on the elections. Its activities became louder on the eve of elections, leading to communal tensions and violence in sensitive towns and localities.

The VHP in its work during the late 1980s and early 1990s drew on the agendas of earlier Hindu organisations such as the Arya Samaj, the Hindu Mahasabha and, more directly, the RSS. It also looked to the legacies of the nineteenth-century socio-religious reform movement and the Indian National Congress–led freedom/nationalist struggle. The writings and speeches of the socio-religious reformers and those engaged in the national movement provided the VHP with a rich ideological source on which to base its movement. This background proved especially useful to the VHP when it began to restrict its definition of the nation, categorising the Muslims and the Christians as the social "other."

To take its perspective on nationalism to a wider audience and create a space for a new ideological understanding, the VHP modified traditional concepts and practices. This is clear when one looks at the specific use of the symbolism of Rama, Bharatmata, Gangamata and Gaumata, the rallying of ascetic forces, and the evolving of paravartan by the VHP in pursuit of its activities. The activists of the

VHP admitted that these varied strategies of mobilisation gave it an extended popularity, broadened its social base and led to the BJP's electoral successes in various regions. In addition, the involvement of Dalits and the OBCs in the movement to build the Rama temple, and as such the moves to cement the various castes and jatis, can be seen as the VHP's attempts to extend its mass base with an aim to build a numerically and ideologically strong Hindu nation.

In addition, one must see these developments in the light of the changing contours of Indian politics, where the Congress-I was rapidly losing its hegemonic presence in North India. The issues of radical social transformation and social justice which had dominated Indian politics in the early 1970s, leading to the Emergency and the protest against it, faded. These have been replaced by issues of socio-political identity at the political level and issues of growth and productive efficiency at the level of the economy. The emergence of the BJP as an important electoral alternative to the Congress, both in terms of economic policy and social base, also gave a much-needed impetus and stability to the agitation.

The Ramjanmabhoomi movement led by the VHP brought it immediate publicity and helped its ally, the BJP, electorally. However, the movement's success in mobilisation remained broadly confined to the North-Indian Hindi-speaking regions. The political impact of this agitation was much wider, but that did not necessarily translate into an expansion of the VHP's organisation or into tangible votes for the BJP in southern India. The degree of agitation over the Ramjanmabhoomi issue can also be attributed to a confused response from other political groups, and a compromising stance by the central government.

The VHP has varied significance in the understanding of its activists. To some of its activists it is a body working for Hindu nationalism, to some it is going to lead the country to the status of *jagat guru* (world leader), to some it is a forum for Hindu self-assertion working for their legitimate rights, and to others it is a movement for consolidation of the "Hindu community" against secular, communist, Muslim and Western attacks. Central to all these concerns are two related goals of the VHP: one, that it is working towards a Hindu political awakening, and two, more importantly, it is making efforts at building a Hindu nation. It is felt within the VHP that a Hindu cultural awakening is essential for real development, prosperity, safety and indivisibility of the country. It is also believed that the moves towards a Hindu nationalism are a sure guarantee of real progress. The activists of the VHP contest rival conceptions of nationalism, which they think enfeeble the real idea of nationalism. The building of this ideology involves an invention of history that is based on a very selective reading of events and facts, and at times is constituted by general ignorance. It also involves intertwining of history and mythology for political goals.

The nature of the VHP overseas, however, is quite different from what it is within India. The support which it has built for itself abroad demonstrates that the question of religio-cultural identity and bonding is the main motivational force which draws Hindus to its fold. Abroad, the VHP is engaged largely in fostering a religious and cultural consciousness among migrant Hindus, and its role as a political activist is marginal. It is engaged in conducting classes on Hindi language, Hindu dharma, takes a lead in organising marches, community sports and "cultural" programmes. As such it differs in character from its counterpart in India, but definitely feeds into the aggressive political posturings it maintains in India.

At present, the VHP as an autonomous organisation may not become a part of the political power structure of the BJP, and it may publicly assert that it is a non-political organisation. The BJP in turn may try, as a part of its strategy of broadening its support base, to distance itself from the VHP on public platforms. But, as is apparent, the latter's importance as a mobilising force which directly translates into votes for the BJP has not declined. It is likely that the local presence of the VHP in urban areas will strengthen, and it is from this base that the organisation will exercise its clout. The BJP's presence at the centre and state levels is helpful for the VHP to move forward with its various programmes, though without overt support of the BJP-led government. At this juncture this symbiotic relation looks politically promising.

In this context, the VHP's call, for example, to examine the Indian Constitution has been heeded by the BJP government at the centre, for it has decided to study the Constitution and bring about changes wherever it deems necessary. Also, the BJP has taken up the ahistorical "Hinduisation" of school curriculum on the pretext of revising the textbooks. The BJP's being in power augurs well for the VHP as it gives the VHP's perspectives on governance and majority-minority relations, that have already gained some form of legitimacy in urban middle-class India, added support. It is this clear statement of a militant Hindu nationalism and the increased religious polarisation and schism, which is the VHP's contribution to political discourse in contemporary India.

Appendix I

A Note on the Interviews

The interviews for this study were conducted at Baroda (also called "Vadodara"), Ahmedabad, Delhi, Allahabad, Lucknow and Faizabad (the district which includes Ayodhya). The first two are important commercial and industrial centres within the state of Gujarat, in western India; Delhi, the Indian capital, is where the headquarters of the VHP are located; and the last three are districts of Uttar Pradesh in North India. Faizabad is a small town and hardly boasts any industrial development, as Baroda and Ahmedabad do, but has been the focus of VHP activity due to the location of Ayodhya, believed to be Rama's birthplace, within its administrative boundaries. Baroda is known for its erstwhile princely Gaikwad tradition and its petrochemical heavy industries, and Ahmedabad for its cotton textile mills and its serene Sabarmati ashram. Lucknow is the capital city of Uttar Pradesh, a hub of vigorous political activity, and with a culture which traces itself to the rule of the Muslim nawabs of Shi'ite belief. Allahabad, besides being an important Hindu pilgrimage centre, historically known as "Prayag," has been an important administrative and educational centre since colonial times with the High Court located there.

The choice of these places for fieldwork was based on the VHP's intense activity in these areas, the BJP's strong support base here, a spate of the most gruesome communal violence here over the years, the demolition of the Babri mosque at Ayodhya, and my familiarity with some of these places. I lived successively at Allahabad, Baroda and Delhi for some years, and had visited them from time to time since childhood. My familiarity with the language spoken in some of these areas, i.e., Hindi, also prompted their choice. Baroda and Ahmedabad are primarily Gujarati-speaking areas, but I had no difficulty in conversing with people there, as most of them seemed quite comfortable conversing in Hindi, and some in English. I am able to follow the Gujarati language, though not as well as Hindi; however, this shortcoming of mine was offset by the VHP's general policy of conducting all its programmes, camps and meetings in Hindi. This has to do with its programmatic decision to promote Hindi in the Devnagari script as the national language.

The study has a definite urban bias, and this has much to do with the nature of the VHP. The VHP can be understood as an organisation having a predominantly urban character, and a strong presence in mofussil towns and cities rather than a rural base. The people I interviewed have all been long-term residents of the places mentioned above. The printed primary material, too, has been collected from these areas, and the problems addressed in it relate to questions usually arising in urban situations rather than in a rural environment. The VHP originated in the city of Bombay (now "Mumbai") with the purpose of carrying forward the RSS agenda in the context of growing industrialisation and urbanisation, and resultant migrations both from the countryside to towns and from India to other countries. The VHP was formed to ensure that these changes did not push the RSS world view into oblivion. The steadily modernising socio-economic milieu within a larger secular outlook was seen as a fearful challenge to Hindu ideological politics that needed to be countered by all means. The VHP was seen as an entity to take on this challenge, and to check it through a carefully chalked-out identity politics of its own. It was formed by those who were themselves established in an urban culture and were political or religious activists—or both—drawing sustenance from a largely middle-class urban base.

I conducted most interviews in India between September 1995 and April 1996. One important interview, that with Ashok Singhal, the chief of the VHP, took place in February 1997 at New Delhi. Two interviews were conducted in London. Some interviews done in November 1993 for my MPhil study have also been used as source material to substantiate the arguments in this study. Most of the interviews were recorded, but some could not be, in which case handwritten notes were made during the course of the interviews. The number of those interviewed is fifty—a figure arrived at by coincidence rather than a deliberate decision. The interviews were useful as they provided information on the VHP's past and present that could not be obtained from its publications. The interviews also gave sociological insight into the nature of the organisation, its leaders, its programmes, planning and support base. The number of individuals interviewed and their organisational affiliations at the time of the interviews are as follows:

Table 4: Number and Organisational Affiliation of Interviewed Activists

Organisational Affiliation of Activists	Number of Activists
An RSS background, but working as VHP activists and holding posts in the VHP organisation	19
VHP (without an RSS background)	10 (three of these are sadhus)
RSS (without affiliation to any other organisation)	2
Bajrang Dal (VHP)	2
Durga Vahini (VHP)	4 (one of these is a former BJP activist and one is a sadhvi)
Mahila Vibhag (VHP)	2
Rashtra Sevika Samiti	6
Sadhus who are not members of the VHP	3
A newspaper editor at Faizabad	1
National Hindu Students Forum (several members of which have an affiliation to the VHP or the Hindu Swayamsevak Sangh in Britain)	1
TOTAL	50

The following three tables state the names and occupations of the interviewed activists, classified according to age groups.

Table 5: Names and Occupations of Interviewed Activists

Section 1: Age group 20 to 40 years

Name	Occupation
Arvind Brahmabhatt	Full-time activist
Sadhvi Rithambhara	Sadhvi
Anil Mehrotra	Advocate
Atul Awasthi	Corporator
Awadh Kishor	Full-time activist
Janhavi Ambekar	Student

Section 2: Age group 40 to 60 years

Name	Occupation
Praveen Togadia	Surgeon
Jaishankar Singh Gaekwad	Full-time activist
Bina Sharma	Full-time activist
Vijay Parnami	Small-scale industrialist
Harish Sharma	Technician
Saroj Mazumdar	Non-working activist
Sushma Rana	School teacher
Hemlaxmi Chawla	Non-working activist
Malti	University lecturer
Shyam Sunder Agarwal	Goldsmith
Ramchandra Upadhyay	College teacher
Sahayji	Retired government servant
Om Prakash Dubey	Personnel management officer
Harijeevan	Cloth trader
Mahesh Narayan Singh	Full-time activist
Purshottam Nayak Singh	Full-time activist
Vinod didi	Non-working activist
Kishor Ruparelia	Trader

Section 3: Age group 60 and above

Name	Occupation
Chunnibhai Patel	Automobile trader
Chiman Mararia	Automobile tyre and tube trader
Prof. Javadekar	Retired professor
Damodar Nene	Physician
Pramila Bede	Full-time activist
Rukmini Akka	Full-time activist
Rajendra Singh	Full-time activist
Ashok Singhal	Full-time activist
Surya Dev Tripathi	Retired government servant
Muktananda Saraswati	Sadhu
Raghunandan Prasad Sharma	Retired government servant
Deoki Nandan Agarwal	Retired judge
A. B. Saran	Senior advocate
Girija Singh	Non-working activist
Gurujan Singh	Full-time activist
B. L. Agarwal	Physician
Gulab Singh Parihar	Retired school teacher
Shanti Devbala	Retired professor
Ramchandra Paramhamsa	Sadhu
Nrittya Gopal Das	Sadhu

The interviews were conducted either in the VHP offices or at the homes of the activists at an appointed hour. Almost all of these activists are or were in leadership positions either at the central, state or district levels. Only those in such positions have authority from the organisation to give interviews or generally give information about the organisation and its working. The general membership usually does not give interviews because first, it is not encouraged by the leadership to do so, and second, the information at its disposal seems limited because the membership is floating and usually gets together and meets regularly only when some high-profile campaign or programme is organised.

The fact of their contributing immensely to the Hindutva project, their background in the RSS and their socio-economic and educational background have been some major factors in leaders assuming their posts in the VHP and its subsidiary organisations such as the Bajrang Dal and the Durga Vahini. The number of VHP leaders, those interviewed or otherwise, who have a firm base in the RSS is substantial. This serves to indicate the strong ties between the two organisations and also gives some clue to the RSS's hold over the leadership and ideology of the VHP.

Contacting and meeting the activists was not a problem. The interviews also went on smoothly. However, the overenthusiasm of some members to talk made it difficult at times to direct the conversation along lines relevant to the research; hence, conducting the interviews was laborious in some cases. Many of the interviews were more in the nature of conversations and general discussions, rather than formatted question-answer sessions. There was a lot of enthusiasm among some activists for giving interviews, which might be because they saw these interviews as a channel for disseminating their world view. Only once did an activist remark a bit suspiciously that nothing should be written against the VHP organisation. At times the interviewees mistook me for a journalist and responded somewhat rudely before I made it clear that I was a research student.

Limited information and lack of time at the disposal of some of the interviewees did pose a problem sometimes. Some activists were able to give information regarding only certain issues and not others. One activist, for example, could tell me more about the legal matters surrounding the Ramjanmabhoomi dispute, and did not have much information about the more recent activities of the VHP. Another activist had more information about the cow-protection activities in which he is engaged in his village, and knew little about the VHP's differences with other Hindu bodies or its legal stand on the Ayodhya issue. Also, the interviews never began at the scheduled time. The activists were often late for interviews though they were the ones who had set the appointed time.

Some of the answers to my questions seemed rehearsed, indicating that they had been patterned and shaped to be so delivered in all kinds of interviews and discussions; interestingly, some of these answers remained unchanged from activist to activist. Such responses suggested that the language and the style of the answers were consciously cultivated and disseminated through meetings, formal discussions in training camps and even through seemingly harmless social mingling. This was most apparent in the case of the issue of secularism. What Ashok Singhal and Sadhvi Rithambhara had to say about the Indian state's policy of secularism was echoed in more or less the same form and language by the regional and district-level activists.

While on fieldwork, I had the opportunity to attend some meetings and one camp of the VHP and its associate organisations. These included a meeting of the Rashtra Sevika Samiti at Baroda on 15 September 1995; a gathering of the members of the Durga Vahini at Baroda on 23 December 1995; and the RSS's international camp at Kayavarohan (in Baroda district), held every five years in India, which besides being addressed by the RSS leaders was also addressed by senior leaders of the VHP such as Ashok Singhal, Sadhvi Rithambhara and Giriraj Kishor. I visited this camp on the same day, that is, 23 December 1995. I also visited the Sri Jageshwar Mahadev temple at Lucknow on February 1996 with a member of Mahila Vibhag. The temple property and its management are controlled by the VHP.

In the cities of Gujarat, as compared to Delhi and Uttar Pradesh, the VHP activists were less hesitant in their responses, less cautious, readily giving information and inviting me to their various programmes. Their enthusiastic response during interviews was something that I felt much less in talking to activists in Uttar Pradesh. Delhi in this regard can be placed somewhere between Gujarat and Uttar Pradesh. I feel that such an attitude was present in UP primarily because of an atmosphere of extreme political uncertainty in the state. A brief description of the political background at the time when the interviews were conducted would give some clues to the responses of the interviewees. In the aftermath of the November 1993 assembly elections in Uttar Pradesh, the Samajwadi Party in alliance with the Bahujan Samaj Party formed the government, with Mulayam Singh Yadav as chief minister. However, this coalition could not last for very long, and was succeeded in government by the Bahujan Samaj Party with Mayawati as chief minister. The Bharatiya Janata Party supported it from outside without becoming part of the government. This partnership also collapsed after four months due to political disagreement. The resulting political uncertainty led to the imposition of president's rule, and I felt that in this politically precarious atmosphere the VHP activists were always on their guard while talking to me.

The March 1995 elections in Gujarat brought the Bharatiya Janata Party to power with an enormous majority of 121 seats out of a total of 182. However, a tussle between the state general secretary of the party, Narendra Modi, and the former state party chief, Shankersinh Vaghela, brought about some fluctuations in Gujarat politics. This resulted in the expulsion of Vaghela from the party on 29 September 1995, and the stepping down of Chief Minister Keshubhai Patel, whose place as the chief minister was taken by a consensus candidate, Suresh Mehta. However, this change of leadership did not calm the dissidents, and Gujarat continued to witness problems at the leadership level throughout 1995 and the first half of 1996.

The BJP also came to power at Delhi in November 1993 where a state assembly had recently been instituted. Madan Lal Khurana assumed office amidst much jubilation and enthusiasm in the BJP ranks. However, Khurana resigned office in February 1996 after allegations of involvement in the financial misdemeanour known as the Jain Hawala case. Thereafter, the chief ministership was taken over by another senior BJP leader, Sahib Singh Verma.

Appendix II

The Vishva Hindu Parishad Abroad

The VHP has branches in eighty countries, but out of these it has a significant presence mainly in Britain and in the United States of America. It is one among many Hindu organisations working abroad; some of the others are the Swaminarayan mission, the Pushtimargis, the Arya Samaj and the Council of Hindu Temples. The VHP, however, is one of the largest and most active, and "appears to be a highly respectable organisation" (Sahgal 1996: 141). In places such as Britain and the United States, the VHP has acquired quite a significant following amongst Hindu residents, and has established close links with Hindu temples. Cordial ties have also been formed with religious groups working among the Sikh, Jain and Buddhist communities abroad. In fact, Sikh, Jain and Buddhist organisations are encouraged by the VHP to affiliate with it and imbibe its interpretation of Hinduism.

There are four main issues which the VHP abroad tries to deal with, all concerned with the question of religious identity: the media image of the community, the perception of Hindus in academia, lack of confidence among Hindus as a religious community and the issue of conversion to Islam and Christianity.[1] The VHP insists that Hindus abroad should be conscious of their religion and culture, and should not forget their roots however

[1] I am discussing these questions because they were specified by Kishor Ruparelia and Janhavi Ambekar in the course of my interviews with them in London on 27 July 1996 and 17 September 1997, respectively. The former is the general secretary of the VHP of Britain and the latter is the chairperson of the National Hindu Students' Forum in Britain. The National Hindu Students' Forum is ideologically close to the VHP and the Hindu Swayamsevak Sangh (the branch of the RSS abroad), and its members are permitted to hold membership of either of the two organisations. Janhavi herself belongs to the Hindu Swayamsevak Sangh, and I first met her at Baroda at the VHP-RSS-organised international camp in December 1995. At that time I was on fieldwork in India.

much they integrate with their country of residence. It also takes upon itself to "correct" what it considers to be the incorrect image of Hindus among the media and academia.

I was told that during the *Satanic Verses* controversy Asians, and as such also Hindus, were branded fanatics, especially in the United States and Britain. The National Hindu Students' Forum (NHSF) in Britain as well as the VHP took upon themselves to correct the "false" impression that Hindus are "fanatics." They also took upon themselves to improve the VHP's image among "the academics who hold a view that the VHP is bad and communal," but "do not investigate or substantiate their opinion before they come to acquire it."[2] Another important question which is sought to be dealt with is a perceived lack of confidence among Hindus about their religious identity and their culture. This is sorted out through organising discussion groups and meetings where such problems are thoroughly discussed and counselling provided. Another matter where the VHP and NHSF feel that they have an important role to play is the checking of conversions of Hindus abroad to Islam and Christianity, where the former is felt to be more threatening than the latter. It is said that Islamic groups target Hindus, and in particular Hindu girls, who are talked into marriage and thereafter converted.

The VHP's activities in Britain commenced in 1972.[3] In 1989 it organised a Virat Hindu Sammelan at Milton Keynes, drawing together all Britain's big Hindu organisations. This programme had an attendance of 55,000[4] (70,000 according to VHP estimates).[5] According to 1989–90 estimates, the VHP has fourteen branches and a membership of about 2,000 in Britain.[6] The highest proportion of membership is formed by the Gujaratis, primarily those who migrated to Britain from Africa.[7] I was told that in Britain, the VHP work has

2 Janhavi Ambekar, in a personal interview in London on 17 September 1997.

3 Hari Babu Kansal, "Vishva Hindu Parishad Abroad," *Hindu Vishva*, silver jubilee issue 1989–1990, 94, English edition.

4 Information from Rachel Dwyer (1994: 185–86).

5 Hari Babu Kansal, "Vishva Hindu Parishad Abroad," *Hindu Vishva*, silver jubilee issue 1989–1990, 94, English edition.

6 Ibid.

7 This was corroborated by Janhavi Ambekar, personal interview in London on 17 September 1997.

> more of an intellectual character—to make Hindus conscious of their identity and aware of their culture—rather than a violent or extremist make-up.[8]

The VHP takes a special interest in the religious education of children. It took a lead in demanding that a "Hindu" syllabus prepared by Hindus themselves should be recognised by the official body that decides school curriculum in Britain, to be taught to students as part of their religious education. There was a committee of six members that was given the responsibility to prepare a "Hindu" curriculum. Out of the six, two were members of the VHP. The preparation of the Hindu syllabus was completed by 1996, and it was brought out in the form of a book to be used as a guide for teaching Hinduism in schools.[9]

The VHP runs Gujarati and Hindi language classes as a part of its programmes. It also conducts classes to impart religious instruction, the lessons of which include a study of the Mahabharata and Ramayana. Narration of stories of the lives of Buddha and Mahavira, and even of Mahatma Gandhi and Sardar Patel, form a part of the instruction; and these classes are opened with a prayer (Jackson and Nesbitt 1993: 149). The main aim in holding these classes is to make Hindu children aware of their Hindu identity and to organise them as members of a Hindu community.

The VHP aims to promote a broad definition of Hinduism transcending regional, doctrinal and ritualistic differences (Jackson and Nesbitt 1993: 8). Through such a broad definition it tries to bring all religious groups on one platform and promote coordination among them. According to Hari Babu Kansal, a VHP leader,

> There are places of worship and cultural centres which have been serving the Hindu Society in their own way. But generally there had been no coordination and unity of purpose among such organisations. With the establishment of VHP abroad, coordination among them has been facilitated.[10]

The VHP has maintained cordial relations with various religious groups, although it claims that while the other groups are more in the nature of sects and sampradayas, it is a broad organisation with

[8] Ibid.

[9] Kishore Ruparelia, general secretary of the VHP of Britain, in a personal interview at London on 27 July 1996.

[10] Hari Babu Kansal, "Vishva Hindu Parishad Abroad," *Hindu Vishva,* silver jubilee issue 1989–1990, 93, English edition.

an overall "cultural thrust."[11] Sympathisers and members of the VHP of Britain frequently refer to it as an "umbrella organisation"[12] which is "looked up to by other Hindu organisations such as the Swaminarayan sect and the Council of Hindu Temples, because it helps them to solve and manage their problems."[13] It appears that there is an ambition within the VHP to attain this umbrella-like character and to envelop within its fold the various religious groups.

The Swaminarayan mission seems to be quite close to the VHP in terms of following the latter's programme, although such links are invariably denied by the former (Dwyer 1994: 186). During the inauguration of the Swaminarayan mission's colossal temple complex at Neasden (London) in August 1995, VHP's Ashok Singhal and BJP's L. K. Advani were the specially invited guests.[14] I was told in the course of an interview that in the last *shiksha shibir* held in 1997 (training camp held annually by the Hindu Swayamsevak Sangh, the RSS branch in Britain) the Swaminarayan sect took charge of providing food to those attending the camp.[15] The various Hindu organisations in Britain usually come together when any one of them organises a programme—which can range from a training camp for students to a sports meet or a religious march or the celebration of a Hindu festival.

In the United States, the VHP started its work in 1970, and it has its branches in forty states.[16] It had in Swami Chinmayananda a very active and influential sadhu to spread its message there. He stressed the importance of inculcation of Hindu traditions and cultural values in the younger generation.[17] Emphasis was laid on organising Hindu youth and involving them in the perpetuation of Hindu dharma through various programmes and projects. In the United States, as in Britain, the VHP began its work with the aim of uniting and perpetuating different strands of the Hindu religious tradition. It was felt that in order to "solidify Hinduism" in the United States it was

[11] Kishore Ruparelia, in a personal interview at London on 27 July 1996.

[12] Janhavi Ambekar, in a personal interview at London on 17 September 1997.

[13] Ibid.

[14] Reported in *Hindu Chetna*, 16 October 1995, 24.

[15] Janhavi Ambekar, in a personal interview at London on 17 September 1997.

[16] Hari Babu Kansal, "Vishva Hindu Parishad Abroad," *Hindu Vishva*, silver jubilee issue 1989–1990, 93, English edition.

[17] Swami Chinmayananda on occasion of the Tenth Hindu Conference at New York in 1984. Reported in *Shraddhanjali Smarika*, 198.

necessary to strengthen links between all Hindu organisations in that country.[18] The VHP's concern about the religious and cultural education of children in the United States led it to start learning groups and workshops—teaching elementary yoga, basic lessons on Hindu scriptures, religious stories and its perspective on Indian history (Fenton 1988: 125–27). It felt that Indian children in America did not get an opportunity to "breathe in the values of Hindu life" as they did in India, and also that the cultural system they were exposed to in a foreign land was "not congenial to the Hindu way of life" (Fenton 1988: 127).

The VHP of America has held several countrywide conferences; one of the most widely publicised was the Global Vision 2000 on 6–8 August 1993 in Washington DC, on the occasion of the centenary of Swami Vivekananda's address to the Parliament of Religions in Chicago. This show was received with great enthusiasm by an audience of about three thousand. VHP leaders such as Ashok Singhal, Vishnu Hari Dalmia and Uma Bharati hailed the day of the demolition of the Babri mosque as "a great and memorable day" which should be inscribed in "letters of gold," amidst cheers from the audience.[19] Swami Chinmayananda had been invited to this conference as a guest of honour, but had died a few days before the commencement of the conference.

As mentioned earlier, the VHP's foremost goal on its formation was the cultivation and preservation of Hindu dharma among Hindus who had migrated to foreign countries. In other words, the VHP's international agenda was given topmost priority. In later years, however, especially after the Ramjanmabhoomi–Babri Masjid issue became politicised and immensely publicised, the "national" agenda was given much more importance.The international programmes and functions were seen merely as vehicles to garner verbal and monetary support from the migrant Hindu community. In one of my interviews I was told that the VHP of Britain is just an off-shoot of the organisation in India and all decisions come from the "top," that is, the VHP leadership in India.[20] Moreover, as early as 1984, a committee constituted to examine the relationship between the VHP in India and the units abroad recommended that the central office at New Delhi should be made the head office of the entire VHP

[18] Karan Singh on occasion of the Tenth Hindu Conference at New York in1984. Reported in *Shraddhanjali Smarika*, 198.

[19] N. Ram, "Global Vision 2000 Indeed," *Frontline*, 10 September 1993, 15.

[20] Kishore Ruparelia, general secretary of the VHP of Britain, in a personal interview at London on 27 July 1996.

organisation, and units abroad should either become branches or be affiliated to the central VHP office. It also recommended that an affiliation fee should be decided in consultation with the foreign units. These recommendations were more or less accepted by the senior leadership of the VHP.[21]

The VHP, along with the RSS, regularly holds camps in India for its international membership. These camps give the activists from abroad an opportunity to keep in regular touch with political events in India, and to know the VHP's perspective on them. The camps are very well organised in terms of facilities, and follow a very disciplined daily schedule. What is interesting is that they become centres for crash courses in political education for students, professionals and businessmen from abroad. The camps are regularly visited by the VHP and RSS leaders, such as Ashok Singhal, Sadhvi Rithambhara and Rajendra Singh, whose speeches and addresses form an important part of the programme. Poster and photo exhibitions of the activities of the VHP, RSS, Rashtra Sevika Samiti and Durga Vahini are held, and posters of quotations from the speeches and writings of Savarkar, Vivekananda, Tilak, Golwalkar, Hedgewar etc. are elaborately displayed. Video shows are held of events such as the demolition at Ayodhya and the VHP yatras to make the activists familiar with the VHP perspective on these. [22]

Despite the VHP's apprehension in the early years of its formation that Hindu emigrants might lose contact with their culture, because of their long absence from India and thinning of ties with their kin, the migrants have "remained culturally conservative and intensely religious" and have maintained "some of the fundamental traditions with which they migrated from India" (Bhachu 1991: 61).[23] The perpetuation of

[21] J. R. Gupta, "The Evolution of a Fullfledged Organisation," in *Hindu Vishva*, silver jubilee issue 1989–1990, 21, English edition.

[22] I had an opportunity to visit one of these camps at Kayavarohan in Baroda district on 23 December 1995. The camp, called the "Vishva Sangh Shibir," was organised under the aegis of the RSS and was attended by about sixty members from abroad, mainly from Britain, United States and East Africa. Such an international camp is held once every five years in India.

[23] Bhachu says this of the East African Sikh and Gujarati diaspora, but it can be extended to those Indians as well who have migrated to other countries directly from India, i.e., who are not "twice migrants" to use Bhachu's own terminology. My observation of some Hindu families in London and particularly my visits to a local body in south London called "Hindu Society," which has an active membership of mainly Punjabi and Gujarati families both from India and East Africa who live in Tooting, Balham, Clapham and Streatham, substantiates this.

some pivotal religio-cultural values—ceremonies, rites and rituals that have to do with birth, marriage and death as also the Indian harvesting seasons—have occurred despite such features as the existence of a culturally different environment, tendency towards nuclear and not extended families, the entry of women in large numbers into the labour market, permanent settlement abroad and loosening of kinship ties and control (Bhachu 1991: 62).

Appendix III

Resolution Passed by the VHP's Board of Trustees at Tirupati on 13 January 1988

Reproduced from Vishva Hindu Parishad ke Prastav *(The Resolutions of the Vishva Hindu Parishad), edited by Raghunandan Prasad Sharma (New Delhi: Vishva Hindu Parishad Publication, n.d.), 72–73. The original text of the resolution is in English.*

After anxious consideration in all its perspective of the recent resolution passed at Bangalore by the National Executive of the Janata Party, regarding the Ram Janma Bhoomi and all such other places of religious worship, this meeting of the Board of Trustees of Central Vishva Hindu Parishad without reservations,

(a) Strongly condemns the approach and policy of the said Janata Party, of appeasement of fanatic and fundamentalist Muslims for attracting their en bloc votes to gain narrow political advantages, and
(b) focuses the attention of all Hindus irrespective of the political party to which they belong, to the grave implications of such stance of restoring the status quo-ante as on 15th August 1947 of all such places of religious worship viz.

(i) undoing of what has been achieved at Somnath Mandir by the efforts of Sardar Patel and Cabinet of the Central Government and restoring the mosque there, which will be a fresh great blow to the "Hindu Asmita" and aspirations of Hindus who constitute 85 percent population of Bharat.
(ii) giving up at all times the cherished dreams of the Hindu society to restore to their original grandeur the sacred places of religious worship such as Shri Ram Janma Bhoomi, Shri Krishna Janma Bhoomi, Kashi Vishwanath Mandir etc.

(iii) Keeping the bleeding wounds inflicted on Hindu society, its Maan-Bindus, Culture and way of life, alive so as to demoralise the values which we respect most, etc.

VHP Board of Trustees warns all political parties that Hindus who are awake, will not tolerate any such nonsense any further from any quarters; and shall continue their fight to the last, to annihilate such tendencies detrimental to the Hindu aspirations and to regain and to restore to the Hindu society and its culture; its honourable position.

This meeting of Board of Trustees of VHP reiterates its previous resolutions regarding the solution of the Ram Janma Bhoomi Mukti; and directs all the VHP units whether in this country or outside to mobilise the public opinion at all levels against the short-sighted policies of political parties as mentioned above and to marshal the strength of Hindus to achieve our goals in this behalf and to be prepared for come what may.

Appendix IV

Strategies of Mass Mobilisation and "Hinduisation" Proposed by the Dharma Sansad

Proposed in the Dharma Sansad's convention of January 1989. Reproduced here from Hindu Vishva, *January 1989, 60–64, English edition.*

Ways and Means for Mass-Awakening

—Well planned *chaturmas* programmes [four months of the monsoon season are called *chaturmas* in Hindi; italics mine] by the Saints in all districts of Bharat.

— After chaturmas "Padyatras" to be chalked out systematically by the saints, each adopting a particular district.

— At the centres of pilgrimages and on the auspicious occasions, discourses of these saints espousing the cause of re-establishing the Hindu Rashtra.

— In temples, educational institutions, scarcity areas and other public places exhortations by saints.

— Meaningful guidance by the top leaders of social, religious and caste organisations.

— To enlighten the masses with the help of literature, exhibition, video cassettes and other modern methods of propaganda.

—To hoist Saffron flag atop the houses of all Hindu families residing in urban rural and tribal areas of Bharat.

Ways and Means for Hinduisation

— The Hindu society should send such persons to legislative assemblies and Parliament, who will guarantee to protect the just rights of the Hindus.

— Only such persons of sterling character be elected who are above any affinity for sect, caste, language or region.

— Political leadership should be bestowed only on such persons, who are capable of determining the national policies on the basis of Hindu dharma, Sanskriti and Hindu values of life.

— In future, the society at large should beware of such politicians who indulge in appeasement of the minorities and accede to their anti-national demands at the cost of national interest, only aiming to fulfil their personal or party ends.

— Politicians in their election manifestoes [*sic*] guarantee to protect the under-mentioned just interest of the Hindus and those who will not agree should be opposed by all Hindus unitedly:

1. Return of Ramjanma Bhoomi, Sri Krishnajanma Bhoomi and Kashi Vishwanath Temple to the Hindu society.

2. The Muslim infiltrators from Bangladesh and Pakistan be sent back and concrete steps be taken to prevent future infiltration.

3. Under the guise of aid, but actually for encouraging conversions, the funds that are flowing from foreign countries should immediately be stopped.

4. Legal restraints on the conversion of Hindus.

5. Common Civil Code for the whole country in keeping with the Bharatiya tradition.

6. The special rights conferred on minorities under section 29 and 30 of the Constitution which are not available to Hindus, should be available to them.

7. Special status given under Sections 370 and 371 of the Constitution to certain States should be withdrawn forthwith.

8. Central Act for prohibiting the slaughter of cow and its progeny.

9. To stop the indiscriminate taking over of the temples and religious places of Hindus.

10. Compulsory teaching of Sanskrit language and Yog training side by side of moral and spiritual education to be included in the national education policy.

Appendix V

The BJP's Position in the Lok Sabha Elections

The following tables, showing the Lok Sabha election results, give some clue to the expanding electoral base of the BJP vis-a-vis the Congress from the late 1980s, when the VHP, the RSS and the BJP closely allied with each other.

Lok Sabha Elections[1]

(Seats won and contested by three all-India parties—Indian National Congress, Bharatiya Janata Party and Janata Party/Janata Dal—in nine major states)

Table 6: 1984

State	Total seats	INC	BJP	JP
Bihar	54	48(54)	0(32)	1(31)
Gujarat	26	24(26)	1(11)	1(12)
Haryana	10	10(10)	0(6)	0(7)
Himachal	4	4(4)	0(3)	0(2)
MP	40	40(40)	0(40)	0(23)
Maharashtra	48	43(47)	0(20)	1(15)
Rajasthan	25	25(25)	0(24)	0(15)
UP	85	83(85)	0(50)	0(45)
Delhi	7	7(7)	0(5)	0(1)
Total won		284	1	3
All-India seats won		415	2	10

[1] Sources: Roy et al. 1995; Singh 1994; Poll Analysis, *India Today*, 31 May 1996.

Table 7: 1989

State	Total seats	INC	BJP	JD
Bihar	54	4(54)	9(25)	31(37)
Gujarat	26	3(26)	12(12)	11(14)
Haryana	10	4(10)	0(2)	6(8)
Himachal	4	1(4)	3(4)	0(2)
MP	40	8(40)	27(33)	4(11)
Maharashtra	48	28(48)	10(33)	5(23)
Rajasthan	25	0(25)	13(17)	11(13)
UP	85	15(84)	8(31)	54(69)
Delhi	7	2(7)	4(5)	1(3)
Total won		65	86	123
All-India seats won		197	88	142

Table 8: 1991

State	Total seats	INC	BJP	JD
Bihar	52	1(52)	5(51)	31(36)
Gujarat	26	5(16)	20(26)	0(24)
Haryana	10	9(10)	0(10)	0(7)
Himachal	4	2(4)	2(4)	0(4)
MP	40	27(40)	12(40)	0(37)
Maharashtra	48	38(48)	5(31)	0(32)
Rajasthan	25	13(25)	12(25)	0(22)
UP	84	5(82)	51(84)	22(73)
Delhi	7	2(7)	5(7)	0(7)
Total won		102	112	53
All-India seats won		244	120	59

Table 9: 1996

State	Total seats	INC & allies	BJP & allies	JD & allies
Bihar	54	2(54)	24(52)	26(54)
Gujarat	26	10(26)	16(26)	0(17)
Haryana	10	2(10)	7(10)	0(10)
Himachal	4	4(4)	0(4)	0(10)
MP	40	8(40)	27(39)	3(40)
Maharashtra	48	15(48)	33(48)	0(48)
Rajasthan	25	12(25)	12(25)	1(25)
UP	85	5(85)	53(85)	20(85)
Delhi	7	2(7)	5(7)	0(7)
Total won		60	177	50
All-India seats won		139	194	179

Glossary

Adivasi	tribal
akhara	monastic order; an alternate meaning refers to a wrestling pit. This indicates the dual character of these.
Aryavarta	the land of the Aryans
ashram	hermitage
baudhik	intellectual
bhajan-kirtan	devotional Hindu songs
Bharatiya	Indian
chhattra-chaya	shelter
Dalit	those placed outside the classical Hindu Varna hierarchy — the "untouchables"
darshan	to visit and pay respects to a seer or shrine
dashbhuja	one with ten arms
devata	Hindu divinity
Devnagari-prachar	popularisation of the Hindi language in the Devnagari script
dharma	religion; moral code; duty; the higher purpose of one's life
dharmacharya	religious leader or guru
dharmasatta	power which comes by virtue of possessing spiritual knowledge
Dharmashastras	the varied Hindu religious texts
dharmik	religious
ekatmata	unity
garbha griha	sanctum sanctorum
garibi hatao	eradication of poverty
gau-raksha	cow protection
guru	teacher
Gurumukhi	variation of Devnagari script, used for Punjabi
hawala	transfer of money across borders without use of the modern banking system
Hindutva	coined by V. D. Savarkar to indicate Hinduness. He meant it to be a broader term than Hinduism, which referred only to the Hindu religion. Hindutva also included Hindu cultural practices, means of conduct and communication, a particular form of nationalist ideology and political practice whose end was the formation of a Hindu nation-state in India.

jagat guru	world leader
janmasthan	birthplace
jati	sub-caste
kalank	blot
karseva	manual work, in service of a cause, usually a religious cause
karya	work or duty
karyashala	workshop
Khalsa Panth	the community of Sikhs
krantikari	revolutionary
lok drohi	one who betrays people
lathi	wooden stick
madrassas	Islamic religious schools
mahatama	great soul; a saintly personality
majlis	congregation
maktab	religious school
mandir	temple
maryadapurshottam	*purshottam* means the perfect man, one who is not given to digression or provocation, who is restrained in temperament and displays equanimity of behaviour; and *maryadapurshottam* means the actions and thoughts of the perfect man, which uphold the "honour" of his position
masjid	mosque
moulavi	Muslim religious leader
mukti	liberation
nawab	honorific generally bestowed upon a Muslim noble, courtier or feudal potentate
namaz	prayers
nirman	construction
nyaya	justice
paduka pujan	prayer offered to slippers
parasti	appeasement
parivar	family
pooja or *pujan*	prayers
pracharak	unit organisers at the provincial level in the Rashtriya Swayamsevak Sangh
rajguru	Brahmin advisor to the king
Ramrajya	mythological kingdom of the divine king Rama; also indicates a utopia in common use
rashtrapurusha	national man/hero
rashtriya	national
rathyatra	literally, "chariot-march"
sabha	congress or conference
sadhu	Hindu monk; an ascetic

sadhutva	qualities of a sadhu
sadhvi	female ascetic
salamati	security
samabhav	oneness
samaj	society
sammelan	meeting or gathering
sampradayas	sect or religious denomination
samskara	cultural and moral conduct, specifically includes training and discipline in tradition
samskarsheel	of a good moral character, adhering to the values of Hindu dharma
Sanatan Dharma	orthodox Hinduism, which does not accept the various socio-religious reform endeavours of the nineteenth century
sanatani	follower of Sanatan Dharma
sangathan	organisation
sant	saint
sanyasi	one who has renounced the world
Sarsanghchalak	head of the RSS
sarva	all
sati	self-immolation by a widowed Hindu woman on the funeral pyre of her husband
satyagrah	literally, truth-force; a method of public action developed by Mahatama Gandhi during the freedom struggle, meant to embody a higher moral purpose. Presently used to describe various shades of mass agitations.
seva	service
shakha	branch
shankaracharya	religious head of one of the four shaivite religious centres established by Adi Shankara in the eighth century AD
shanta rasa	calm demeanour
shastra	scripture
shila	foundation stone (or brick)
shilanyas	laying of foundation
shuddhi sabhas	gatherings at purification/conversion ceremonies to take non-Hindus into the Hindu fold
suba	a distinct area for a particular group
suraksha	protection, defence
swabhiman	self-respect
swayamsevak	literally, a volunteer; RSS activist
taziya	procession taken out by Shiite community in reverence for Imam Hussain
trinetra	one with three eyes

ugra bhava	angry and aggressive disposition
ulema	Muslim clergy
vananchal	tribal area
varna	caste
Vedanta	one of the six schools of traditional Hindu philosophy, which captures the essence of the Vedas
Virat Hindu Sammelan	Grand Hindu Conference
virat purusha	Hindu concept of a primeval man
virodh	opposition
yagna	fire sacrifice; oblation
yatra	pilgrimage; march

Bibliography

PRIMARY SOURCES

Newspapers and magazines circulated/published by the Vishva Hindu Parishad and the Rashtriya Swayamsevak Sangh

Hindu Chetna, New Delhi.
Hindu Vishva, Allahabad.
Masurashram Patrika, Mumbai.
Organiser, New Delhi.
The Motherland, New Delhi.
Vandematram, Varanasi.

Publications popularised or/and published by the Vishva Hindu Parishad

Agarwal, Vamandas. 1992. *Bharat main secularism ki vikriti*. New Delhi: Vishva Hindu Parishad Publication.

Bharatiya Janata Party (BJP). 1991. *Mid-Term Poll to Lok Sabha, May 1991: Our Commitment Towards Ram Rajya*. Bharatiya Janata Party.

(By an) "Angry Hindu". 1988. *Angry Hindu? Yes, Why Not*. New Delhi: Suruchi Prakashan.

Deoras, Madhukar Dattatreya (Balasaheb Deoras). 1997. *Hindu Sangathan Aur Sattawadi Rajniti*. Noida: Jagriti Prakashan.

Dubey, Om Prakash. n.d. but in print in 1995. *Hindu Dharma*. Kitwe: Mission Press.

Ekatmata Yajna 1983. 1984. New Delhi: Vishva Hindu Parishad Publication.

Goswami, Parshuram. 1991. *Hamari Manyatayen*. Lucknow: Lokhit Prakashan.

Integral Approach. 1991. New Delhi: Suruchi Prakashan.

Jai Sri Rama Satsang Mandal. n.d. but in print in 1993. *Prashna Anekon Uttar Ek*. Allahabad: Vishva Hindu Parishad Publication.

Muktananda Saraswati. n.d. but in print in 1993. *Vartman Indian Samvidhan*. Vrindavan: Akhil Bharatiya Sant Samiti.

Rajeshwar. 1992. *Paravartan: Kyon aur kaise?* (Conversion: Why and how?). New Delhi: Suruchi Prakashan.

RSS Resolves....Full Text of Resolutions from 1950 to 1983. 1983. Bangalore: Prakashan Vibhag (RSS).

RSS: Spearheading National Renaissance. 1985. Bangalore: Prakashan Vibhag (RSS).

Sagar, Krishnananda. 1988. *Samvidhan ki bhavana aur Rashtriya Swayamsevak Sangh*. Okhla: Jagriti Prakashan.

Seshadri, H. V. 1988. *RSS: A Vision in Action*. Bangalore: Jagrana Prakashana.

Sharma, Raghunandan Prasad. 1992. *Shipra aur Saryu ki tarangon ke disha-nirdesh*. New Delhi: Vishva Hindu Parishad Publication.

———. 1996. *Nagpur main dwitiya ekatmata yatra ka samapan samaroh*. New Delhi: Vishva Hindu Parishad Publication. January.

———. n.d. but in print in 1995. *Marg darshak mandal ki vibhinn baithakain chhati dharma sansad ke aayojan par*. New Delhi: Vishva Hindu Parishad Publication.

———. n.d. but in print in 1995. *Satat sadhna yatra ke tees varsh 1964–1994*. New Delhi: Vishva Hindu Parishad Publication.

———, ed. n.d. but in print in 1995. *Vishva Hindu Parishad Ke Prastav*. New Delhi: Vishva Hindu Parishad Publication.

Shraddhanjali Smarika (Commemorative Volume to Pay Homage to. . . .). 1987. New Delhi: Vishva Hindu Parishad Publication.

Singh, Ganesh and Vireshwar Diwedi. n.d. but in print in 1992. *Mandirnirman ka pratham charan purna: Mandir "vahin" banane ki kyon shapath hai hamari?* Lucknow: Lokhit Prakashan.

Vajpayee, Suresh. 1992. *Laksha Ek: Karya Anek*. New Delhi: Suruchi Prakashan.

Vanavasi Kalyan Kendra. 1992. Sonbhadra (U.P.): Vishva Hindu Parishad Publication.

World Hindu Conference 1979. 1979. Bombay: Vishva Hindu Parishad Publication.

Other publications

Sadhnaji, Brahmacharini. *Short Biography of Swami Chinmayananda*. Internet, http://www.tazoat.com/-bnaik/biograph.html.

Golwalkar, M. S. 1939. *We or Our Nationhood Defined*. Nagpur: Bharat Publications.

———. 1966. *A Bunch of Thoughts*. Bangalore: Vikrama Prakashan.

Madhok, Balraj. 1969. *Indian Nationalism*. New Delhi: Bharatiya Sahitya Sadan.

Prakash, Indra. 1966. *Hindu Mahasabha: Its Contribution to India's Politics*. New Delhi: Akhil Bharat Hindu Mahasabha.

Savarkar, V. D. 1949. *Hindutva*. Poona.

Vajpayee, Atal Behari. 1993. *Hindus Betrayed*. New Delhi: Suruchi Prakashan.

Election data and other reports

Singh, V. B. 1994. *Elections in India*. Vol. 2, *Data Handbook on Lok Sabha Elections 1986–1991*. New Delhi: Sage.

Roy, Prannoy, David Butler and Ashok Lahiri. 1995. *India Decides: Elections 1952–1995*. New Delhi: Books and Things.

Poll Analysis. 1996. *India Today*, 31 May.

Citizen's Commission on Persecution of Christians in Gujarat. 1990. *Violence in Gujarat: Test Case for a Larger Fundamentalist Agenda*. N.p.: National Alliance of Women. April.

Private papers

Munshi, K. M. Nehru Memorial Museum and Library, New Delhi.
Savarkar, V. D. Nehru Memorial Museum and Library, New Delhi.

Interviews

A. B. Saran, adhyaksha, Allahabad unit, VHP. Allahabad, October 1995.

Anil Mehrotra, mantri, Hanumannagar (Allahabad), VHP. Allahabad, October 1995.

Arvind Brahmabhatt, sangathan mantri, Baroda, VHP (RSS background). Baroda, December 1995.

Ashok Singhal, adhyaksha, VHP (RSS background). New Delhi, February 1997.

Atul Awasthi, activist of the Bajrang Dal. Lucknow, February 1996.

Awadh Kishor, member of the VHP (RSS background). Ayodhya, February 1996.

B. L. Agarwal, upadhyaksha, Allahabad unit, VHP. Allahabad, October 1995.

Bina Sharma, South Gujarat mahila pramukh, Durga Vahini (VHP), has a BJP background. Baroda, September 1995.

———. Baroda, December 1995.

Chimanbhai Mararia, vibhag mantri, Baroda and Bharuch districts, VHP (RSS background). Baroda, September 1995.

Chunnibhai Patel, adhyaksha, Baroda and Bharuch districts, VHP. Baroda, December 1995.

Damodar Nene, RSS swayamsevak. Baroda, September 1995.

Deoki Nandan Agarwal, former upadhyaksha of the VHP. Allahabad, November 1993.

———. Allahabad, February 1996.

Dr Malti, member of Durga Vahini (VHP). Delhi, March 1996.

Girija Singh, former upadhyaksha, Uttar Pradesh, VHP. Allahabad, November 1993.

Gulab Singh Parihar, Awadh prant sangathan mantri, VHP (RSS background). Lucknow, February 1996.

Gurujan Singh, sangathan mantri, VHP, Uttar Pradesh (RSS background). Allahabad, November 1993.

Harijeevan, nagar mantri, Lucknow, VHP (RSS background). Lucknow, February 1996.

Harish Sharma, chief of Bajrang Dal, Baroda (VHP). Baroda, December 1995.

Hemlaxmi Chawla, member of Rashtriya Sevika Samiti. New Delhi, February 1996.

Jaishankar Singh Gaekwad, activist of the VHP with an RSS background. Baroda, December 1995.

Janhavi Ambekar, chairperson, National Hindu Student's Forum, London. London, September 1997.

Kiladheesh Baba, member of the Congress-I-formed trust to build the Rama temple at Ayodhya (sadhu). Ayodhya, November 1993.

Kishor Ruparelia, mahamantri, VHP, London. London, July 1996.

Mahesh Narayan Singh, mahamantri, Ayodhya, VHP (RSS background). Ayodhya, February 1993.

Muktananda Saraswati, chairperson of Akhil Bharatiya Sant Samiti (VHP). New Delhi, February 1993.

Nrittya Gopal Das, member of VHP and of the Ramjanmabhoomi Nyas formed by it (sadhu). Ayodhya, November 1993.

———. Ayodhya, February 1996.

Om Prakash Dubey, trustee, formed VHP units in Zambia and South Africa. Allahabad, October 1995.

Phalahari Baba, member of the Congress-I-formed trust to build the Rama temple at Ayodhya (sadhu). Ayodhya, November 1993.

Pramila Bede, all India general secretary, Rashtriya Sevika Samiti. Baroda, September 1995.

Praveen Togadia, mahamantri, Gujarat, VHP (RSS background). Ahmedabad, December 1995.

Prof. Javadekar, former adhyaksha of the Baroda unit of the VHP (RSS background). Baroda, October 1995.

Purshottam Nayak Singh, kshetra mantri, Lucknow, VHP (RSS background). Lucknow, February 1996.

Raghunandan Prasad Sharma, mantri in charge of the Publications Department of the VHP (RSS background). New Delhi, October 1995.

———. New Delhi, January 1997.

Rajendra Singh, sarsanghchalak, Rashtriya Swayamsevak Sangh. Allahabad, November 1995.

Ramchandra Paramhamsa, chairperson, Ramjanama Bhoomi Nyas, VHP (sadhu). Allahabad, November 1995.

Ramchandra Upadhyay, secretary, Allahabad unit, VHP (RSS background). Allahabad, November 1995.

Ramsubhag Das, a well-known Ayodhya sadhu, but not a VHP member. Ayodhya, February 1996.

Rukmini Akka, all India joint general secretary, Rashtriya Sevika Samiti. Baroda, September 1995.

Sadhvi Rithambhara, sanyojika, Durga Vahini (VHP). Baroda, December 1995.

Sahayji, member of VHP (RSS background). Allahabad, November 1995.

Saroj Mazumdar, member of Rashtriya Sevika Samiti. Baroda, September 1995.

Seetla Singh, editor of *Janmorcha,* newspaper published at Faizabad. Faizabad, November 1993.

Shanti Devbala, all India joint secretary, Mahila Vibhag (VHP). Lucknow, February 1996.
Shyam Sunder Agarwal, former mantri, Allahabad unit, VHP (RSS background). Allahabad, November 1995.
Surya Dev Tripathi, mahamantri, Indraprastha unit, VHP (RSS background). Delhi, April 1996.
Sushma Rana, activist of Durga Vahini (VHP). New Delhi, March 1996.
Vijay Parnami, mantri, Baroda, VHP (RSS background). Baroda, September 1995.
Vinod didi, member of Mahila Vibhag (VHP). Lucknow, February 1996.

SECONDARY SOURCES

Newspapers and magazines

National Herald, Lucknow.
Asian Age, New Delhi, London.
Hindustan Times, New Delhi.
Leader, Allahabad.
Pioneer, New Delhi.
Statesman, New Delhi, Calcutta.
Telegraph, Calcutta.
Times of India, Bombay, Ahmedabad, New Delhi.
Frontline.
India Today.
Outlook.
Sunday.

Books and articles

Agnes, Flavia. 1995. Redefining the Agenda of the Women's Movement within a Secular Framework. In *Women and the Hindu Right: A Collection of Essays,* eds. Tanika Sarkar and Urvashi Butalia. New Delhi: Kali for Women.
Ahmad, Aijaz. 1993. Fascism and National Culture: Reading Gramsci in the Days of Hindutva. *Social Scientist* 21 (3–4): 32–68.
———.1994. Nation, Community, Violence. *South Asia Bulletin* XIV (1): 24–32.
Alam, Javeed. 1989. Search for an Indian Renaissance. *Social Scientist* 17 (1–2), January–February: 72–78.
———. 1993. Democracy and Rights in India in the Wake of Ayodhya. *Social Scientist* 21 (7–8): 49–62.
Anderson, Benedict. 1991. *Imagined Communities: Reflections on the Origin and Spread of Nationalism.* London: Verso.
Andersen, Walter K., and Sridhar D. Damle. 1987. *Brotherhood in Saffron: The Rashtriya Swayamsevak Sangh and Hindu Revivalism.* Boulder: Westview Press.

Appadorai, Arjun. 1993. Number in the colonial imagination. In *Orientalism and the Post-colonial Predicament: Perspectives on South Asia*, eds. Carol Breckenridge and Peter van der Veer, 314–39. Philadelphia: University of Pennsylvania Press.

Arslan, Mehdi, and Janaki Rajan, eds. 1994. *Communalism in India: Challenge and Response*. New Delhi: Manohar.

Aurobindo, Sri. 1952. *Speeches*. Pondicherry.

Ballard, Roger, ed. 1994. *Desh Pardesh: The South Asian Presence in Britain*. London: Hurst.

Basu, Tapan, Sumit Sarkar, Tanika Sarkar, Pradip Datta and Sambuddha Sen. 1993. *Khaki Shorts and Saffron Flags*. New Delhi: Orient BlackSwan

Baxi, Upendra, and Bhikhu Parekh, eds. 1995. *Crisis and Change in Contemporary India*. New Delhi: Sage.

Bayly, C. A. 1973. Patrons and Politics in Northern India. *Modern Asian Studies* 7: 349–88.

Bhachu, Parminder. 1991. The East African Sikh Diaspora. In *Aspects of the South Asian Diaspora*, ed. S.Vertovec, 57–85. Oxford University Papers on India, vol. 2, part 2. Delhi: Oxford University Press.

Bhargava, Rajeev. 1994a. How Not To Defend Secularism. *South Asia Bulletin* XIV (1): 33–41.

———.1994b. Secularism, Democracy and Right. In *Communalism in India: Challenge and Response*, eds. Mehdi Arslan and Janaki Rajan, 61–73. New Delhi: Manohar.

Brass, Paul R. 1994. *The Politics of India since Independence*. The New Cambridge History of India. Cambridge: Cambridge University Press.

Breckenridge, Carol, and Peter van der Veer, eds. 1993. *Orientalism and the Post-colonial Predicament: Perspectives on South Asia*. Philadelphia: University of Pennsylvania Press.

Chandra, Bipan, Mridula Mukherjee, Aditya Mukherjee, K. N. Panikkar and Sucheta Mahajan. 1988. *India's Struggle for Independence 1857–1947*. New Delhi: Penguin.

Chatterjee, Partha. 1994. Secularism and Toleration. *Economic and Political Weekly* XXIX (28): 1768–77.

———. 1995. History and the Nationalization of Hinduism. In *Representing Hinduism: The Construction of Religious Traditions and National Identity*, eds. Vasudha Dalmia and Heinrich von Stietencron, 103–28. New Delhi: Sage.

Chaturvedi, Sitaram. 1988. *Madan Mohan Malaviya*. New Delhi: Publications Division, Ministry of Information and Broadcasting, Government of India (first published in 1972).

The Citizen's Commission. 1999. Special Report on Violence in Gujarat. *Indian Journal of Secularism* 3 (2).

Dalmia, Vasudha, and Heinrich von Stietencron, eds. 1995. *Representing Hinduism: The Construction of Religious Traditions and National Identity*. New Delhi: Sage.

Das, Durga, ed. 1974. *Sardar Patel's Correspondence*. Vol. 9, *1945–1950*. Ahmedabad: Navajivan.

Das, Veena, ed. 1990. *Communities, Riots and Survivors in South Asia*. Delhi: Oxford University Press.

Datta, Pradip K. 1993. VHP's Ram: The Hindutva Movement in Ayodhya. In *Hindus and Others: The Question of Identity in India Today*, ed. Gyanendra Pandey, 46–73. New Delhi: Viking.

Desai, A. R., ed. 1979. *Peasant Struggles in India*. New Delhi: Oxford University Press.

Deshpande, Satish. 1995. Communalising the Nation-Space: Notes on Spatial Strategies of Hindutva. *Economic and Political Weekly* XXX (50): 3220–27.

Diehl, Anita. 1977. *E. V. Ramaswami Naicker-Periyar: A Study of the Influence of a Personality in Contemporary South India*. Lund (Sweden): Lund Studies in International History.

Dua, Bhagwan D. 1992. Problems of Federal Leadership. In *Foundations of India's Political Economy: Towards an Agenda for the 1990s*, eds. Subroto Roy and William E. James, 93–112. New Delhi: Sage.

Dubashi, Jay. 1992. *The Road to Ayodhya*. New Delhi: Voice of India.

Dutt, Nripendra Kumar. 1931. *Origin and Growth of Caste in India*. London: Kegan Paul *et al.*

Dwyer, Rachel. 1994. Caste, Religion and Sect in Gujarat. In *Desh Pardesh: The South Asian Presence in Britain*, ed. Roger Ballard, 165–90. London: Hurst.

Elst, Koenraad. 1990. *Ram Janmabhoomi vs. Babri Masjid: A Case Study in Hindu-Muslim Conflict*. New Delhi: Voice of India.

Engineer, Asghar Ali. 1995. *Lifting the Veil: Communal Violence and Communal Harmony in Contemporary India*. Hyderabad: Sangam Books.

Engineer, Irfan. 1995. Religion, State and Secularism. *Economic and Political Weekly* XXX (43): 2726–28.

Erdman, Howard L. 1967. *The Swatantra Party and the Indian Conservatism*. Cambridge: Cambridge University Press.

Farmer, B. H. 1993. *An Introduction to South Asia*. New York: Routledge.

Fenton, John Y. 1988. *Transplanting Religious Traditions: Asian Indians in America*. New York: Praeger Publishers.

Frietag, Sandria. 1980. Sacred Symbol as Mobilising Ideology: The North Indian Search for a "Hindu" Community. *Comparative Studies in Society and History* 22 (4): 597–625.

Gangadharan, K. K. 1970. *Sociology of Revivalism: A Study of Indianization, Sanskritization and Golwalkarism*. New Delhi: Kalamkar Prakashan.

Gopal, Sarvepalli. 1979. *Jawaharlal Nehru: A Biography*. Vol. 2, *1947–1956*. London: Jonathan Cape.

Gould, Harold A. 1993. Patterns of Political Mobilization in the Parliamentary and Assembly Elections of 1989 and 1990. In *India Votes: Alliance Politics and Minority Governments in the Ninth and Tenth General Elections*, eds. Harold A. Gould and Sumit Ganguly, 14–49. Boulder: Westview Press.

Gould, Harold A., and Sumit Ganguly, eds. 1993. *India Votes: Alliance Politics and Minority Governments in the Ninth and Tenth General Elections*. Boulder: Westview Press.

Goyal, D. R. 1975. *RSS: Indian Version of Fascism*. New Delhi: Ministry of Information and Broadcasting, Government of India.

———.1983. Ekatmata Yagna Yatra-I: RSS Attempts to Hinduise Politics. *Mainstream*, 26 November, 31–34.

Graham, Bruce D. 1988. The Congress and Hindu Nationalism. In *The Indian National Congress: Centenary Hindsights*, ed. D. A. Low, 170–87. Delhi: Oxford University Press.

———. 1993. *Hindu Nationalism and India Politics: The Origins and Development of the Bharatiya Jana Sangh*. Cambridge: Cambridge University Press.

Hansen, Thomas Blom. 1999. *The Saffron Wave*. New Delhi: Oxford University Press.

Hansen, Thomas Blom, and Christophe Jaffrelot, eds. 1998. *The Bharatiya Janata Party and the Compulsions of Politics in India*. New Delhi: Oxford University Press.

Hardgrave, Robert L., and Stanley A. Kochanek. 1986. *India: Government and Politics in a Developing Nation*. Orlando: Harcourt Brace Jovanovich Publishers.

Hasan, Mushirul, ed. 1981a. *Communal and Pan-Islamic Trends in Colonial India*. New Delhi: Manohar.

———. 1981b. Communal and Revivalist Trends in Congress. In *Communal and Pan-Islamic Trends in Colonial India*, ed. Mushirul Hasan, 199–223. New Delhi: Manohar.

Heimsath, Charles H. 1964. *Indian Nationalism and Hindu Social Reform*. Princeton: Princeton University Press.

Hellman, Eva. 1993. Political Hinduism: The Challenge of the Vishva Hindu Parishad. Ph.D. diss., Uppsala University.

Jackson, Robert, and Eleanor Nesbitt. 1993. *Hindu Children in Britain*. Stoke on Trent: Trentham Books.

Jaffrelot, Christophe. 1993. Hindu Nationalism: Strategic Syncretism in Ideology Building. *Economic and Political Weekly* XXVIII: 517–24.

———. 1996. *The Hindu Nationalist Movement and Indian Politics: 1925 to the 1990s*. London: Hurst.

Jhangiani, Motilal. 1967. *Jana Sangh and Swatantra: A Profile of the Rightist Parties in India*. Bombay: Manaktala and Sons.

Jones, Kenneth W. 1989. *Socio-religious reform movements in British India*. The New Cambridge History of India. Cambridge: Cambridge University Press.

Juergensmeyer, Mark. 1996. *Religious Nationalism Confronts the Secular State*. New Delhi: Oxford University Press.

Kapur, Anuradha. 1992. Militant Images of a Tranquil God. In *Politics of Confrontation: The Babri Masjid Ramjanmabhoomi Controversy Runs-Riot*, ed. Asghar Ali Engineer, 45–48. New Delhi: Ajanta Publications.

———. 1993. Deity to Crusader: The Changing Iconography of Ram. In *Hindus and Others: The Question of Identity in India Today*, ed. Gyanendra Pandey, 74–109. New Delhi: Viking.

Kaviraj, Sudipta. 1995. Religion, Politics and Modernity. In *Crisis and Change in Contemporary India*, eds. Upendra Baxi and Bhikhu Parekh, 295–316. New Delhi: Sage.

Keer, Dhananjay. 1988. *Veer Savarkar*. Bombay: Popular Prakashan.

Khan, Mumtaz Ali. 1991. Mass Conversions of Meenakshipuram: A Sociological Inquiry. In *Religions in South Asia: Religious Conversions and Revival Movements in South Asia in Medieval and Modern Times*, ed. G. A. Oddie, 47–63. New Delhi: Manohar.

Kohli, Atul, ed. 1988. *India's Democracy: An Analysis of Changing State-Society Relations*. Princeton: Princeton University Press.

Kothari, Rajni. 1967. The Congress 'System' in India. In *Party System and Election Studies*, Rajni Kothari et al. New Delhi: Allied Publishers.

———. 1970. *Politics in India*. Boston: Little Brown.

———. 1988. *State Against Democracy: In Search of Humane Governance*. Delhi: Ajanta Publications.

——— et al. 1967. *Party System and Election Studies*. New Delhi: Allied Publishers.

Low, D. A., ed. 1988. *The Indian National Congress: Centenary Hindsights*. Delhi: Oxford University Press.

Ludden, David, ed. 1996. *Contesting the Nation: Religion, Community and the Politics of Democracy in India*. Philadelphia: University of Pennsylvania Press.

Lutgendorf, Philip. 1997. All in the (Raghu) Family: A Video Epic in Cultural Context. In *Media and the Transformation of Religion in South Asia*, eds. Lawrence A. Babb and Susan S. Wadley, 217–53. Delhi: Motilal Banarsidass.

Madan, T. N. 1987. Secularism in Its Place. *Journal of Asian Studies* 46 (4): 747–59.

Malik, Yogendra K., and V. B. Singh. 1994. *Hindu Nationalists in India: The Rise of the Bharatiya Janata Party*. New Delhi: Vistaar.

Malkani, K. R. 1980. *The RSS Story*. New Delhi: Impex India.

Manor, James. 1988. Parties and the Party System. In *India's Democracy: An Analysis of Changing State-Society Relations*, ed. Atul Kohli, 62–98. Princeton: Princeton University Press.

———, ed. 1994. *Nehru to the Nineties: The Changing Office of Prime Minister in India*. London: Hurst.

Marty, Martin E., and R. Scott Appleby, eds. 1991. *Fundamentalism Project*. 3 vols. Chicago: University of Chicago Press.

Mehta, Ved. 1994. *Rajiv Gandhi and Rama's Kingdom*. New Haven and London: Yale University Press.

Nandy, Ashis. 1990. The Politics of Secularism and the Recovery of Religious Tolerance. In *Communities, Riots and Survivors in South Asia*, ed. Veena Das. Delhi: Oxford University Press.

Narang, A. S. 1983. *Storm Over the Sutlej: The Akali Politics*. New Delhi: Geetanjali Publishing House.

Nayar, Baldev Raj. 1966. *Minority Politics in the Punjab*. Princeton: Princeton University Press.

Noorani, A. G. 2000. *The RSS and the BJP: A Division of Labour.* New Delhi: Leftword Books.

Oddie, G. A., ed. 1991. *Religions in South Asia: Religious Conversions and Revival Movements in South Asia in Medieval and Modern Times*. New Delhi: Manohar.

Omvedt, Gail. 1995. *Dalit Visions: The Anti-Caste Movement and the Construction of an Indian Identity*. New Delhi: Orient BlackSwan

Pal, Bipin Chandra. 1910. *The Spirit of Indian Nationalism*. London: Hind Nationalist Agency.

Pandey, Gyanendra. 1990. *The Construction of Communalism in Colonial North India*. Delhi: Oxford University Press.

———. 1993a. The 'New' Politics of Late Twentieth Century India and the World. In *Hindus and Others: The Question of Identity in India Today*, ed. Gyanendra Pandey, 1–23. New Delhi: Viking.

———. 1993b. Which of us are Hindus? In *Hindus and Others: The Question of Identity in India Today*, ed. Gyanendra Pandey, 238–72. New Delhi: Viking.

Parthasarathi, G., ed. 1989. *Jawaharlal Nehru: Letters to Chief Ministers, 1947–1964*. Vol. 5, *1958–1964*. New Delhi: Government of India.

Parvate, J. V. 1958. *Bal Gangadhar Tilak*. Ahmedabad: Navajivan Publishing House.

Rai, Alok. 1993. Religious Conversions and the Crisis of Brahaminical Hinduism. In *Hindus and Others: The Question of Identity in India Today*, ed. Gyanendra Pandey, 225–37. New Delhi: Viking.

Raj, S. Albones. 1981. Mass Religious Conversion as Protest Movement: A Framework. *Religion and Society* XXVIII (4): 58–66.

Rajagopal, Arvind. 2001. *Politics after Television: Hindu Nationalism and the Reshaping of the Public in India*. Cambridge: Cambridge University Press.

Renan, Ernest. 1882. *Qu'est-ce qu'une nation?* Trans. Ida Mae Snyder. Paris: Calman-Levy.

Roy, Subroto, and William E. James, eds. 1992. *Foundations of India's Political Economy: Towards an Agenda for the 1990s*. New Delhi: Sage.

Sahgal, Gita. 1996. Diaspora Politics in Britain: Hindu Identity in the Making. In *In Quest of a Secular Symbol: Ayodhya and After*, ed. Rajeshwari Ghose, 140–56. Perth, Curtin University of Technology: Indian Ocean Centre and South Asian Research Unit.

Saraswati, Muktananda. 1993. Muktananda Saraswati on Muslims: Interview. *Mainstream* XXXI (51): 16–18.

Sarkar, Sumit. 1989. *Modern India, 1885–1947*. London: Macmillan.

———. 1993. The Fascism of the Sangh Parivar. *Economic and Political Weekly* XXVIII (5): 163–67.

Sarkar, Tanika. 1994. Educating the Children of the Hindu Rashtra: Note on RSS Schools. *South Asia Bulletin* XIV (2): 10–15.

———. 1995. Heroic Women, Mother Goddesses: Family and Organisation in Hindutva Politics. In *Women and the Hindu Right: A Collection of Essays*, eds. Tanika Sarkar and Urvashi Butalia. New Delhi: Kali for Women.

Sarkar, Tanika, and Urvashi Butalia, eds. 1995. *Women and the Hindu Right: A Collection of Essays*. New Delhi: Kali for Women.

Sharma, Jagdish Saran. 1972. *The National Biographical Dictionary of India*. New Delhi: Sterling.

Sharma, R. S. 1980. *Sudras in Ancient India: A Social History of the Lower Order Down to Circa AD 600*. Delhi: Motilal Banarsidas Publishers.

Sharma, Suresh. 1996. Savarkar's Quest for a Modern Hindu Consolidation. *Studies in Humanities and Social Sciences* II (2): 189–215.

Sikand, Yoginder, and Manjari Katju. 1994. Mass Conversions to Hinduism among Indian Muslims. *Economic and Political Weekly* XXIX (34): 2214–19.

Singh, Iqbal. 1960. *Facts about Akali Agitation in Punjab*. Chandigarh: Fairdeal Press.

Singh, Karan. 1974. *Towards a New India*. Delhi: Vikas Publishing House.

———. 1983. Hindu Renaissance. *Seminar* 284: 14–17.

———. 1993. Crisis in Hinduism. *Seminar* 402: 43–44.

Thapar, Romila. 1985. Syndicated Moksha. *Seminar* 313: 14–22.

———. 1989. The Ramayana Syndrome. *Seminar* 353: 71–75.

———. 1991. A Historical Perspective on the Story of Rama. In *Anatomy of a Confrontation: The Babri Masjid–Ramjanmabhumi Issue*, ed. Sarvepalli Gopal, 141–63. New Delhi: Viking.

Tilak, B. G. n.d. *His Writings and Speeches*. Madras: Ganesh.

Vanaik, Achin. 1985. The Rajiv Congress in Search of Stability. *New Left Review* 154: 55–82.

———. 1992. Reflections on Communalism and Nationalism in India. *New Left Review* 196: 46–47.

———. 1997. *Communalism Contested: Religion, Modernity and Secularization*. New Delhi: Vistaar.

Van Dyke, Virgina. 1997. General Elections, 1996: Political Sadhus and Limits to Religious Mobilisation in North India. *Economic and Political Weekly* XXXII (49): 3149–58.

Veer, Peter van Der. 1987. 'Gods must be liberated!' A Hindu Liberation Movement in Ayodhya. *Modern Asian Studies* 21 (2): 283–303.

Verma, Brajlal. 1987. *Hanuman Prasad Poddar*. New Delhi: Publications Division, Ministry of Information and Broadcasting, Government of India.

Vertovec, S., ed. 1991. *Aspects of the South Asian Diaspora*. Oxford University Papers on India, vol. 2, part 2. Delhi: Oxford University Press.

Vivekananda. *The Complete Works of Swami Vivekananda*. 1922–59. Almora: Mayavati Memorial Edition.

Vyas, H. K. 1983. *Vishva Hindu Parishad: The RSS Broad Outfit for Spreading Militant Aggressive Hindu Communal Poison*. New Delhi: Communist Party of India Publication.

Yang, Anand. 1980. Sacred Symbol and Sacred Space in Rural India: Community Mobilisation in the "Anti–cow killing" Riot of 1893. *Comparative Studies in Society and History* 22 (4): 576–96.

Index

Advani, L. K. 65, 66, 67, 98, 114, 115, 157
Aiyar, C. P. Ramaswamy 9, 19, 23
Akali Dal 24, 25
Akhila Bharatiya Pratinidhi Sabha (of the RSS) 24
Apte, S. S. 5, 9, 10, 12, 14, 19, 20, 29
Arya Samaj 15, 24, 26, 34, 96, 128, 143, 154
Ayodhya 37, 46, 49, 50, 52, 55, 56, 57, 65, 66, 67, 72, 73, 74, 75, 78, 92, 98, 99, 101, 103, 104, 105, 109, 110, 111, 112, 113, 114, 115, 134, 146, 151, 159

Babri Masjid Co-ordination Committee 53
Babri mosque 4, 30, 45, 50, 52, 53, 57, 58, 66, 72, 88, 98, 99, 100, 101, 102, 103, 111, 115, 134, 146, 158
Bahujan Samaj Party 41, 64, 152
Bajrang Dal 3, 51–53, 56, 67, 71, 84, 89, 90, 99, 100, 102, 107, 109, 113, 121, 129, 134, 135, 136, 137, 138, 148, 151
Bharat 6, 19, 35, 38, 44, 58, 70, 72, 73, 81, 82, 100, 110, 115, 116, 161, 163
Bharatiya Janata Party (BJP) 2, 3, 4, 15, 39, 41, 44, 57, 58, 59, 62, 63, 64, 65, 66, 67, 72, 74, 75, 76, 96, 99, 107, 108, 113, 114, 115, 117, 119, 137, 139, 140, 142, 144, 145, 148, 152, 153, 166, 167, 168
Bharatiya Vanvasi Kalyan Ashram 27
Bharatmata 42, 43, 49, 105, 112, 138, 143
Buddhism 7, 26, 81, 96

Chinmayananda 5, 8, 11, 12, 20, 21, 27, 28, 44, 157, 158
Christian missionaries 4, 12, 13, 14, 27, 34, 35, 38, 51, 73, 74, 82, 84, 129, 130, 131, 132, 134, 137, 138, 140
Christianity 2, 4, 6, 8, 10, 12, 14, 15, 27, 28, 29, 39, 44, 82, 123, 128, 130, 131, 133, 139, 140, 154, 155
Christians 11, 12, 14, 30, 73, 75, 82, 83, 94, 110, 115, 117, 120, 121, 124, 127, 129, 130, 131, 132, 133, 134, 135, 136, 137, 138, 139, 140, 143
Congress 1, 2, 6, 9, 10, 11, 16, 17, 21, 22, 23, 24, 25, 27, 28, 30, 40, 41, 44, 45, 53, 55, 57, 59, 61, 62, 63, 64, 65, 92, 94, 95, 97, 101, 107, 108, 115, 127, 129, 134, 135, 139, 142, 143, 144, 166
Congress's Nagpur Resolution 21, 25
cow protection 136, 151

Dharma Sansad 35, 45, 59, 60, 70, 71, 72, 77, 78, 79, 143, 163
dharmacharyas 18, 71, 73, 74
Durga Vahini 71, 84, 88–93, 102, 148, 151, 152, 159

Ekatmata Yatra 3, 38, 43, 44, 45, 76, 110, 112, 113, 143

Gandhi, M. K. 16, 156
Gandhi, Rajiv 53, 54, 63, 64
Gandhi, Sonia 129, 139
Gangamata 42, 43, 143
Gaumata 42, 43, 143
Giriraj Kishor 110, 152
Gita 16, 20
Gita Press' 16
Golwalkar, M.S. 5, 7, 9, 16, 17, 18, 20, 26, 29, 30, 78, 93–95, 159

Hindu dharma 4, 7, 8, 9, 11, 12, 13, 18, 20, 25, 26, 29, 30, 39, 45, 76, 80, 81, 82, 86, 89, 121, 123, 130, 131, 133, 142, 143, 145, 157, 158, 164
Hindu Mahasabha 15, 16, 28, 63, 143
Hindu nationalism 4, 9, 25, 28, 30, 45, 47, 50, 52, 59, 61, 64, 69, 88, 93, 108, 127, 144, 145
Hindu society 6, 7, 10, 12, 13, 14, 17, 18, 19, 24, 25, 26, 27, 28, 29, 34, 41, 43, 44, 49, 57, 68, 71, 73, 75, 76, 82, 83, 85, 86, 93, 96, 102, 106, 110, 118, 122, 123, 124, 138, 156, 159, 161, 162, 164
Hinduisation 3, 51, 59, 70, 73, 127, 128, 130, 131, 141, 145, 163, 164
Hinduism 3, 5, 7, 8, 13, 15, 20, 26, 28, 29, 31, 33, 34, 40, 50, 58, 62, 69, 75, 81, 82, 83, 84, 85, 96, 123, 126, 128, 129, 130, 131, 132, 133, 136, 154, 156, 157
Hindutva 4, 26, 28, 51, 52, 53, 55, 64, 67, 76, 80, 81, 82 88, 91, 92, 93, 96, 98, 105, 107, 108, 109, 110, 113, 114, 115, 116, 121, 122, 125, 126, 127, 150

Islam 6, 8, 10, 11, 28, 29, 33, 39, 44, 82, 83, 92, 100, 123, 128, 130, 133, 140, 154, 155

jagat-guru 70, 144
Jainism 7, 26, 81, 96
Jana Jagrana Abhiyan 34
Jana Sangh 1, 2, 15, 16, 23, 24, 25, 26, 27, 28, 30, 45, 63, 96
Janata party 27, 79, 161, 166

Kalyan 16, 48
Karan Singh 8, 30, 31, 158
Krishnajanmabhoomi 74, 79, 161
Kumbha 5

Mahila Vibhag 89, 90, 91, 92, 148, 152
Malaviya, Madan Mohan 16, 62
Marg Darshak Mandal 35, 57, 69, 70, 79, 98
Meenakshipuram 33–36, 41, 98, 136, 143
minorities 3, 44, 50, 61, 75, 77, 114, 118, 120, 121, 122, 129, 135, 139, 141, 164
Modi, Narendra 153
Mookerjee, Ramaprasad 23
Mookerjee, Shyama Prasad 23
Muktananda Saraswati 85, 115, 150
Munshi, K.M. 5, 9, 19, 21, 22, 23
Muslims 1, 11, 12, 22, 30, 34, 37, 38, 41, 49, 54, 55, 61, 62, 64, 75, 82, 83, 84, 87, 92, 93, 94, 101, 105, 106, 107, 109, 110, 111, 114, 115, 117, 118, 119, 120, 121, 122, 124, 127, 129, 130, 132, 133, 134, 135, 137, 138, 140, 143, 161

Nagaland 1, 2, 14, 27
Nehru, Jawaharlal 15, 21, 22, 24, 61, 93, 120, 127

paravartan 127, 128–34, 143
Patel, Sardar 22, 61, 156, 161
Pawaiyya, Jaibhan Singh 109, 110
Poddar, Hanuman Prasad 16, 48
pracharak 19, 68
Punjabi suba 23, 24, 25

Ramjanmabhoomi 37, 45, 48, 50, 51, 53–60, 63, 67, 70, 72, 74, 79, 84, 99, 101, 102, 114, 123, 136, 144, 151, 158, 161, 162
Ram Janmabhoomi Nyas 72, 100, 102
Rama 17, 45, 46, 47, 48, 49, 50, 51, 52, 53, 55, 57, 58, 66, 67, 70, 72, 76, 79, 99, 102, 103, 109, 111, 112, 134, 143, 144
Ramayana 47–50, 57, 60, 109, 156
Ramrajya 48, 55, 57
Rao, P. V. Narsimha 72, 100
Rashtriya Swayamsevak Sangh (RSS) 1, 25, 136
reconversion 107, 127, 128, 129, 132
Rithambhara, Sadhvi 55, 88, 110, 149, 152, 159

sadhus 4, 7, 15, 17, 18, 19, 35, 40, 44, 68–74, 77, 78, 96, 99, 102, 103, 132, 148
SAHMAT 109
Sampurnananda 19
Sandipini ashram 5, 6, 19, 22, 26
Sanskriti Raksha Yojana 34, 143
Sant Tukdoji 8
sants 7, 17, 18, 19, 35, 68, 70, 71, 72, 73, 78, 79, 99, 102
sarsanghchalak 17, 18, 59, 68, 76, 97
Savarkar, V.D. 28, 81, 159
secularism 1, 53, 54, 62, 108, 115, 116, 117–21, 124, 137, 151, 152
Shah Bano 53, 118
Shankaracharyas 96, 103
shila pujan 57, 112
shilanyas 52, 55, 56, 57, 88, 92, 104
Shiv Sena 53, 59, 99
shuddhi karan 128
Sikhism 2, 7, 26, 81, 96
Singh, Fateh 24, 25
Singh, Gurujan 19, 83, 150
Singh, Kalyan 65, 74
Singh, Rajendra 18, 19, 68, 76, 97, 150, 159
Singh, Tara 23, 24, 25, 26
Singhal, Ashok 21, 39, 43, 44, 45, 55, 57, 59, 68, 70, 71, 78, 80, 97, 98, 109, 110, 129, 131, 133, 139, 140, 147, 150, 152, 157, 158, 159
Sushil Muni 8
Swatantra Party 1, 21
swayamsevaks 2, 68, 97, 98

Tandon, Purshottamdas 16
tolerance 108, 115, 121–24, 125

Uma Bharati 88, 105, 107, 110, 158
untouchables 33, 34
Upanishads 16, 20

Vanvasi Kalyan Kendra 26, 27, 36, 130
virat purusha 86
Vishva Hindu Parishad (VHP) 2, 7, 10, 12, 13, 15, 23, 27, 29, 35, 37, 38, 54, 69, 75, 79, 81, 85, 128, 130, 138, 154, 155, 156, 157, 161

Wadiyar, Jaya Chamraj 13
World Hindu Conference 5, 6, 11, 13, 20, 21, 27, 28, 29